BY A NOSE

FRED SMERLAS
and
VIC CARUCCI

SIMON AND SCHUSTER

New York   London   Toronto   Sydney   Tokyo   Singapore

Simon and Schuster
Simon & Schuster Building
Rockefeller Center
1230 Avenue of the Americas
New York, New York 10020

Copyright © 1990 by Fred Smerlas and Vic Carucci

Designed by Irving Perkins Associates
Manufactured in the United States of America

1 3 5 7 9 10 8 6 4 2

Library of Congress Cataloging in Publication Data

Smerlas, Fred.
By a nose / Fred Smerlas and Vic Carucci
p.   cm.
1. Smerlas, Fred.   2. Football players—United States—Biography.
3.   Tackling (Football)   4. Buffalo Bills (Football team)
I. Carucci, Vic.   II. Title.
GV939.S615A3 1990
796.332'092—dc20   90-10080
[B]   CIP
ISBN 0-671-70532-6

Fred Smerlas

To my lovely wife, Kristine, the woman who breathed life back into me; to my parents, Peter and Catherine, aka Harry and Mary, for keeping me well fed.

Vic Carucci

To Rhonda, for her unwavering love, support, and tolerance; to Kristen and Lindsay, whose bright, beautiful faces remind Daddy of what's truly important in life.

ACKNOWLEDGMENTS

The authors wish to thank the following for their contributions to the production of this book: Scott Berchtold, Chris Berman, Rhonda Carucci, Kristen Depowski, Mike Dodd, Larry Felser, Warner Hessler, Kevin Hughes, Denny Lynch, Michael Madden, Will McDonough, Milt Northrop, Reid Oslin, Jim Perry, Scott Pitoniak, Leo Roth, Joe Shaw, Jason Sherwood, Kay Smerlas, Kristine Smerlas, Peter Smerlas, Howard Smith, Rick Woodson, and Paul Zimmerman.

We would also like to give very special thanks to Jeff Neuman and Stuart Gottesman, our editing team at Simon and Schuster, for applying their great skill to our manuscript and being patient through a long and difficult process, and to our literary agent, Basil Kane.

CONTENTS

CHAPTER

ONE

ON THE NOSE

I MAKE A LIVING as a nose tackle. This should tell you right away that there are a few loose toys in my attic. No one in his right mind would spend more than a single play there. I've been in my wrong mind for eleven years and 162 NFL regular-season games, including 149 consecutive nonstrike starts. There isn't another player in league history who has spent more time at that position. I guess that makes me a nose for the ages.

A nose tackle has a lot in common with a pinball. After the snap, you don't really get very far, but you're bounced around in every possible direction. Then, having done your job, which is to occupy the center and a guard or two long enough for someone else to make the tackle, you disappear into a hole of obscurity until the next play. The difference is, a little steel ball doesn't crack or tear on the inside, or get bumped, bruised, sliced, and diced on the outside.

It also doesn't have to try to lift itself out of bed Monday morning.

When people who don't know football meet me for the first time, they're always puzzled by my job title. I'm sometimes introduced as a "nose man," and they immediately assume I'm a doctor who specializes in sinus problems or a plastic surgeon. When they find out I play football, they ask how the position got such a goofy name. I try to explain that, just as your nose is smack in the middle of your face, the position, in a 3-4 defensive alignment, is smack in the middle of the line, between the two ends. And if they still don't understand, I just point to my nose. When they see the size of it, they nod and say, "Yeah, Fred, I guess you could make a tackle with that thing."

Sure, there are more glamorous ways to pick up a paycheck in the NFL. You have running backs . . . wide receivers . . . the kids who collect dirty laundry in the locker room.

And of course, there are those TV talk-show hosts who moonlight as quarterbacks. Who has it better than they do? For a couple million bucks a year, they get to entertain the media, make commercials, ride in limousines, sign autographs, pose for pictures. And every now and then, when the mood strikes them, they throw a pass. The league even rewrote its rule book to help prevent those poor babies from getting hurt by big meanies like me. Plays are whistled dead when the quarterback is "in the grasp" of a defender. Give me a break! Pass rushers can take only one step after the QB unloads the ball before they unload on him. Do you believe that? I just know that one of these days I'm going to take the field and find a barbwire fence surrounding the pocket.

A whole generation of nose tackles could go down with injuries, and the people who ran the NFL would say, "Gee, that's too bad. Let's just hope they didn't fall on any quarterbacks."

There are also more glamorous positions than mine on defense, such as end and outside linebacker. Those guys do the sacking and dancing; nose tackles do the pushing and grunting.

But I wouldn't want to be anywhere else. For one thing, I've never been anywhere else, at least not in the NFL. I think it's a little too late for me to start learning how to play receiver. For another, I can honestly say I love being a nose tackle. I love being right at the heart of the action. When I'm on the field, I'm involved in every single play, whether it's a run or a pass, whether it's coming straight at me or going somewhere else. There are times when, if a play is headed away from him, a defensive end becomes so uninvolved he might as well be watching the game on TV along with the rest of the couch potatoes.

My primary job is to penetrate. If it's a pass, I'm trying to collapse the front of the pocket, so the ends and linebackers can make the sack. If it's a run, I'm trying to move the pile forward, so the ends and linebackers can make the tackle. Stopping the run is the key. If you can stop another team cold on the ground, you can usually start making arrangements for the postgame party. If the opponent is running wild, you'd better put away the party hats and break out the ice bags.

At nose tackle, every snap is like walking through an intersection during rush hour in Manhattan. With your eyes closed. Vehicles, disguised as blockers, come at you from all directions. It could be one of the guards, each with a clear shot at your legs while you're tangling with the center. It could be a fullback. It could be a halfback. Or maybe, just when you think you've broken free from that 280-pound, once-deprived child in the middle of the offensive line, a tight end or wide receiver will come flying out of nowhere and try to stuff himself into your earhole. And let's not forget about the linebackers from your own team. While in hot pursuit of the ball, they have a way of forgetting about everything in their path—including the back of your legs.

With all that traffic, and all those reckless drivers, there's bound to be an accident. It's just a matter of time. That's why, on every snap, I'm going full tilt. My legs are going a hundred miles per hour. The more you keep your legs moving, the less chance you have of leaving one or both in the wrong place at the wrong time, and going off the field on a golf cart. Football players learn fast that that's one limousine ride they never want to take. As it is, I've suffered injuries on both knees and had an ankle swell to the size of a basketball. My ribs have been cracked. My right elbow has been operated on twice. I've had a wrist sprained so bad, I couldn't bend it. I've broken or dislocated all of my fingers and have had fingernails torn off. I've had a pinched rotator cuff. I don't know how many times I've had to pull that big schnozz of mine back to where it belongs. My eyes have been gouged and poked. And I've been the victim of five knockouts—at least, that's how often I remember thinking I was back at my alma mater, Boston College, and not in the NFL.

"What they do to that guy," Hall of Fame defensive lineman Alan Page once said of the nose tackle, "it's bordering on criminal."

Believe me, that border is crossed many times. But the pain only lasts for a second. You can't dwell on it any longer than that. It's not like you have two or three hours or two or three weeks to research it. If you get knocked down, you bounce back up. If your fingers are out of joint, you pop them back in. If your nose is broken, you straighten it out. You gather whatever body parts you've left on the field, return them to their proper place, and wander into that intersection again. You've heard of Zorba the Greek? I'm Absorba the Greek.

For me, there's nothing that compares to the weekly challenge of battling with the center—one-on-one, facemask-to-facemask.

Except, of course, when the guy has garlic breath. Or when he misses his monthly shower. (Do you have any idea how bad a 280-pound body can smell when it starts baking in the sun?) Or when he loses his breakfast all over the football. That's happened more times than I care to remember. You do the best you can to ignore it and go about your business. But it's not always easy. I once got into my stance and stuck my hand into what I could only assume had been a large plate of bacon, eggs, and hash browns. I turned toward the

ref and said, "This deserves a time-out, don't you think?" I
had to laugh in meetings the next day when the coach
pointed to the screen and yelled, "Why the hell are you so
far off the ball on this play, Smerlas?"

At 6'3" and 300 pounds, I guess you could say I have the
perfect build to play nose tackle. True to my Greek heritage,
I have relatively short legs and a large upper body. Picture
a jukebox covered with hair. Will Grant, a former teammate
of mine with the Buffalo Bills, once told me, "Fred, when
you were born, God stamped 'Nose Tackle' on your forehead." When you look at the prototype for the position, what
you have is a guy who's too bulky and slow to play defensive
end, and not quite tall enough to play defensive tackle in a
four-man front. So, as a public service, the NFL created another spot on the defensive line just to keep freaks like me
from roaming loose in society.

The most important asset for an effective nose tackle is
power, which is why the weight room has been like a second
home to me throughout my professional life. It's pretty amus-
ing when people come up to me and ask, "How'd you get
all those muscles? Did you lift a lot of weights?" What do
they think, I wrapped cookies?

Other important qualities are quick feet and quick hands,
because the first thing you do when the ball is snapped is
engage the center (I hope my wife, Kris, doesn't take that the
wrong way). The faster you can fire your hands into the plates
of his chest, the harder it is for him to block you. Your hands
also serve as a guide to where the center's going, which,
usually, is the first sign of what the entire offense is up to.
You feel the direction he's headed, and then it's up to your
feet to get you there before him. My hands are like another
pair of eyes. So if the center happens to complain that I'm
handling him a little too aggressively, I can always say I'm
just compensating for poor "vision."

Sometimes the battle with the center bears a close resemblance to a wrestling match. And that's perfect for me, because I was an all-American wrestler in high school. I highly
recommend wrestling to anyone playing high school foot-

ball, because it helps improve your quickness, toughness, and tenacity. I don't recommend playing nose tackle, however.

Besides having the right physical tools for the position, you also have to be in the proper frame of mind. In this case, the frame is very bent and very twisted. When I go on the field, my hair's messed up, I need a shave, my shirt's out, I have old shoes on, I have blood all over my hands. I look ugly and I play ugly.

It shouldn't come as any surprise that I've received my share of letters from NFL headquarters for uniform violations. One said I was showing too much skin between the top of my socks and the bottom of my pant legs. Can you believe that? Me receiving an X-rating?

Another letter actually mentioned that the red wasn't bright enough in my red-and-white socks. As if, an hour before kickoff, I'm going to pause in the middle of working myself into a frenzy to check something like that. I always thought what we were involved in was a football game, not a fashion show.

There are some people who might say my off-field appearance isn't a whole lot better, especially when we play on the road. Dress codes for road trips are silly, but most coaches want their players wearing suits or sports jackets and ties. The thinking is, if you look and feel like a pro, you play like a pro. But I can't understand why coaches spend all week preparing us to act like primal beasts; then, just because we take a plane to the game, they want to make us look civilized. And the thing that gets me is, no one really sees us on those trips until we're on the field in our uniforms. Our chartered flight leaves from a private airport. After we land, we board chartered buses that pull up right next to the plane. We're shuffled through the back door of the hotel with our room keys waiting for us. We spend most of our time at the hotel meeting with our coaches. And chartered buses take us to and from the stadium, which we enter and exit through well-hidden tunnels.

The only thing I can figure is that a bunch of NFL head

coaches got together and bought stock in big-men's clothing stores.

In case you haven't guessed by now, I'm not a suit-and-tie type of guy. I like to be comfortable, and the only suits I find comfort in are the kind you wear for jogging, not funerals. So I compromise. I wear one of the two rumpled sports jackets I own—white or light blue—with a Hawaiian shirt and a red tie I haven't unknotted in about five years. The tie's a real time-saver, and that's important to me because I tend to pull into the airport just as the pilots are completing their final checks.

Engines, check. Flaps, check. Fuel, check. Fat Greek on board, check.

My showdown with an opposing center begins the moment I press the play button on my VCR and his image appears on the TV screen. Next to *Star Trek* reruns, videotape of centers, guards, and other nose tackles around the league is my favorite form of viewing. I'll sit there for hours, watching every single thing they do and working the remote control until I develop calluses on my thumb. When it comes to preparing for a center, I'll search for the tiniest details I can find, right down to the brand name of the towel hanging from the back of his pants. (I've always wondered about those towels. The only thing I can figure is the quarterback insists on having one handy just in case there's another kind of disagreement between the center and his pregame meal.)

The closer it gets to game day, the more consumed I become with my opponent. At a certain point, I don't need the VCR anymore; the guy is showing up in my dreams. I'll actually start playing the game while I'm asleep. On more than a few occasions, I've opened my eyes to find myself pumping my legs furiously because I'm convinced it's Sunday, 80,000 maniacs are screaming, and the ball has just been snapped in front of my face. A couple of times, I've pumped my legs so hard I've driven my skull into the headboard. As if that isn't enough to scare the daylights out of my poor wife, there has been a time or two when, believing I was in midbattle with the center, I've grabbed her out of a sound sleep and shaken her before finally hearing her scream, "Fred! Stop! It's me, Kris!" I have to say she handles it pretty well. Of course, I still haven't quite gotten used to kissing her good-night through that facemask.

The first thing I do when I take the field is call the defense together for the huddle. I yell, "Huddle!" and all of a sudden ten guys appear around me, waiting for instructions from the defensive coaches on the sideline. Yelling "Huddle!" might seem like a trivial thing, but if I don't do it, there's no huddle. It gives me a real sense of power.

Without fail, someone will look around the circle at all of these bug-eyed psychopaths and say, "Okay, boys, let's get out of here in three." Early in my career, it was one of my favorite lines—three plays and out. But since I turned thirty, I say, "Screw that. Let's get out of here in one." I don't want to be on the field any longer than I have to. That's the beautiful thing about playing defense; the offense wants to be out there all day long, plowing up and down the field and scoring a zillion points, but if we do our jobs right on defense, we get to spend most of the day *off* the field, drinking Gatorade and waving to the fans. And if things are really going good, some of us have been known to send out for hot dogs—and eat them while watching from the bench.

After we break our first defensive huddle of the game, I go through a ritual I call The Stare. I stand about two yards behind the ball, place my hands on my hips, and watch the center as he makes his way toward the line of scrimmage. I'm looking right into his eyes, and more often than not, they'll tell me what I'll be dealing with for the next sixty minutes. If they have that "I wish I were anyplace but here" expression, and the guy is breathing heavily and trying his best not to look into my facemask, I know it's going to be a fairly easy time. I'm going to play it clean, as I always do, but I might throw him down a little harder if I get the chance and make some funny noises so he'll think I'm really mean. You have to remember, some of these guys were in elementary school when I started playing. The first time they saw my face, I was on a bubble-gum card and they were just reaching puberty.

On the other hand, if the center's eyebrows are bent, his pupils are glazed, and he's foaming at the mouth, I know I'm in for a long day. Now, there are some guys who try to look mean, who grit their teeth and snarl and say things like, "I'm going to kill you." But I've given The Stare enough times to know that somewhere inside that Godzilla costume is a trembling Bambi.

Having played my little mind game with the center, the next step is to get myself in the best position possible to conquer him physically. That's why, before every single snap, I go through a mental checklist that would put NASA to shame. First, I get my feet slightly wider than my shoulders, so I have a good, solid base to work from. Second, I bend my knees to a half-squat, just low enough to get the greatest amount of power from my legs; in a full squat, you lose a little power. Third, I rest my forearms on my knees to establish a sense of balance. Fourth, I turn my toes in just a hair, because that helps me to push off with the balls of my feet rather than the insteps, which don't give me nearly as much explosion. Fifth, I put my right foot a little bit farther forward than my left. Being right-handed, I have a tendency to push off with my left foot first, so I've found if the right foot is ahead of the left, I tend to push off with both feet and that increases my lateral movement. Sixth, I drop my right hand to the ground, assuming a three-point stance. Seventh, I put my left hand as close to the center's right shoulder as I can without being offsides—that improves my chances of engaging him before he engages me. And finally, I arch my back so I'm locked in a position that makes it harder for the center to move me backward and gives me maximum thrust from my hips and legs.

Once I have my mechanics straight, I study how the center has positioned himself. The first thing I look for is the way he distributes his weight on the ball. If he keeps it closer to his body and he's leaning back, I know from watching all that video that a pass is coming. If the ball is way out in front of him, and he's leaning forward, I know it's going to be a run. Sometimes his foot placement will indicate if he's going to go right or left. And if he smiles the moment the quarterback slips his hands under his buns, that says something, too. It says I'd better be extra careful *he* doesn't get any wrong ideas when we become engaged.

You have to remember that all of these thoughts are racing through my head in a matter of seconds. And when you consider how critical it is for me to beat the center off the ball and my normal hyperactive tendencies, I'm pretty much wired to the hilt—especially before the first snap of a game. Picture a guy who gets up in the morning, drinks four quarts of coffee, smokes four packs of cigarettes, and then sits in an isolated room for a while. How wired am I? Sometimes I drive to the stadium without ever starting my car.

Hunched over the ball, I make sure I keep my eyes as wide open as they can be. That way, after the snap, I don't miss any of the countless things that are happening at the speed of light. It also helps me maintain my aggressiveness. For some reason, I used to wince on the first hit after the snap, and I found it actually caused me to let up a little bit, to be more tentative than I was when my eyes were opened wide. So now it looks like I've constantly got my finger stuck in an electrical outlet.

That first hit clears up everything. You find out right away what your battle with the center is going to be all about. For an entire week you asked yourself, "Is he going to try to beat me with quickness? Is he going to try to dominate me with strength?" Now you have your answer. At the same time, you realize the guy's just as human as you are—even if he does shower only once a month. You realize playing well against him is not going to be such an insurmountable task after all. You've done it all a thousand times before; you can do it again. Even if the guy knocks you on your ass, you don't feel all that bad, because that first snap is behind you. You know exactly what you did wrong, and you can correct it. Of course, if you knock him on his ass on that first hit, the second one can't get there fast enough.

But victory at nose tackle isn't always measured by giving the center an unwanted seat on the field. For me, the greatest thrill is being able to get my hands up fast enough so that I can grab his shoulder pads and lock him out. At that moment, I have complete control. I'm in total command. He can't do a thing until I let him. If the ball carrier comes my way, I just flip the center to one side and take off after the ball-carrier. Controlling the center is a lot more gratifying than making a tackle, because anyone can make a tackle just by being in the right place at the right time. But to physically control a guy who's as big and as strong as you are, to know you can do anything you want with him, is the highest of highs. That's my touchdown. After a play like that, my chest is puffed out and peacock feathers are sprouting from my rear end.

Because of my personality, a lot of people have told me I should have worn the silver and black of the Raiders—that is, when wearing those colors stood for something other than "have team, will travel."

I wore the red, white, and blue of the Bills from 1979, when they made me a second-round draft pick, until March of 1990, when I signed with the San Francisco 49ers as a Plan B free agent. Not counting the three games I missed in 1987, because I wouldn't cross the picket line during the strike, I started every game the Bills played in the 1980s. I was with them through the best of times—1980, when they were 11-5, won their first division championship since '66, and made the playoffs for the first time since '74; 1981, when they were 10-6 and made a strong run at Super Bowl XVI; 1988, when they were 12-4, won the AFC East again, and came within 11 points of reaching Super Bowl XXIII; and 1989, when they slipped to 9-7, but still won their third division title of the decade. And the worst of times—1984, when they were the laughingstock of the NFL at 2-14, and 1985, when, after another 2-14 finish, it seemed as if they had fallen off the face of the earth.

In Buffalo, I played for four head coaches and enough defensive coordinators to fill an entire coaching staff. Or two. Or three. Yet my peers still voted me to five Pro Bowls, equaling a Bills record shared only by O. J. Simpson and offensive guard Joe DeLamielleure.

More importantly, I've managed to have a hell of a lot of fun.

A football team is made up of a variety of characters, and humor has a way of bringing everyone together. No matter how bad things are going, there's always something you can laugh about, and I have a pretty good nose for finding it. In the locker room. On the practice field. Even in the huddle on game day. I love to crack jokes in the huddle—providing, of course, I'm still conscious—because that loosens everyone up so they can think more clearly about what they have to do on the next play.

I remember one game in 1988 when Buffalo's great inside linebacker, Shane Conlan, was playing for the first time after missing a couple of games with a foot injury. There's a real disparity between Shane's head, which is huge, and his legs, which are skinny enough to belong to a cheerleader. I mean, the kid is one giant head with little legs coming out from under his chin. So, as we got into our first huddle, I told Shane, "You wouldn't believe how many reporters came up to me this week asking if you were going to play today."

"What did you tell them?"

"I said, 'I'm really not sure if he's going to play or not. But I did see three guys carrying his helmet to practice, if that's any indication.'"

Everyone broke into laughter.

Sometimes we laugh at each other. Sometimes we laugh at ourselves.

One of the first lessons my father taught me while I was growing up in Waltham, Massachusetts, was that I shouldn't take life too seriously.

"If you do," he said, "it'll eat you alive."

I guarantee you, this is one Greek entree that won't ever be served.

TWO

BETWEEN THE LINES

ALTHOUGH WE'RE ONLY INCHES APART on the field, when it comes to our personalities, defensive linemen and offensive linemen might as well be on different planets.

When a defensive lineman walks into someone's house, regardless of how well he knows the person, he kicks off his shoes, puts his smelly feet on the coffee table, and takes control of the clicker for the TV set. He clicks and he clicks until he finds a wrestling match or a horror movie. Then he'll sit there for hours, munching potato chips, sucking down beers, being loud, and generally making a nuisance of himself.

An offensive lineman always wipes his feet before entering anyone's home, including his own. And if he takes his shoes off, you can bet he'll have a pair of slippers to wear. He'll sit quietly on the couch, hands folded in his lap, and say, "Pardon me, would you mind changing the channel? I be-

lieve there's a National Geographic special on tonight."
That's the kind of program offensive linemen love to watch.
And they can't get enough of game shows, such as *Concentration* and *Jeopardy*, that involve a lot of thinking. Their
idea of excitement is thumbing through do-it-yourself home-
improvement books.

Defensive linemen? Give us Freddy Krueger and a few
dismembered bodies and we're happy.

We drive motorcycles, Jeeps, and 4x4 trucks—anything
that can go anywhere and go fast. One of my favorite pastimes
used to be driving my Jeep through creeks and riverbeds. I
wasn't hunting (that's something offensive linemen like to
do), just thrill-seeking. The only drawback was, every so
often the Jeep would sink. I remember, during a midnight
cruise through a creek near Rich Stadium, I hit a patch of
water six feet deep and wound up swimming out of the
driver's seat. On another midnight excursion, through a riv-
erbed, I got stuck so deep in sand, a big truck had to come
and haul me out. Then, it retrieved the Jeep.

The trouble spots are a lot harder to avoid in the dark,
which, of course, is part of the thrill. Anybody can drive in
daylight. And anybody can drive on a road. Creeks and riverbeds make it so much more challenging. So do sidewalks.
One night, I was out with some friends in Boston, and in
the particular neighborhood we were driving through, there
was plenty of light—suffice to say most of it was red. We
noticed quite a few women in ultrashort skirts going up and
down the sidewalks, stopping every so often to "chat" with
men who walked or drove by. Curious to see how fast these
ladies of the evening could move with a Jeep chasing them,
I jumped the curb and started roaring down the sidewalk. I
must say, we were quite impressed with their speed, especially in those high heels.

But our fun was quickly halted by the flashing lights of a
police car.

"What the hell's wrong with you?" the cop demanded.

I stumbled for a few seconds and finally said, "But Officer, we were just doing our part to help clean up the streets of Boston."

He didn't buy it and wrote me a ticket. So much for our impromptu vice raid.

My favorite means of transportation is a motorcycle. Well, not just any motorcycle. I have a Harley-Davidson FXRS Super-Glide. Thirteen hundred and forty cc. Rubber-mounted engine. The ultimate experience on two wheels. People can't help but do a double take when they see a 300-pound guy on a 700-pound motorcycle—especially when the light turns green and he's pulling a wheelie down the street. I just love the freedom I get from driving a bike, whether it's on a city street, down a highway, or through a hotel lobby. Uh, yeah, a hotel lobby. I was at the Pro Bowl in Hawaii, and I'd rented a motorcycle for the week. The AFC squad was staying at a hotel with an open-air lobby, so one day as I was driving back from practice, I decided to take a shortcut to the beach. The suitcases on the floor made for a neat little obstacle course, which I negotiated to perfection. I'm not so sure the bellhops appreciated my maneuvering, though. I couldn't understand what they were yelling, but I don't think it was Hawaiian for "Way to go, Freddy!"

Another time, while making the 500-mile trip from my off-season home in Waltham to Buffalo, I stopped at a Howard Johnson's to grab a bite to eat. I was dressed completely in black: black helmet, black leather jacket, black leather gloves, black leather chaps, black leather boots. I walked inside, and as I pulled off my helmet, revealing a bushy black mustache on a windburned face and black hair going in all directions, everyone looked at me as if they were about to witness a holdup. At first the waitresses wouldn't come within ten feet of my table. When I assured them I was not on the FBI's most-wanted list, I finally got some service. But in case they had any lingering doubts, I was careful to include a side order of quiche along with my cheeseburger and fries.

Once, while I was stopped at a light, a bunch of fellow Harley riders pulled up next to me. Judging by their tattoos and missing teeth, I'd say they definitely were most-wanted material. They looked over and immediately knew who I was. Lucky me.

"Are we glad to see you on a Harley, man," one of them said, sounding relieved. "I'd be really bummed out if someone like you was on a Jap bike."

You have to understand that, to a Harley owner, even the tattooed and toothless variety, a Japanese-made motorcycle is a lower form of life. I'd rather walk than drive one. If a guy on a Yamaha, or worse, a Honda, pulls up next to me, I'll shut my bike off until he leaves. I refuse to let my Harley run in the company of such inferior machines. That's one of my two rules of the road. The other? Never drive my Harley faster than it will go.

Everything offensive linemen drive has four wheels and four doors. They're big on station wagons, vans, any family vehicles you'd expect to find in Mister Rogers's neighborhood. And their speedometers never venture past 55.

Defensive linemen and offensive linemen don't see eye to eye on furniture, either. In my rookie year, my furniture consisted of two black couches with fake fur and little mirrors on them, and my "entertainment center"—a portable TV on a cardboard box. I inherited the couches from one of my teammates, ex-Bills linebacker Shane Nelson, who, in his rookie season two years earlier, inherited them from a veteran teammate, tight end Paul Seymour. Most guests wouldn't sit on them, at least not before putting down a handkerchief or anything else they could find to protect their clothing.

Offensive linemen would never be caught dead with stuff like that. All of their furniture is nicely upholstered, with cloth covers on the armrests and plastic over the sofa and lampshades. If you didn't know better, you'd swear you were in your grandmother's home.

Defensive linemen love to sprawl on the floor, even to eat

their meals. If you ever find yourself knee-deep in empty pizza boxes and Chinese-food containers, odds are you're in the living room of a defensive lineman. Offensive linemen always eat at the table, with linen napkins on their laps and monogrammed place mats under their dishes.

Offensive linemen have the cleanest and most organized lockers in the dressing room. Everything, from jocks to socks, is hung in orderly fashion. Jim Ritcher, the Bills' veteran left guard, keeps a can of Lysol on his top shelf. He sprays his locker once a day—twice if he knows a defensive lineman has been within five feet of his personal belongings.

If you're brave enough to stick your head into a defensive lineman's locker, you never know what you'll find. A mouse used to hang out in mine, but he didn't stay very long. There was stuff in there even *he* wouldn't eat. A few seasons back— during the one time in my eleven-year career that I cleaned it—I found about fifty pairs of football shoes (some didn't even belong to me), ten T-shirts, ten pairs of shorts, all sorts of unopened mail, an uncashed per diem check from a training camp two years earlier, twenty pencils, countless photographs, all kinds of wrappers, old and yellow newspapers, and even older and yellower socks.

I had about seven different lockers with the Bills. I did so much traveling in that dressing room, I should have qualified for a free airline ticket. Ironically, I spent the last two and a half seasons in the same area as the offensive linemen. I suppose it wouldn't shock you to learn they tried pretty hard to evict me. I showed up for a meeting one morning and found my locker had been "quarantined." Using athletic tape, the offensive linemen had made a huge X in front of it and hung signs all around it that said "Warning! Do Not Enter" and "Caution! This Area Is Hazardous to Your Health." They went as far as to relocate all of my stuff. One time I found it piled in the middle of the floor. Another time, I found it in an unused locker at the other end of the dressing room.

Would I take the hint? Never. If anything, they made me

even more determined to stay and bring down the value of their "property."

When you consider the differences in our jobs, the differences in our personalities are understandable.

Defensive linemen get in the huddle and say things like, "Rip off his arms! Tear off his head! Make him wish his mother and father never met!" We want to do everything we can to leave the field as quickly as possible. All we want to do is break in, kick some ass, get out, and get some rest. As a rule, we aren't the kind of guys most girls would want to bring home to mom and dad. That is, unless home happens to be a prison and mom and dad are doing twenty years to life.

Offensive linemen are clean-cut and clean-shaven. They get in the huddle and say, "Okay, guys, let's put together a nice, twelve-play drive, eat up the clock, and try and score." Before the game, they draw up these neat little X's and O's, along with all sorts of lines and arrows. Then they snicker and say, "Boy, are we ever going to trick those guys today." Everything offensive linemen do is diagrammed precisely. They don't go to the bathroom without first consulting their playbooks.

We defensive linemen have our little techniques and strategies, too. But most of the time, we play it off the cuff. And we sure as hell don't need to be told what to do when we get to the man with the football. We want to search and destroy, splatter and trample, rape and pillage. After that, we *really* get nasty.

Generally, offensive linemen don't have as much God-given athletic ability as defensive linemen, or for that matter anyone else on the team. (I guess that means I've been on the wrong side of the ball all these years.) Because of that, they tend to be the biggest overachievers in the world. They lift the most, run the farthest, practice the hardest, study the longest. They measure their advantages in unbelievably minute terms. They'll say, "Now, if I eat one-tenth less fat than my opponent, I'll have that much of an edge on the field."

Whereas a defensive lineman will say, "If I can break the quarterback's leg, he'll be a lot easier to catch."

No players on the team are more self-made than offensive linemen. They have to be. In addition to compensating for whatever they might lack athletically, they're also trying to master one of the more difficult positions in the game. After all, it takes time to learn how to hold without being caught.

The trickery offensive linemen use doesn't stop with X's and O's. They wear jerseys that are fourteen sizes too small so defensive linemen have nothing to grab. And if that isn't enough, they put two-way tape on their shoulder pads so the fabric molds right around them. And if *that* isn't enough, they spray the upper part of their jerseys with silicone or coat them with Vaseline. You try and grab them, and it's like having a 300-pound wet bar of soap squirt through your fingers.

Among the first things rookie defensive linemen learn is that veteran offensive linemen are part octopus. Because the officials don't watch interior-line play as closely as everything else on the field, they only see a fraction of the rampant holding that goes on. For one thing, there are too many bodies in the way. For another, things are happening too fast for their slow-motion eyes to follow. Experienced offensive linemen know how to get away with holding; that's how they survived long enough to become experienced. When they engage you, they try and grab you between the armpits, rather than outside the shoulders where their hands would be more visible. Then they try and pull you in as tight as possible, so the officials won't see the clumps of your jersey in their fists. At the same time, defensive linemen use their hands and arms to try and separate themselves from offensive linemen. By creating that distance, offensive linemen are forced to reach and, you hope, stretch your jersey far enough so the penalty becomes too obvious for the zebras to miss.

Most of the time, though, your shirt has to be practically torn off before a flag will drop. I remember a game against

San Diego a few years back when my jersey was just about gone. I turned to the ref and said, "Do you think I had it custom-made like this, or is it possible someone has been holding me today?" He gave the usual response: "I didn't see it."

"Well, maybe the next time you'll hear it," I said. "Because I'm sure everyone else in the stadium has heard something go riiiiiip!"

Centers always try and do things to pull nose tackles off-sides, taking advantage of the fact they have complete control of our trigger—the football. They'll give it a little squeeze. Or they'll nudge it forward, just a hair. Or they'll twist it, ever so slightly. If I take the bait, the only thing the officials see is me flying out of my stance before everyone else. The next thing that flies is a yellow flag, which is followed by the referee's turning on his wireless microphone, clearing his throat, and telling the entire world: "Offsides, number seventy-six, defense . . ." God, I hate those wireless mikes. In one of my early seasons, I must have jumped prematurely twenty times. I think it's an NFL record, although I've never bothered to check.

And I don't think I ever will.

Another trick centers use to get the upper hand is drawing you into friendly conversation before the snap. That's probably the toughest one for me to avoid, because I'm a pretty talkative guy. As long as someone's cordial to me, I'll be cordial in return. The only problem is, in the middle of a game, it can become a real distraction. I learned that the hard way a long time ago. We were playing the Los Angeles Rams, and the first time they had the ball, their former standout center, Rich Saul, said, "Hi, Fred, how ya doin'?"

"Pretty, good, Rich," I said. "How 'bout yourself?"

"Great. Boy, are you playing well this year."

"Gee, Rich, that's really—"

And before I could get the rest of the sentence out, choonk, he snapped the ball. I wasn't ready for it. I mean, I thought the guy was my best buddy, and the next thing I knew, the ball was gone and Rich was blocking the hell out of me.

Of course, there aren't any rules against that sort of distraction. But Ken Mendenhall, a former center for the then-Baltimore Colts, certainly was in the wrong when he would bark signals at the line of scrimmage, right along with the quarterback. The quarterback's cadence alone is tough enough to follow without letting it pull you offsides. But there would be Mendenhall yelling, "Hut! *Hut! Hut!*" directly into my face at the same time the quarterback yelled it above us. Once again, the ref was a big help.

"Didn't hear a thing," he said.

"You mean to tell me you didn't hear him yelling in my face? What do you think, the quarterback's a ventriloquist or something?"

The ref didn't answer. Not that it made much difference, because Mendenhall was a far better signal-caller than center.

Unfortunately, I haven't had the luxury of facing Ken Mendenhall every week since. In eleven years, I've faced some of the best centers in the league—guys who block with the tenacity of defensive linemen.

For instance, in my first NFL game, the Bills' 1979 preseason opener against the Pittsburgh Steelers, the man across from me was none other than Mike Webster. My first NFL game, and I'm taking on a guy who already had three Super Bowl rings, was six months away from getting his fourth, and was coming off the first of eight consecutive Pro Bowl seasons. I mean, Webby was a rookie when I was still in high school. My buddies and me used to marvel over the way those thick arms of his would bulge from under the rolled-up sleeves of his jersey. He barely stood 6'2" and weighed 260 pounds, but he just had so much power and knew how to get that all-important leverage on his opponent. So you could understand why my white pants almost turned brown before I stepped onto the field. I just knew I was going to get beat so bad, even my parents weren't going to like me anymore.

At the time, I was still struggling with the transition from defensive end, which I played in my final two years of college, to nose tackle, which I knew nothing about. I was just relying on brute strength and raw talent. But I didn't do nearly as badly as I expected. If I saw the film of that game today, I'd probably think I looked like Bozo the Clown. Back then, however, it did wonders for my confidence.

The following year, Webby and I were Pro Bowl teammates in Honolulu. Besides those huge arms, I noticed when I saw him on the beach one day without shoes and socks that he had the largest toes I'd ever seen. He looked like a muscular Barney Rubble. But Webby was hardly a caveman where his game was concerned. He was really ahead of his time. Before most teams switched from the 4-3 to the 3-4 defense and centers began facing nose men on a regular basis, he already had the strength, quickness, and know-how to adjust to everything that came his way. That's why he was still playing in the '89 season, his sixteenth in the NFL, for the Kansas City Chiefs. Incredible!

At one time during my career, the AFC East was home to some of the premier offensive linemen in the NFL. Because we faced each division team twice a season, I could count on feeling as if I had played two games in one for at least half of our schedule. Never was that truer than after spending a day on the field with New England Patriots guard John Hannah. Like Webster, he's a shoo-in for the Pro Football Hall of Fame. But it'll be interesting to see what they do about making his bust; given the size of Hannah's head, it's going to require more bronze than the Free World has to offer. And even if it does get made, the Hall is going to have to build a separate wing to display it.

The first time I saw John in a game, I thought I was on the set of a science-fiction movie. It looked as if someone had taken his helmet, filled it with wax, and placed it in the middle of his shoulders. Without the helmet, his head looked like a giant hunk of flesh with eyes. And on the field, Hannah sounded every bit as frightening as he looked. When he pulled out to block on a running play, you could actually hear him coming. He'd snort (thus his nickname, "Hog") and

growl, getting louder as he got closer: "ArrrrrrRRRRRRGH!"
And when he lowered that big coconut of his, defenders in
his path would just explode and go flying in every direction.
It should have been registered as a lethal weapon.

Early in our careers, Jim Haslett, a former inside linebacker
for the Bills and my off-field partner in crime, and I were
designated "choppers" on the field-goal defense team. Our
job was to chop down the protection, while Sherman White,
our 6'5" defensive end, jumped over the top of us and tried
for the block. One time, we both happened to crash down
on one of Hannah's knees. He was furious. "You son of a
bitches! You bastards! That's my bad knee you hit!" he
screamed. Figuring he was just trying to intimidate us—and
being a couple of young punks who thought we were real
tough—we ignored him and didn't give his outburst another
thought. But when Hannah came to the line for another field-
goal attempt, his face was beet red and steam was blasting
from his nostrils. Never able to recognize danger when we
saw it, Haz and I tried chopping him again. This time, as we
began to dive, Hannah wound up with both of his giant
forearms and fired them into our facemasks, denting each
one. It took about a minute or two for us to find our way
back to the sidelines.

After about a half hour, we remembered our names.

The AFC East was also home to some great centers. One
of the very best in the game today is the Bills' Kent Hull.
And I'm not saying that just because we were teammates. I
faced the guy every day in practice from 1986, when he came
to Buffalo from the USFL, to 1989—I was lucky to have
anything left by Sunday.

Kent stands 6'5" and weighs 275 pounds. But when he
joined the Bills, he was a lot closer to 260. The first time I
saw him, I thought he was a tall, slender tight end. When I
found out he had been an all-USFL center, I said, Oh, yeah?
I'm going to give him a welcome to the NFL he's never going
to forget.

During my initial practice against him in training camp, I

threw a double-fisted punch at his facemask that was so hard, I lifted him right off the ground. Most guys would have crumbled the instant contact was made, but Hull kept his balance and kept pushing. I thought, this kid's not bad. I'd better use some technique on him. So the next time, I jammed him in the plates of his chest and locked him out, but he kept moving, kept giving me trouble. Then, on a pass rush, he locked me out. After a while, I said, this guy's got something.

Not only is he tough, but he's gutsy. Since his first NFL season he has made himself bigger and stronger and has become more comfortable with everything he does. Now, he is an absolute terror. Besides having a very quick first step, Kent has great leg-strength and body-lean, which allows him to maintain balance. The fact he has been twice voted to the Pro Bowl speaks volumes, because a lot of NFL players resent USFL refugees. They had to be really impressed to put his name on their ballots.

Kent is known among his football playing friends as "Montana Mare." The nickname came from one of his former General teammates, quarterback Gene Bradley, also an ex-Bill. Gene was a tobacco chewing country boy from Arkansas who had all sorts of little lines like, "You're about as useful as a one-legged man in an ass-kicking contest." One day Bradley was watching from the sidelines as Kent snapped to another Generals quarterback, Doug Flutie. And when he saw Kent's butt come chin-high to the 5'10" Flutie, Bradley cracked, "Flutie looks like a fly on the ass of a Montana Mare."

My all-time nemesis was Joe Fields of the New York Jets. I called him the master of the half inch. If he was able to get that half inch on you off the snap, he'd work his hips around, feel the way you were moving, and just throw you the other. In his prime direction, Joe was a magician—the craftiest guy in football and best undetectable holder in the league.

I'll never forget my first confrontation with him in my rookie year. I looked at him before the game, and he was wearing his jersey real tight. But even at that, his arms looked as if they'd been stolen from Woody Allen. He just wasn't very big (6'2", 250 pounds) and he had kind of a baby face. Being a lot bigger and stronger, I said to myself, "I'm going to kill this guy. He doesn't have a prayer against me."

Famous last words. From the opening snap, I couldn't get near Fields, yet he was all over me. He was like a piece of flypaper—on my hip, my back, my shoulders. I just couldn't figure out his style. I couldn't lay a glove on him to save my life. At one point, he yelled, "I'm still here, you son of a bitch!" I became more frustrated with each play until, finally, I threw a punch at him. What did he do? He swung right back. The next thing I knew, we were both down in the mud of Shea Stadium, going after each other like a couple of wild dogs. Talk about your great deceptions! The guy may have looked like a poodle, but he played like a pit bull.

Before he tore up his knee a few years ago, Dwight Stephenson of the Miami Dolphins was the best center in modern-day football. He was the first guy who actually forced me to get away from my street-fighting approach by developing the technique of holding the ball way out in front of him and after the snap leaping from side to side instead of going head-up with me. Even if you beat Stephenson on the snap count, you still had extra distance to cover because of his long, long arms. And he was so fast, he'd use my momentum against me, throwing me to whichever side I was going so I would take myself out of the play. That made it especially important for me to get my hands on him as quickly as I could. The only way to counter his style was to keep him from moving laterally.

I had some of my better games against Stephenson, but they came in the latter portion of my career. When he first came into the league, no one knew too much about him. I didn't have the slightest idea how to play him, and in his first start against Buffalo he just kicked my ass all over the field. As we watched film of the game the next day, Chuck Knox, our head coach at the time, came up to me and said,

"Jesus Christ, Smerlas! You let that Stephenson guy block you like that? He couldn't block my grandmother."

"God, Chuck," I said. "I'd sure as hell hate to meet your grandmother."

Stephenson was one of the two all-time great centers I faced when we played the Dolphins. The other was Jim Langer, who is now in the Hall of Fame. His last year with the Dolphins was my rookie season. Langer was about Fields's size, being another smallish center who flourished when there were hardly any grizzly bears like me at nose tackle. But Langer could beat you with his tremendous quickness and played a major role on those dominant Dolphins teams of the 1970s.

Another memorable AFC East center was Pete Brock, formerly of the Patriots. Nothing fancy about him. Peter just came off the ball low and tried to kill you. On the opening play of our first game against each other, he hit me so hard he broke my facemask. I got up and it felt as if I were dreaming—as if I were having an out-of-body experience. I shook my head and thought, Oh, my God! The first play of the game and I'm already half knocked out? This has got to be a nightmare. I know, when I wake up, everything will be okay.

Much to my chagrin, when I finally came to my senses, Brock was still there, looking to break another piece of my equipment. And when it came to trying to break my concentration before the snap, Peter had a style all his own. There we were, our nose hairs almost touching, and he'd be winking and puckering his lips as if he wanted to kiss me. Seeing a big lug like that winking and puckering, it was all I could do not to fall down laughing and get an offsides penalty.

Most exchanges during a game aren't so friendly, however. Linemen will say anything to get into each other's head. You'll hear insults about your mother, your wife, your sister, your dog, your cat, your goldfish—any subject the other guy thinks will strike a nerve. If you don't get rattled right off the bat and are able to maintain your aggressiveness, the conversation dies right down. But if you make it obvious he's gotten the better of you with that crack about one of your female relatives and a fire hydrant, you'll get a dissertation for the rest of the game.

I've gotten my share. I've given my share.

Chris Ward, a former tackle for the Jets, thought he was really going to get Haz and me to tremble when we faced him as rookies. We had chopped him two or three times on field-goal defense, and he was becoming increasingly annoyed with us. Not so much because of the chopping, but because in addition, Haz kept poking him in the eyes and punching him in the stomach. After one chop/poke/punch too many, Ward snapped.

"I'm going to get a knife and stab you guys," he said. "When I get off this field, I'm going to grab a knife and stab you."

Once again, we weren't impressed.

On the Jets' next field-goal attempt, we grabbed his ankles and buried him.

This time, Ward really lost it.

"After this game's over, I'm going to drive up to Buffalo and kill both of you guys," he yelled from the ground. "I'm going to stab you when you're not looking."

Ward never made the trip. I never became Greek shish kebab.

I went completely off the deep end myself while getting the better of Green Bay Packers' guard Ron Hallstrom in a 1988 game. At one point, I followed him all the way back to his huddle, growling and snorting and screaming a few choice words not suitable for printing in this or any other book. I was so out of control, the referee finally said, "Calm down, Smerlas. Please, calm down." I pretended not to hear him and kept yelling and screaming at Hallstrom, who by that time was looking at me like I'd just climbed out of the laboratory of a mad scientist. Finally, the ref turned to Art Still, the Bills' free-spirited left end in 1988 and 1989 and said, "Would you tell him to shut up?"

"I'm sorry, Mr. Official, sir," Arthur said. "But I think Fred

had a little too much coffee this morning. I've been trying
to get him to switch to decaf, but as you can see, he isn't the
easiest guy to talk to."

That can also apply to when I'm on the receiving end of
defensive signals. Before each snap, one of our inside linebackers is supposed to relay the calls that are signaled to
him from the sidelines. The terminology is pretty basic: Rose
and Rip refer to different assignments on the right side, Lou
and Liz refer to different assignments on the left. The linebacker has the leeway to change the call, depending on what
happens on the other side of the line. But I can think of one
time when I wished that weren't the case. Ray Bentley, our
defensive signal-caller, kept noticing formation adjustments
and switching our defense accordingly. First he yelled,
"Rip!" That meant, as soon as the ball was snapped, I would
step to my right on a stunt. Then he yelled, "Liz!" Now I'd
be stepping to my left. A couple of seconds later, he made
it a "Rip" call again. He kept going back and forth like that:
"Liz! Rip! Liz! Rip!"

Finally, enough was enough. I turned around and
screamed, "What the hell's wrong with you, Ray? Make
up your mind!" The ball was snapped, and I was certain, any minute, Liz and Rip Taylor would come charging
onto the field to help us make the tackle. Well, maybe Liz
would make the tackle. Rip would be there to throw the
confetti.

Among my chores during a game is calling signals at the
line. Being in the middle, I have the best vantage point to
see how the offensive line is positioned and anticipate how
it's going to block, which I then relay to the ends. I make
up my own terminology, based on a person's physical and
psychological makeup. I used Figment, Earring, and King to
identify Arthur; Chicken Wings, McDonald's, and Reindeer
for Bruce Smith, Buffalo's All World right end.

Figment is from a bizarre conversation I had with Arthur
at our '88 training camp. We were practicing, and I turned
to him and said, "Hey, Arthur . . ." He wouldn't answer me.

So I kept yelling, "Arthur! Arthur! What the hell's wrong with you?"

"Arthur's not here today," he finally said. "He's back at the dorm, sleeping. I'm just a figment of your imagination."

For the rest of the day, I had to call him *Figment* to make him respond to me. *Earring* and *Ponytail* are from a Pro Bowl we were in together when he played for Kansas City. In those days, Arthur wore a pair of earrings and a ponytail. *King*, of course, is for King Arthur—except in this case the Round Table is located on Mars.

Fried chicken wings, smothered in hot sauce, are the spicy Buffalo delicacy that Bruce consumes in mass quantities, along with just about everything McDonald's has to offer. *Reindeer?* A few years ago, Bruce totaled his Mercedes when, during the middle of the night, he skidded off a highway to avoid what he said looked like a reindeer. I guess he figured his $60,000 car was a small sacrifice to be sure Santa Claus could make his rounds on Christmas Eve.

I refer to myself as Oregano, the Greek spice. I think that speaks for itself.

Here's an example of how it worked with the Bills. When I said, "Chicken Wings," that meant I wanted Bruce to go to his left and crash down on the opponent's left guard, while I went behind him to my right and covered the end. If I said, "Chicken Wings, Oregano," that meant I was going toward the left guard and Bruce was coming behind me to cover the middle. We had a lot of fun with it, and because we did, it made it that much easier to remember. Besides, all of that talk about food could be a real distraction for offensive linemen. You know how those hogs love to eat. Sometimes it was so bad, we'd strap saliva buckets around their necks so we didn't get flooded off the field.

Talking with the opposition can be an effective way of establishing ground rules when you go against notoriously dirty players. With all of the videotape we watch, we know well in advance how much of that sort of thing we're going to see in a given game. Sure, there are penalties and officials to keep everything honest. But if someone's made up his mind he's going to take a shot at your knees, he won't be stopped by the fear of having a little yellow flag thrown at him. He needs a far greater consequence to ponder. So, when we face a team with a dirty offensive lineman or two, those of us on the defensive line clear things up right from the start—just as Bruce Smith did one time against Chicago. Tom Thayer, the Bears' right guard, is among the dirtier SOBs in the league. He always goes for the legs, trying to hurt you with cut-blocks and legwhips and any other low-down tactic he can think of. He isn't satisfied with taking you out of the play; he wants to take you out of the game. Which was why, as we got to the line for the first snap, Bruce said, "Okay, Thayer, what's it going to be today? You want to play it your way, we can play it that way, too. But if you plan to take anybody's knees out, you'd better not miss. Because after that, it's going to be open season on your knees." Thayer got the message and played it pretty clean that day. If he hadn't, I was prepared to throw some hot sauce on his legs, and tell Bruce it was time for lunch.

At one time, the Patriots were among the dirtier teams around. Their offensive linemen would dive for your legs on cut-blocks, and if they missed, they'd start rolling and try to knock you down that way. Quite often they'd take out some of their own guys and even hurt them in the process. Teams like Denver, Seattle, Cincinnati, Chicago, and Green Bay are known for frequent cut-blocking.

We're not talking about your typical day at the office here. When we report to work, we're looking to beat our opponent through any means possible—physical or mental. If someone wants to get an edge at the office, all he has to do is tear up the other guy's copy of the *Wall Street Journal*. On the football field, what you tear up may consist of living tissue.

There wasn't a team that worked harder at trying to gain that edge than the Raiders. Everyone knows about the criminal element they had playing defense, but they also had some pretty intimidating people on their offensive line. My

first encounter with them came as a rookie, and was that
ever an education. Their center, Dave Dalby, welcomed me
to the NFL by punching me in the chin on each of the first
five plays of the game. He was just out of his mind. (Luckily,
it wasn't long before he punched himself out, and I had an
easier time with him as the game progressed.) A short while
later, Gene Upshaw, the Raiders' Hall of Fame guard, cut-
blocked me on the side of my legs while they were planted
and the most vulnerable to injury.

"What the hell was that for?" I snapped. "You trying to
end my career before it starts?"

Upshaw just shrugged, as if to say, "This is the NFL kid.
Your Boston College days are over." Maybe that's why he
wore padding on every inch of his body, including his fingernails.

Another Hall of Famer, Art Shell, who became the NFL's
first black head coach when he took over the Raiders in 1989,
was playing tackle in the same game. The first time he parked
his 6'5", 285-pound frame in front of me, I swore I was wit-
nessing an eclipse. All I saw was a giant silver-and-black
shadow.

One of the game's foremost intimidators, of course, was
my ex-teammate Conrad Dobler. Although he spent his ten-
year career at offensive guard, Connie truly played with a
defensive lineman's mentality. In fact, I don't know if there
has ever been a defensive lineman as despicable as the man
who wore the label "dirtiest player in professional football"
with pride. He was nasty before anyone knew what nasty
was—the classic example of a guy who would do anything
to beat his opponent, whose entire game was based on sur-
vival. He'd kick, punch, poke, bite. You name it, Conrad did
it. And he didn't just do it in games. There were more than
a few practices in the two seasons he spent as Buffalo's right
guard (1980 and 1981) when he tried those tactics on me.
Of course, by that time he was at the end of his career and
his legs were pretty well shot. Being in my second and third
seasons, I had enough quickness to stay away from him most

of the time. It almost became a joke. He'd be yelling, "You son-of-a-bitchin' Greek! I'll kick your ass! I'll tear your heart out!"

"Yeah," I said, "but you've got to catch me first." Most of the time, he couldn't.

He did, however, catch another of our nose tackles, Charlie Davis. Charlie and Conrad had been teammates in St. Louis, where Connie began his reign of terror in the NFL. During the first practice of their first training camp together in Buffalo, Charlie started to beat Conrad to the outside on a pass rush, and just as Charlie was getting past him, Conrad jumped and gave him a swift kick to the instep, sending Charlie flying to the ground.

"Goddamn you, Conrad!" Charlie yelled. "Now, don't be starting that crap here. I thought we left that in St. Louis."

Conrad just smiled and walked back to the huddle. Charlie got up and got in his stance for the next play. Once again, it was a pass. Once again, he started beating Conrad to the outside. Once again, Conrad gave him a kick and put him on the ground. This time, Charlie tore after him, and during their brief scuffle, I thought to myself, You would think someone who had been Conrad's teammate before would know better than to think the man was actually going to change his style just because he changed uniforms.

During another training-camp practice, a rookie defensive end named Darrell Irvin jammed Connie real hard and got around him without any problem. Conrad stormed back to the huddle, his eyes bugging out of his facemask, and you just knew, somehow, he was going to get back at the kid for making him look bad. Sure enough, on the next play, he jammed his thumb into Darrell's esophagus and, when Darrell raised his arms to protect his throat, Conrad fired a punch into his solar plexus. Poor Darrell was on the ground gasping for air, and for a moment we all thought he was dead. It took a good fifteen minutes before he got up.

Connie injured his share of opponents, but he also did quite a bit of damage to his own body. All of those legwhips he threw—planting with one foot while swinging the other around his back and smashing it into the legs of a pass rusher—were more crippling to him than they were to the other guy. By the time he got to Buffalo, his knees and ankles were destroyed by all of the dirty deeds he had performed in St. Louis and New Orleans. And in the final two seasons of his career, every official in the league kept an extraclose watch on him. He couldn't resort to any of his tactics without being penalized, and he was too broken down physically to play it straight. He had no choice but to retire.

Joe Devlin, who ended a thirteen-year career with the Bills after the '89 season, was another example of an offensive lineman with the killer instinct usually found on the other side of the ball. He wasn't dirty, far from it. But he was a master at the art of intimidation. I know almost everyone in our dressing room feared him, including yours truly. Joe's not the type of person to say idly, "I'll kill you." If he says it, you'd better reserve a cemetery plot.

I'll never forget the first time I met Joe. He had the look of death in his eyes—the kind of look a shark gives its next meal. I had noticed that everyone kind of avoided him, that he sat alone at his own table during meals, that he hardly ever spoke. And the better I got to know him, the better I understood why everyone avoided him. Here's a guy whose idea of a vacation is sitting in a tree for three days waiting to kill an animal. How serious is Joe about hunting? Not only does he wear camouflage on his hat, jacket, and pants, he also has camouflage paint on his face. One time, he made a citizen's arrest, escorting some other hunters at gunpoint to a ranger's station because they had broken the law by using the wrong kind of weapon during deer season. Not that the deer were any safer; Joe can hear them breathing from a mile away.

For as long as I've known him, he has worn a black string around each wrist. Early in my career, I asked him why. He didn't answer. He just gave me those shark eyes.

"Well," I said to myself, "maybe I'll ask him another time, when I get to know him better."

I've known Joe for eleven years. I still don't have the answer.

His house is in the middle of the woods, and the driveway is a mile long. When I visit him, I make sure he knows it's me and not some stranger whose head might look good over his fireplace. I start honking my horn and yelling, "Don't shoot, Joe! It's Freddy, Joe! We used to be teammates. Remember?" Devlin likes his privacy so much, he wants to make "targets" out of trespassers. That's why, all the way down the driveway, you see only one postage-stamp-sized sign to warn away would-be intruders. But he does have a soft side. I've never seen a parent show a child as much affection as Joe shows his son, Troy. He treats him like a gem.

At thirty-six, Joe's still one of the strongest and best-conditioned athletes around. Staying in shape isn't simply part of his job; it's a way of life. Just before our '89 training camp, he and one of Buffalo's fullbacks, Jamie Mueller, whose nickname is Norman (as in Norman Bates of *Psycho* fame), wore harnesses attached to their Jeeps and pulled them across Joe's sprawling property. They'd do that a few times in the morning, lift weights until lunchtime, and spend the afternoon pushing their Jeeps. In a 1983 preseason game against Detroit, Joe suffered a broken ankle that sidelined him for the rest of the year. The trainers gave him a rehabilitation program to follow, and Joe threw it away. He had his own program. Once his cast came off, he woke up at five o'clock every morning, ate breakfast, packed a lunch, and spent the entire day walking through the woods. He walked for miles and miles, usually not getting home until dark. The following season, he was back at full strength.

Joe rarely lost his cool on the field. If you took a cheap shot at him, he didn't start ranting and raving. He'd just study your body, quietly figuring out how he was going to retaliate on the next play. He'd look at your stomach, your throat, your elbows, your knees, and zero in on the spot or spots he was going to attack. So, on the next play, you'd make a move on him and *boom*, Joe'd punch you in the stomach. You'd start yelling and screaming and calling him every name in the book. And he'd just turn around and walk back to the huddle. On the next play, you'd still be talking to him, and after the ball was snapped, *bang*, he'd punch you in the throat. This would keep up until you'd finally say to yourself, "I'm not dealing with a normal guy here. I thought I intimidated him, and he just put me in the hospital."

For all that is uncommon between defensive and offensive linemen, the one thing we share is the place we work. It's called The Pits. Now, I'm not sure if that's another way of saying *line of scrimmage*, or a very accurate description of what it's like to play there. Think about it. You're taking the largest and strongest players from both teams, putting us in a confined area, and telling us to spend an hour or so beating each other's brains out.

Everyone else gets to operate in space. Quarterbacks have the pocket. Running backs have holes. Receivers have pass routes. Linebackers and defensive backs have areas of the field to cover. Linemen? We may flip-flop and change assignments every now and then, but it always comes down to hitting, hitting, and more hitting—the entire game. There isn't a more violent place on the field. And there isn't another place that has a greater influence on the final score.

The next time you're at a football game, try, for a moment, to unglue your eyes from the quarterback. Do the same with the halfback, fullback, and wide receivers. Never mind the linebackers, forget about the safeties, ignore the cornerbacks.

For once, just once, focus on The Pits. You won't see anything flashy. You won't see anything pretty. You won't, depending on your angle, see anything, except a pile of tangled bodies.

But you will see where the *real* football is played.

CHAPTER

THREE

THE HEAD OF THE BEAST

IF THE NOSE tackle is football's ultimate grunt, the quarterback is its ultimate VIP. He is *the* playmaker; I'm the guy who does things so others can make the plays. He hands the ball off and starts clapping and jumping and signaling for the first down or the touchdown; I'm at the bottom of the pile, staring at insects and hoping I can still walk when everyone finally gets off. His face and physique inspired the creation of Barbie's boyfriend, Ken; I can't nap at picnics because I'm afraid someone might mistake me for a beer keg and I'll wake up with a tap sticking out of my skull.

But I don't begrudge him for all of his glory or the fact he picks up his paycheck in an armored truck. He should be the highest-paid guy on the field, because, for all of his accolades, there's just as much criticism—if not more. No one is under greater stress, including the head coach. The field is the quarterback's Oval Office.

I have a lot of respect for the ones who've been able to keep their minds and bodies intact long enough for their careers to be measured in double digits. There is something special about them, something that goes well beyond the ability to throw a football.

They also have enough money to pay off the national debt.

But given the fact we're conditioned to see them with bull's-eyes on their chests, it is only natural for a little tension to exist between defensive linemen and quarterbacks. That goes for teammates, as well. During training-camp practices, they wear red vests that are supposed to remind everyone on defense, "Look, but don't even think about touching!" Coaches tell us to get off the line as quickly as possible, rush full speed, then pull up at the last moment to avoid hitting the Golden Child. Talk about frustration. That's like telling a kid to run as fast as he can toward a big pile of candy, but just before he gets there, he must veer toward a heaping plate of spinach.

Sometimes, quarterbacks believe so strongly in the protective power of those vests, they'll go through practice with their chin straps unbuckled. They'll also convince themselves the 300-pound maniacs screaming past them, without delivering so much as a nudge, are invisible. On top of that, when they complete a few passes, they'll act as if they've done something special, as if they've just won the Super Bowl. Who couldn't make a completion under those conditions? So, every once in a while in practice, my make-believe arm will *accidentally* connect with the quarterback's real-live helmet.

It's just my way of saying, "Wake up and smell the nose tackle."

Frank Reich, the Bills' No. 2 man behind Jim Kelly, has a tendency to leave his chin strap unbuckled in camp drills. I like Frank a lot; we're good friends. But one time, I simply couldn't resist the temptation of knocking his helmet off. Frank's eyes popped out as he watched his helmet rolling on the grass. He grabbed for his neck to make sure his head was still attached.

"What the hell are you trying to do, Fred, decapitate me?" he yelled.

"Buckle your chin strap and maybe it won't happen the next time," I said with a wry smile.

Even when you're trying, it isn't always easy to pull up at the last moment. Once in a while, the quarterback gets knocked to the ground. Hard. And boy, does that ever piss off the head coach. When that happened, Marv Levy, who was normally pretty reserved, started freaking out as if someone had committed murder right before his eyes. But if, while I was rushing the passer, someone smashed into my knee and I was on the ground writhing in pain, the only thing you'd hear would be, "Okay, men, let's move over to the next drill. And please be careful not to trip over Fred. I wouldn't want any of you to get hurt."

After practice, I stagger into the dressing room. I'm hot, tired, sore, muddied, and bloodied. The quarterbacks? They swagger in looking just as neat coming off the field as they do going on. It's kind of hard to get dirty when all you have to do is stand back and throw without ever having to worry about getting knocked on your ass. Even kickers work up more of a sweat.

Walking out of the dressing room, the quarterbacks are on their toes, with their legs together and shoulders back, as if they've just bench-pressed 500 pounds. Young women come rushing over for autographs and you hear a quarterback, in the deepest voice he has, say, "Did you see me throw that ball today, baby?"

During a game, there isn't anyone I hate more than the opposing QB. And that includes the farm animals on the other side of the ball. As far as I'm concerned, the QB's sole purpose in life is to make me suffer. If the temperature's 115° above, he is trying to keep me out there until the plastic from my helmet starts dripping onto my shoulder pads. If it's 20° below, he tries to keep me out there until ice forms an eye shield over the top of my facemask. If you're getting tired, he's throwing screen passes that force you to turn around and chase the back. You're dying to get off the field, and he keeps getting first downs.

With every completed pass or big run, he becomes more and more confident. So much of his game involves thinking, and when he feels good about himself, his thoughts are crystal clear. He's executing the right plays, making the right reads, calling the right audibles. And worst of all for a nose tackle, while barking signals directly over your head, he's comfortable enough to vary his cadence and draw you offsides. He'll also dip his head a little bit, aiming his voice right at your eardrums. And if he can't get you to jump with his vocal cords, he'll try to do it by subtly rolling his shoulders, moving his elbows, or bending his knees in rhythm with the cadence. Anything to pick up five free yards that the nose man pays for in embarrassment.

Meanwhile, the offensive linemen see all of this success and start getting pretty pumped up themselves. That's a nightmare for defensive linemen, because the more inspired they become, the harder they block. You want those guys as deflated as possible. You want them wishing they were at home, studying for one of their favorite game shows or remodeling the kitchen.

Everything that is ruining your day begins and ends with the quarterback. He is the head of the beast, and if you can kill the head, the body will usually die shortly thereafter. Get in the quarterback's face a few times, knock him around a little, and the rest of the offense will start to collapse. He makes bad reads, he doesn't audible nearly as much. Even a simple handoff becomes a struggle.

The next thing you know, there's an interception. Then a sack. Then a fumble. It's all falling apart, and his cadence is back to being nice and steady, exactly as you like it.

You glance up at his eyes. You can see he's just begging for a place to fall. Why disappoint the man?

I like to think of the quarterbacks I've faced over the past eleven years as being one of three kinds.

First, there are the elite—the ones who are extremely

gifted, physically and/or mentally. Their arms pack power, touch, or both. Their minds have a built-in radar system that allows them to track everything happening on the field, at all times, and consistently make big plays. When they were born, God said, "Thou shalt throw a football and be paid handsomely."

Next, there are the quarterbacks who might not have the best arms around, but who make the very most of whatever physical tools they do possess. These are guys who over-achieve. They get by on sheer toughness and/or sheer intel-ligence, although few pro football players can survive on brains alone. Brains have a way of being knocked out of one's head. And anyone who's an ultrabrainiac is smart enough to choose another line of work anyway.

Finally, there are those I refer to as crumble guys—the ones who are preparing to run for their lives before they even take the snap. Get close enough to them in the backfield, and you can almost see your highlight film flashing from their pupils. Some crumble guys are just plain afraid to take the punishment. Others are more concerned with protecting the millions they stand to lose by suffering an injury than with doing whatever it takes to win. On game day, the only num-bers I want the quarterback on my team thinking about are the ones on the scoreboard, not his paycheck. He'll have plenty of time to deal with the paycheck the next morning, when he and his armed security men show up to collect.

The very first quarterback I ever faced as a pro—outside of teammates in practice—was from that elite group. We opened the preseason of my rookie year against Pittsburgh, and the thought of going against Terry Bradshaw, with his Hall of Fame throwing arm, and the great Mike Webster at center, was enough to make me sweat off about twenty pounds the night before. When I saw them on the field during the pregame warmups, I felt as if I were back in grade school. I was even tempted to ask for their autographs.

"Hi, Mr. Bradshaw," I said, flashing a goofy smile. "It's a real pleasure to meet you, sir."

"Hi, Fred," he said. "Pleasure to meet you, too."

I couldn't believe it. Terry Bradshaw actually knew my name. I just wanted to sit down and ponder that for a while. In fact, I almost felt like sitting out the entire game. That way, if I did manage to get past Webster and his mountain range of muscles, there'd be no chance of my hurting Bradshaw—even accidentally. I remember thinking, how could I ever live with myself if I broke a legend in two? As it turned out, I never made any serious contact with Bradshaw in that game.

But Jim Haslett, our wacky linebacker who was also a rookie at the time, did in our regular-season finale that year at Three Rivers Stadium. I missed the trip because of a knee injury, and I can't say I truly regretted watching the game on TV. Not because we lost, 28–0, but Haslett nearly touched off a riot when he place-kicked Bradshaw's helmet—with his head still inside. Considering Haz is a Pittsburgh native, you would think he'd have shown more respect for a hometown hero. The NFL called him on the carpet for the incident, and he received tons of hate mail from all over the country. Suffice it to say that some of the letters suggested he do a little coffin-shopping.

In 1982, I had the sad experience of seeing Bradshaw at his worst. Having resumed our schedule after going on strike for eight weeks, we beat the Steelers 13–0 at Rich Stadium. Bradshaw, who was one year away from his retirement, completed only 2 of 13 passes for minus 4 yards and had 2 intercepted. I wound up sacking him twice, and although he remained in one piece, I felt kind of lousy afterward. It was like the first time you beat your father at arm wrestling when you know he's trying. For a second, you're really proud of yourself. Then, you wish you never took him on in the first place. You always want to think of your father as being invincible.

That was how I felt about Bradshaw—even when he wasn't wearing his toupee.

Dan Fouts will always be remembered as one of the purest

of the pure passers ever to take an NFL snap. But don't mistake the former Charger for doing it all with finesse. If Foutsy thought you were roughing him up too much, he wouldn't hesitate to return the favor by giving you a punch or a kick. Or maybe he'd whip the ball off your helmet while screaming a few well-chosen words in your face. I sacked him once, and he gave me a forearm in the facemask. It didn't hurt much, certainly not the way one of John Hannah's beefy forearms did. But I was so stunned that a 180-pound quarterback would have the guts to do such a thing to a 300-pound defensive lineman, I couldn't bring myself to use his legs to make a wish.

Dan was also one of the meaner-looking quarterbacks I've ever gone against. With that bushy beard, he reminded me of a mountain man. I could just see him out in the wilderness, with a big coonskin hat on his head, killing bears with a football and eating them—raw.

At the top of my current and perhaps all-time elite list is one of my new 49er teammates, Joe Montana. The first time I faced him was 1980, when we were both second-year players. It was the final game of the regular season, at San Francisco, and we were in an all-or-nothing situation. If we won, we captured the AFC East championship with an 11-5 record. If we lost, we were out of the playoffs, despite being 10-6, because of a screwy tiebreaker. We weren't expecting the 49ers to give us much trouble. At the time, they had yet to establish themselves as supreme beings of the NFL. They were 2-14 in each of their two previous seasons and had gone through an eight-game losing streak earlier that year. While watching them on film, we laughed so hard it was all we could do to stay in our folding chairs. That's how bad the 49ers were back then.

It was raining that day in Candlestick Park, and the field looked in much better condition for a tractor pull than a football game. You'd take a step and a twenty-pound chunk of sod would fly off your shoe and splatter on another part of your body. I'll never forget being covered from head to toe with so much mud. (In fact, every now and then, I still find a speck of it behind my ears.) I'll also never forget the way Montana played. Before the game, everyone had been saying he wasn't a good passer or a good runner or a good quarterback, period. Soon after the opening kickoff, I found myself saying, everyone's right, this guy isn't good at all. He's great! We had the No. 1 defense in the NFL, and Joe was slicing us up as if we had never played before. Not only could he read the defense and throw, he could run, read, and throw simultaneously. And that, more than anything, is what makes him the deadliest quarterback in the league and one of the greatest of all time.

We barely won the game, 18–13, and it wasn't over until the last of Montana's three Hail Mary passes fell harmlessly into a puddle. The 49ers supposedly had nothing to play for; the Bills were shooting for their first division title since 1966 and first playoff berth since 1974. Yet it took everything we had to beat them. And that was purely because of Joe Montana. He was the light bulb being inserted into a socket that had been empty for the better part of seven seasons. You could almost see little signs taped to his fingers that said, "Reserved for Super Bowl ring."

Montana may not have the top physical gifts at his position, but when you look into his eyes, you can almost see the X's and O's on his mental chalkboard. I don't know if there has ever been another quarterback who played the game with better on-field awareness. As he comes to the line, Montana accounts for every single thing going on. He makes an initial read of the defense. He checks to see how close the cornerbacks are to the line. He looks at the linebackers, to see whether they've walked up or are staying back. He puts someone in motion and watches carefully to see how the defense responds. He knows exactly where each of his ten offensive teammates is at all times.

Total concentration, poise, and composure. Every thought geared toward figuring out how to beat the opponent. And after the snap he's still thinking, still reading as he's moving, even with guys like me looking to rearrange those X's and O's in his brain.

Dan Marino, another great passer, is best known for his release. The NFL has never seen a quicker one. And God, is that ever frustrating for a defensive lineman. No matter how clear a path you have into the backfield and no matter how fast you run, he'll almost always get rid of the ball before you can get your hands on him. It's like being one step from the finish line of a marathon, and someone keeps moving the damn string back.

But it isn't always a simple case of his unloading the ball before someone unloads on him. For accuracy and touch, Marino's in a league by himself. I remember, in a 1986 game against the Dolphins, we were playing zone coverage and he was just tearing us to shreds. One time, after I had gotten close enough to feel the breeze of the ball as it left his hand, Marino turned to me and said, "You can't play zone against me. What are you guys thinking about, anyway?"

We stayed in zone the rest of the day. Marino completed a career-high 39 passes for 404 yards and 4 touchdowns. I'd say he was right, wouldn't you?

Besides his release and marksmanship, Marino also has great field vision. He sees so much in such a short time, you wonder if he has bionic eyes. He can see and throw faster than any human being who ever played the game. I compare him to Larry Bird, the greatest basketball player alive and my only sports idol. Like Bird, Marino almost always knows exactly where every pass rusher is coming from. And I've seen him perform incredible, Bird-like feats. Once, two of our guys were bearing down on him from the front, and Marino threw underhanded, underneath their arms, for a 20-yard completion.

Not a throwaway. A completion.

I got so frustrated in one game, I finally turned to him and said, "Dan, what the hell have we got to do to get to you and the ball at the same time?" He just smiled and walked away. Of course, he didn't have to respond. I knew the answer: wait for his retirement.

His last Super Bowl loss notwithstanding, I still think Denver's John Elway has the NFL's foremost cannon for an arm. If he spots a receiver between two defensive backs, with no more than two yards to spare on each side, he'll try to zing the ball in there. Or if he's scrambling and he's near the sidelines, almost out of bounds, he'll wing it in the opposite direction and upfield. I've seen him complete some ungodly passes, the kind you have to replay on your VCR several times before you're convinced you saw what you thought you saw. I've also seen his confidence in that arm get him into trouble, because he will force the ball and throw an interception.

Besides a big arm, Elway also has the biggest teeth I've ever seen. Why, they're so big . . . he has to floss with a rope . . . he picks them with a broomstick . . . his mouth doubles as a drive-in movie screen . . . when he breaks into that Colgate smile, it makes walruses envious. I've never understood how anyone could look so happy 365 days a year. I suppose if my annual income were several million dollars and everybody adored me and referees constantly watched out for my safety, I'd be smiling, too. But it does sort of tick you off. You wonder if he's quietly having a laugh at your expense. And you can't help being reminded he makes more money in interest than you make in salary.

Funny, but I've never seen Elway eat one of the candy bars he passes to his wife in that TV commercial. I'm sure he realizes he doesn't have the time it would take a dentist to put a filling in one of those "Mr. Ed" teeth. He might not even have the cash.

Elway can also give you major headaches with his legs. So do two other members of that elite group—Randall Cunningham of Philadelphia and Don Majkowski of Green Bay.

You need an extra oxygen tank on the sidelines whenever you go against Cunningham. He makes you spend the day running the equivalent of two marathons, only to discover you've been chasing a ghost. He runs a 4.5 forty, which is why when he sees someone like me lumbering after him, he laughs. I go to wrap my arms around him and the next thing

I know, I'm hugging myself. Most quarterbacks run a little, then step up to throw. When Cunningham runs, he usually doesn't plan to stop until he has slipped a half dozen tacklers and is well beyond the first-down marker. And if you're playing man-to-man coverage against him, he's going to have enough room in the secondary to get twenty yards a crack. Cunningham has a great arm to complement his Road Runner feet. My suggestion would be to let it do more of the work.

Take it from a defensive lineman: too much running is hazardous to a quarterback's health.

I was a big Majkowski fan before the rest of the NFL discovered his Majik last season. He's really a cocky guy, but not obnoxious. He showed me the kind of heart he had in our 1988 game against the Packers. We were on the way to a 28–0 victory, yet he hung tough and never showed signs of being rattled even though we sacked him six times and were in his face almost every play. Majik's hometown is Depew, New York, a Buffalo suburb, and after one play, he told me he'd followed my career since he was in elementary school.

"Well, then you know I'm getting a little old," I said. "So why don't you slow down so I can catch your ass?"

Another ultracool character among the great quarterbacks in the game today is Boomer Esiason of Cincinnati. I'll be lined up, ready to explode as soon as the ball's snapped, and Boomer just sort of saunters out of the huddle. He casually takes his place over center, looks down at me, and says, "Hey, Fred, how you doin'? How's the wife? You know, we got you to jump offsides a whole bunch of times last year. Ha! Ha! Let's see if we can go for the record this year. What do you say, Fred?"

And if, per chance, I do jump, he'll give me a little wink and say, "Gotcha!" My eyes are bugged out, foam's coming out of my mouth, and old Boomer is sauntering back to the huddle like nothing ever happened.

He's sort of a cross between Montana and Marino. He's intelligent enough to anticipate what the defense is going to do, like Montana, and he has a fairly quick release, like Marino. When it comes to personality, I don't know if there's another quarterback who plays with Boomer's enthusiasm. His love for the game and being the center of attention just kind of oozes out of him when he's on the field. He has a lot of fun, whereas Montana and Marino pretty much keep their emotions under wraps as they try to kill you. Esiason tries to kill you, too, but he does so with a smile. And the bigger the crowd, the wider the smile. To Boomer, the field has always been like Carnegie Hall.

But when those of us on defense say, "Break a leg," we mean it—literally.

Of course, there are certain quarterbacks who think in terms of breaking the leg of a defender. And whatever they can't accomplish by throwing the ball, they'll accomplish with their toughness. Just by taking a hammer-headed approach to the game, they'll make something happen on the field and more importantly, light a fire under everyone else on offense.

I can't think of too many quarterbacks who have used toughness to their advantage better than Tommy Kramer, who was released by Minnesota after the 1989 season. He wasn't one of those guys whose helmet was blown dry. He was just a slug-it-out, kick-you-in-the-ass kind of player— the type who, on first and ten, would rather run a quarterback sneak than throw. He didn't try to dissect defenses like Wade Wilson, his former Viking teammate. He tried to put his fist through them. Wilson's a computer analyst. Kramer was a street fighter.

As you tried to take Kramer down, he tried to head-butt you. And if you did take him down, he wouldn't wait for you to get off him; he'd push you off. Knock him down a couple more times, he'd get pissed off and start throwing at your nuts.

Jim McMahon is that way, too. When he was with the Bears, I remember a game when, after blowing right past center Jay Hilgenberg, I smashed McMahon as hard as I

could. He still got the pass off, for a completion, as he fell
to the ground. Then, he got up and said, "Nice hit!" and
went about his business. I respected him for that. A lot of
quarterbacks would have said, "Ouch! If you do that again,
I'm going to send my lawyer after you." Mad Mac under-
stands that if he's in a fistfight, he can't all of a sudden stop
and say, "Wait a minute! I'm Jim McMahon. I'm a multi-
million-dollar quarterback. You can't hit *me*."

In Chicago, he was the classic example of a quarterback
whose attitude set the tone for the rest of the team. The Bears
just aren't the Bears with Mike Tomczak at the controls. For
one thing, Tomczak looks like the Karate Kid. When he
comes off the field after a bad pass, I keep expecting Mr.
Miyagi to be on the sidelines, waiting to deliver some com-
forting words of wisdom. Instead, Mr. Ditka is there, waiting
to chew on his face. McMahon just seemed to give that team
so much of the rough-and-tumble personality it doesn't have
anymore. It's not that Tomczak's a bad player; he's just too
gentle looking and acting to provide the kind of ingredient
that is right for the Bears' chemistry—the kind that makes
them explode.

Doug Flutie's lack of height should never be mistaken for
a lack of toughness. Sure, he scrambles away from a lot of
heat. But Flutie's main concern as he darts around the backfield like a waterbug isn't saving his tootie. He's trying to
come up with a big play. After he had slipped through my
fingers about a half dozen times in a 1988 game against New
England, I finally glared at him and yelled, "You little bastard! When I catch you, I'm going to tear you apart. You hear
me? I'll kill you, you little shit."

Doug just gave me a wink, making it clear nothing I'd said
fazed him in the least. I was dumbfounded, feeling like a
boxer who had just thrown his best punch only to have my
opponent walk away without so much as a scratch. That was
a case of a quarterback's getting into *my* head.

The Patriots have one of the NFL's all-time tough players
at the position in Steve Grogan. Here's a guy who has never

been afraid of anything, who has always taken a headfirst approach to the game, and still managed to survive for fifteen seasons. After he underwent disc surgery, a lot of people wrote him off for good before the 1989 season. Yet he started six games while wearing a neck brace and was never shy about standing tall in the pocket. Need I say more?

Bert Jones, the ex-Colt and Ram, took a lot of punishment, too. But he also gave a lot. He probably would have made a good tight end, because he enjoyed popping people every bit as much as they enjoyed popping him. Maybe more.

Jones's other forte was conning officials. He was the best in the league at that. He'd just constantly talk to them—not yell, but talk. He'd put his arm around them, and they'd be walking and talking and smiling like the closest buddies in the world. And because of that, a lot of calls went his way. I guess Bert spoke the officials' language. I've tried, but I just can't grasp Martian.

Other quarterbacks use intelligence to make the most of their limited athletic ability. Among those currently in the league, I can't think of a better example than Cleveland's Bernie Kosar. Nobody has a more awkward style than this guy. He reminds me of a giant crab when he steps to the line, extending his right leg three feet into the backfield while keeping the left under center as he leans forward to call signals. It looks pretty silly, but Bernie needs that extra step on pass rushers to compensate for his lack of speed.

Actually, the guy is a lot better at avoiding sacks than you might think. He does it with head fakes and pump fakes. You'll be running straight for him, ready to make the sack, and he'll give a little pump that forces you to raise your arms and leave your feet. Then, he just steps to one side and throws. Because of his shoot-from-the-hip, sidearm delivery, the ball often barely clears defenders' armpits on the way to a receiver. If that happens enough times early in the game, the ball starts to smell like Right Guard.

Late in the game, you pray the ref will get a new ball.

Jim Everett has good skills beneath his shoulders, which

he greatly enhances with what he has above them. I don't know if there's a more conscientious quarterback in the league. During our Monday night victory over the Rams in '89, I happened to have one of my better games at beating the center off the ball. A few times, I made contact the exact moment the snap was being delivered, which made it hard for the Rams to get anything going offensively.

After the game, Everett, whom I had never met before, pulled me aside to talk. With his curly blond hair and blue eyes, he looked as if he had just stepped off a surfboard. The next thing I expected to hear was, "Hey, dude, you played a bitchin' game tonight. Wanna party?"

Instead, very businesslike, he asked, "Was I doing something wrong with my cadence that allowed you to guess the snap count and come off so quick?"

I told him he wasn't, although I wouldn't have said if he was, just in case we had to face the Rams again in the near future. But in all my years of playing, I've never been asked such a question by a quarterback. Most of those guys never assume *they* could possibly do anything wrong. And if they do, they sure as hell would never admit it to a defensive lineman.

Bob Griese wasn't an overwhelming physical talent by any means. But I doubt you'll find a brighter quarterback in the history of the NFL. To him, reading a defense provided about as much of a challenge as a *See Spot Run* book. He knew how to take control of a game by attacking weaknesses and demoralizing the opposition. I know, in more than a few encounters with the Dolphins, he made me feel knee-high to a placekicker.

By the time I came into the league, Griese was wearing those big glasses that made him look like a librarian playing quarterback. I couldn't help but feel a little uncomfortable around him, thinking about all of the overdue books I had at home.

I felt even less comfortable trying to follow his cadence. When it came to voice inflection, Griese had no peers. If he knew you were highly aggressive—which, at that time, was the essence of my game—he would promptly go to work at trying to get you to jump offsides. After jumping several times one Sunday, I became so frustrated, I thought about stealing his glasses and hiding them under our bench until the final gun.

But then I thought about all of those overdue books . . .

Danny White did a lot of things well, but nothing great. He threw well, not great. He ran well, not great. Doing things well worked for White because most of the success he experienced came from simply being the main cog in the Cowboys' finely tuned offensive machine. He was a spur on one of Tom Landry's snakeskin boots.

White may not have been the greatest passer in the league, but he certainly was the cleanest. I swear, the guy not only showered before and after each game, but at halftime as well. There was no need to watch where he was running after the snap; all you had to do was follow the scent of Aqua Velva. Danny also had the straightest and brightest teeth I'd ever seen (that is, until John Elway came along). I always thought he was the Man from Glad's younger brother.

One of the all-time overachievers at quarterback was Jim Plunkett. Nothing flashy about him. In fact, until someone pointed him out to me at the Pro Bowl one year, I thought he was just a chunky island person picking up shells along the beach. But with his bombs-away passing, Plunkett was perfect for the Raiders' wide-open offense. He was also the perfect Raider. Not in terms of his personality—he couldn't budge the needle on their wild-and-crazy meter to save his life—but because he joined them after failing to stick with New England and San Francisco. He was another misfit who found a home in Al Davis's silver-and-black orphanage.

Plunkett was fortunate to have a strong enough arm and a quick enough release to make his throws without too much movement, because he was one of the slower quarterbacks ever to play the game. With those tree-trunk legs, even *I* could catch him from behind. His name said it all: he'd just plunkett himself in the middle of the field and let his arm do the rest.

A quarterback operates like the commander of a submarine. When his pocket is airtight, he just looks through that periscope, finds the open receiver, and fires. Bingo. It's when the pocket springs a few leaks that he shows what he's truly made of. Will he keep his cool and try to make the play? Or will his ship become the *Yellow Submarine*?

Tony Eason, whom the Jets picked up in 1989 after he was cut by New England, is the consummate crumble guy. When I think of him, the first image that comes to mind is that chicken-shit look he always has on his face. It's as if he knows, no matter what happens on the play, he's going to get mauled. And he wants no part of it. He's the kind of quarterback a defensive lineman hopes won't ever get yanked or carried off the field. You almost feel like giving him part of your salary for making you look so good.

Ken O'Brien is another Jet I wouldn't mind facing on a weekly basis. Instead of doing the I'm-too-young-to-die two-step, he does something equally beneficial to defenders by sitting in the pocket and taking sacks. In 1985, O'Brien was dumped sixty-two times. Everyone blamed his offensive line, but from what I could see, his protection wasn't nearly as bad as he made it look by holding the ball too long. Rather than stepping up and trying to make something happen, he would just sort of fold over and eat the ball. Considering all of the pigskin he swallowed, I began to wonder whether he was on some special pork diet.

The more sacks O'Brien took, the more criticism his linemen received. The more criticism they received, the angrier they became with him. After one play against us, where O'Brien must have held the ball twelve seconds before being sacked, Jets center Joe Fields was absolutely furious.

"Can you believe that son of a bitch?" he said to me. "He's sitting back there all day, and we've got to take the goddamn blame for it. It's just not fair, Fred."

I think part of O'Brien's problem is he doesn't read coverages quickly enough. He waits for patterns to develop and defenses to react accordingly. In the NFL, a quarterback can't get away with that very often; it's only a blink of an eye before someone is going to be in his face or on his back. I also think O'Brien wants to make the highest-percentage throws possible for the sake of his statistics. Interceptions are ugly blemishes on *his* performance. Sacks reflect badly on the offensive line.

What does he care if those hogs collect a few more warts?

The one Jet quarterback who never seemed to concern himself about interceptions was Richard Todd. As far as he was concerned, everyone on the field belonged to the same team. I mean, the man had the worst field vision of any quarterback I've ever seen. You got the feeling all he did at times was drop back and let the ball fly, regardless of the coverage. Consequently, defensive backs usually looked more like his intended receivers than his intended receivers.

Todd also had a hand in my scoring the first—and only—touchdown of my NFL career. It happened in my rookie season. We were on our way to a 46–31 victory over the Jets when I ran a stunt with our right end, Sherman White. The Jets' offensive linemen bit on it, leaving Sherm to throttle Todd and knock the ball loose. It bounced in front of my feet and into my hands at the Jets' 13-yard line. To give you an idea of my speed, there were two minutes left in the third quarter when I got the ball, and by the time I reached the end zone, time had expired.

Although he received a lot of fanfare as the second coming of Joe Namath, Todd was nothing more than an average quarterback at best, attracting too much media attention. Of course, he wasn't the first professional athlete in New York City to squeeze fame and fortune out of average ability. And he won't be the last.

In New York, average ability gets you All-Pro recognition. In Buffalo, it gets you cut.

Not all of my memorable experiences with opposing quarterbacks have come on the field.

At the Pro Bowl one year, me and a buddy of mine from Waltham, George Martin, were relaxing on rafts in the water one day when, all of a sudden, we heard this high-pitched voice getting closer and closer. At first, we thought someone had spotted a shark. Then, we realized it was Joe Theismann, the talking machine that doubled as a quarterback for the Redskins. He was just wading around in search of a poor, unsuspecting ear to attack. And he went after mine.

I really didn't know him that well, yet he spoke as if we'd been friends since childhood. He talked nonstop for about fifteen minutes while George and I looked on in silence. Then, he just turned around and waded back to shore, still talking.

"Who the hell was that?" George asked.

"I think it was Joe Theismann," I said.

"Is he a rapper, or what?"

Until Flutie came along, the smallest NFL quarterback I had ever gone against was former Cleveland great Brian Sipe. He had this boyish face that made you wonder if he had really spent four years at San Diego State before entering the NFL or if the Browns just kidnapped him from a highschool junior varsity squad.

We never became friends, and it probably had something to do with an embarrassing moment I had with him at the Pro Bowl one year. Walking down the beach, I ran into Tom DeLeone, the Browns' center at the time and one of my teammates on the AFC squad. Tom wasn't very big for an offensive lineman, maybe 6'2" and 245 pounds, and when I saw the guy standing next to him was even smaller and much younger looking, I said, "Gee, Tom, it's pretty nice of you to bring your little brother all the way out to Hawaii to watch you play."

"Uh, no, this isn't my little brother," DeLeone said nervously. "This is Brian Sipe. He'll be our starting quarterback Sunday."

"You're Brian Sipe?" I said. Then, looking for a graceful way out, I said, "Well, you look a lot older in your pictures. Uh, see you at practice."

In the spring of 1989, Boomer Esiason and I were participants, along with a number of other NFL players, in the annual Goofy Games at Disney World. The day before the games began, we were all introduced at a reception, and the master of ceremonies spent at least twenty minutes talking about Boomer. He spent no more than twenty seconds on the rest of us combined, but he couldn't say enough about Boomer.

So, the next morning, as we sat on a bus that would take us to our first set of events, I thought it was a perfect opportunity to let Esiason know how much we all appreciated being part of the "Boomer Games." I grabbed the microphone for the bus's PA system and said, "Jeez, Boomer, since we have a little time to kill here, I think we should cover some facts about your football career we might have missed last night. Would you mind going over your eighth- and ninth-grade statistics for us just one more time, please?"

Always quick with a comeback, Boomer took the mike and said, "Well, Fred, I can't recall those numbers. But I do know how many times I got you to jump offsides last year. Does nine ring a bell?"

CHAPTER

FOUR

THE GOOD, THE
BAD . . . THE UGLY

N<small>FL PLAYERS</small> have a variety of ways to kill time before a game. Some talk, some sleep, some read, some pray, some just sit and stare.

Jim Kelly likes to throw up. Conrad Dobler chain-smoked and filed his teeth.

And with anxiety putting the squeeze on everyone's kidneys, there are constant lines in front of the urinals (except of course, for the one containing Kelly's breakfast).

Me? Around the locker room, I'm known as the Pregame Preacher. I'll preach about anything, from politics to perfume. No subject is too big for me to tackle—especially when it isn't wearing a helmet and shoulder pads. Kent Hull, the Bills' center, once said, "The reason I come in early before a game is just to hear what Fred has to say. I wouldn't miss it for anything."

Once all of the world's problems have been settled to my

satisfaction, I grab a game program, lie down in front of my locker, and carry on with the rest of my pregame routine: looking for the ugliest faces I can find among the opposing players' photographs. You'd be amazed how many you come across without even trying.

Earlier in my career, I would get together each week with Jim Haslett and Shane Nelson, and we'd compare the other team's program mugs with the Bills' to determine, position by position, which were uglier. We circled the losing players in pen, then counted them to establish the overall winner. For some *strange* reason, the Bills never lost the team competition.

And I'll bet you can't guess the only three individuals who went undefeated.

We saved the programs so that by the end of the season we could figure out our ugliest opponent of the year. Although the Patriots were a team we consistently defeated, I'd have to say the Atlanta Falcons were the ugliest of the 1980s. Faces down. I mean, we'd have those guys beat before we even got to the second page.

The Falcons had a defensive lineman who was so ugly, we counted him twice. His head reminded me of a concrete slab. His hair went in every direction imaginable. He had a nose that looked as if someone had gone over it with an iron. He had a beard that was real short along the cheeks and shabby around the chin.

Could there have been any question why he was our clearcut pick one season for MDU—Most Disgustingly Ugly?

Believe it or not, I also judge players around the league on the basis of their football skills. And being my preaching self, I've formed quite a few opinions over the past eleven years.

Among the running backs, you have your slashers, your dashers, and your smashers. Slashing and dashing are a given. Without them, a running back doesn't even set foot in an NFL training camp. The thing that sets apart the great from the good at the position is smashing—the willingness to charge full speed and headfirst into 300-pounders like me or those 240- to 260-pound, half-crazed linebackers. For a lot of running backs, that's an extremely hard thing to do more than once. I can't count the number of plays where, as the whistle blows, I'm holding one of the ballcarrier's arms, someone else has a leg, and someone else has his head. You can actually hear his bones crunching as he's being twisted into a pretzel.

And it never ceases to amaze me when that guy is able to get up, return all of his limbs to their proper direction, and go back to the huddle as if nothing happened. That's when you know he has the courage, the ultimate desire to win, the intangibles that put him a notch above everyone else.

You can see it in his eyes. If he comes at you wincing, you know he's going to go down like a feather. But if he comes at you with his eyes wide open, you're the one who will wince. Try keeping your eyes wide open while on a collision course with a 300-pounder, or almost anyone or anything else for that matter. It isn't easy.

When I think about a running back with slash, dash, and smash, the first name that comes to mind is Walter Payton, probably the most talented athlete with whom I have ever shared a field. He stood all of 5'11" and weighed about 200 pounds. Yet on a lot of his carries, he'd start out left, find nothing, turn to his right, find nothing, then put his head down and barrel straight through anyone in his path. Not only that, but he'd come up with his legs spinning, always going for that extra yard.

Of course, Payton's legs didn't function like those of a mere mortal. Besides being able to churn out speed and cut on a dime, they had the kind of spring capable of turning heads in the NBA. In fact, I'll bet Walter could have dunked his helmet—with his head still inside.

One of the more dramatic touchdowns of his career—and a favorite of NFL Films—came against Buffalo in 1979. The Bears had the ball at our 1-yard line, so those of us up front were digging in, fully expecting Payton to go over the top.

After the snap, I plunged forward, and saw him go airborne. Meanwhile, one of our linebackers, Chris Keating, filled my gap and jumped directly over me. Looking up from the pile, I could see Keating got pretty high off the ground, so I figured he had a shot at keeping Payton out of the end zone. But somehow, Walter managed to increase his altitude—in mid-flight! He must have climbed six feet into the air while crossing the goal line. Like he had a jet-pack under his jersey.

Now tell me, how do you teach that? Better yet, how do you stop that?

Off the field, Payton was Mr. Congeniality. You couldn't find a nicer person. And he had the softest, most pleasant sounding voice. He sounded more like an artist or a dancer than a football player. But when it came time to play, Mr. Congeniality was ready to use your face as his dance floor.

The thing that made Tony Dorsett so effective with the Cowboys was the tremendous burst of speed he could call upon at any given moment. I received a close-up view of it in a 1981 Monday night game at Texas Stadium. Dorsett caught a pass and three of us—myself, Haslett, and line-backer Lucius Sanford—converged on him near the side-lines. Sanford hit him from behind, but Dorsett still managed to explode to an opening and wound up with a 73-yard touchdown. He could change direction and burn as fast as anyone who ever played the game.

During a preseason contest with Dallas, Haslett and I were so excited about tackling him on one play, we got a little carried away with our emotions. We started jumping on him and kicking him, and Dorsett looked up at us as if we were nuts—which we were.

"What the hell are you guys doing?" he yelled. "This is a preseason game, for God's sake?"

"Fuck you," we said. "As far as we're concerned, this is a regular-season game. And we're gonna kick your ass!"

On the next play, Dorsett, who had the necessary intangibles for greatness, ripped off a 30-yard gain. So much for our intimidation tactics.

There aren't many running backs in the game today who make you worry that, regardless of where they are on the field, they're only a handoff away from a touchdown. Eric Dickerson instills that kind of fear in a defense. He doesn't spend too much time butting helmets, though. His whole game is to slip past that first wave of tacklers and wave good-bye to everyone else as he heads for the end zone.

Dickerson has an uncanny sense for finding holes. If he comes to the line and sees two openings, he'll choose the right one 90 percent of the time. A lot of guys are fast, but most can't cut and accelerate the way Dickerson does. He doesn't run so much as float. It's really a thing to behold when you're watching it at field level.

And when Eric gets the ball, the onus is on the defense to put as many helmets on him as possible. With some running backs, you can get away with having one guy act as the cutoff man while someone else makes the tackle or runs the ball-carrier out of bounds. But if you put two guys on Dickerson, he'll make three moves. Put three guys on him, he'll make four moves. And so on. The idea is to get him to make so many moves, he's just running in place.

In addition to talent, Dickerson also has had the luxury of running behind some powerful, dominating offensive lines. The Los Angeles Rams gave him a great one, and Indianapolis's hasn't been too shabby either, especially through his first couple of seasons with the Colts. How does he compare with Payton? He doesn't. No one does. In his early years, Walter was asked to do a lot more than Dickerson with a whole lot less help up front. If Payton started his career with the same line Dickerson had with the Rams, he'd have probably broken Jim Brown's all-time record of 12,312 yards in two seasons rather than ten.

Dickerson likes to use that stiff-arm, and when absolutely necessary, he will put his head down for a collision. But with all that padding he wears, above and beyond standard issue, you can't help but raise an eyebrow sometimes and wonder, just how tough is this guy? The only extra pad that ever accompanied Payton on the field was the launching kind.

No NFL running back opens his eyes wider than San Francisco's Roger Craig. He comes at you like a complete wild man, as if he's looking forward to having his teeth rattled— and rattling yours in the process. No running back in league history has been more versatile, either.

Craig is a great one, make no mistake about that. But he also has the help of Joe Montana and an offensive scheme that takes full advantage of every single thing its star players can do. A lot of running backs aren't so fortunate.

James Brooks of Cincinnati is probably the league's best pure receiver coming out of the backfield. He's one of the few running backs in the NFL who can consistently catch those screen and dump passes on the fly. A lot of backs have to be stationary to catch the ball, but not Brooks. He can catch it over his shoulder or while running laterally. And he can run routes with the best of receivers.

His size makes him a real challenge to bring down. Standing only 5'10", Brooks is easy to lose in a crowd. I always mistake him for the belt buckle of Anthony Munoz, the Bengals' 6'6", 278-pound offensive tackle.

Although he doesn't have the greatest speed in the world, Marcus Allen of the Raiders can be every bit as frustrating as Brooks to would-be tacklers. He makes up for whatever swiftness he lacks with great moves and field savvy; he's one of the smarter runners I have ever seen. In a game three years ago, Allen caught a screen pass and I was charging at him from the side, ready to lower the boom. He never even bothered to turn his head. He just picked me up on his batlike radar, and all of a sudden, poof! He was gone.

The last time I saw someone disappear that fast was on *Star Trek*, after Scotty beamed him up.

I'll take Marcus Allen over his part-time teammate, Bo Jackson, anytime. Bo might know football, but he doesn't know it nearly as well as Allen. And as long as he's going to divide himself between baseball and football, he probably never will because he just can't devote enough practice to it. I've noticed, a lot of times, Jackson has to slow down and take a few extra steps before changing direction. With line-backers possessing as much speed as most running backs, that little delay can be costly. Most of Jackson's big gains come when he collides with defenders and spins off them. He has that straight-ahead power that turns people into bowling pins, as well as a tremendous explosion of speed. But it would make a major difference in his game if he were able to change direction on the fly with Allen's smoothness. Maybe, in terms of getting the most out of his football career, what Bo doesn't know *can* hurt him.

There isn't a great deal to say about Freeman McNeil's career with the Jets, and I think that really sums up the way things have gone for the guy since he entered the league in 1981. It seems, for all of the eye-popping games he has had, there are just as many he has missed because of injuries. Of his nine years in the NFL, the guy has only had one, 1988, in which he remained healthy from start to finish. Think about that.

The ironic thing is, McNeil can slip tacklers as well as anybody. He's known as Crazy Legs, because when you try to tackle him low, his legs go one way and his upper body goes another. Now you have him, now you don't. But his cut-back style, in which he's trying to get the defense to overpursue, has resulted in considerable punishment. I guess you could compare McNeil's career to a temperamental car—when it runs, it runs great, but there are a lot of times you can't get it out of the driveway.

Some running backs have a lot more smash than slash and dash.

The strongest man I've ever hit is former Atlanta running back William Andrews. After one of our collisions, I thought I was going to look around and see pieces of me scattered all over the field. I was also certain William's helmet was protruding from my back.

Even when I saw the play on film, twenty-four hours later,

I felt a jolt. Andrews's body was as hard as a rock. He had muscles in his earlobes.

My first encounter with Larry Csonka came against the Dolphins in the regular-season opener of my rookie year. He had returned to Miami for his swan song after spending three seasons with the Giants. Seeing someone in the offensive backfield covered with as much hair and as many muscles as me was more than a little intimidating. So was the sight of his taking a handoff and plowing through the middle.

The first time he touched the ball, I jumped on his back and felt like a contestant in a rodeo. The same thing happened on several of his other carries. Zonk might not have been the same player he was in his younger days, but you wouldn't have known it by the piggyback rides he was giving that day.

John Riggins was another bulldozer runner, except he had more open-field speed than Csonka and dished out even more punishment. You actually could hear Riggo growling before every snap. There was a glare in his eyes. You just knew he wanted to make you a notch in the back of his Redskins helmet. Csonka was hardly what you'd call an evasive runner, but if it was possible for him to avoid you, he would. Not Riggins. If you were close enough to him as he ran downfield, he'd actually slow down a little to try and give you a shot.

Riggins just enjoyed the sound of crunching bones—especially if they were someone else's.

Ex-Oiler and Saint Earl Campbell ran with the football the way Rocky Marciano boxed—a classic inside banger. Play after play, Earl tucked the ball in his gut and with steam blasting from his nose and ears, whacked you with everything he had. Which was quite a bit. One game for Earl would be like five for a lot of other running backs. One game against Earl would be like five for a lot of defenders, too. He had the speed to take it outside when he had to, but there wasn't even a hint of finesse in his game. He just let it all hang out.

The foremost smasher in the game today is Christian

Okoye of Kansas City. Like Andrews, his body is made of
granite. I have yet to meet him on the field, and can't say
I'm all that eager to. From everything I've seen on video and
heard, Okoye is the only player in the league who wears
pads for the safety of others. Bills defensive end Leon Seals
told me that when he and Okoye were teammates practicing
for the Senior Bowl college all-star game, the defenders all
wore neck braces after the first day of banging heads with
the native of Enugu, Nigeria.

Okoye led the NFL in rushing in 1989, and amazingly,
almost all of those yards came on sheer straight-ahead power.
He doesn't show any tackle-avoidance to speak of, which
could shorten his career.

But while all running backs take their share of punishment, the one skill position with the toughest players, pound
for pound, has to be wide receiver. Think of running downfield and jumping as high as you can, while underneath you
there are eleven maniacs trying to hit your head, your chest,
your back, your legs, your family jewels. Sure, it looks like
a beautiful ballet on television, in super slow motion, as the
receiver flips three times and lands on his head.

But do you have any idea how much that hurts?

Everyone who walks onto a football field is basically tough.
That's a prerequisite. Receivers? Those who stick around for
several seasons, who concentrate on the ball and nothing
else while hanging in midair like a metal duck in a shooting
gallery, are more than slightly insane. I mean, they're such
skinny little shits taking these monstrous shots. So it's very
easy for the great ones to separate themselves from the rest
of the pack. Guys can run and jump all day in training-camp
practices, with no one trying to sample their blood. But when
they get into that first preseason game and Jack Tatum's ghost
is lurking somewhere in the opposing secondary, the true
colors will always show.

If there's a yellow spot in the front and a brown one in
the back, the next thing they're going to see is the waiver
wire.

It's an entirely different game for a receiver coming from college to the pros. In college, he sees mostly zone coverage, which provides plenty of open territory for him to maneuver and avoid taking pops. In the NFL, he has defensive backs practically fused to both hips. Also, the quality of secondaries he sees in college aren't remotely close to what he sees on a regular basis in the NFL.

What's made the game even more dangerous for receivers is the presence of more and more big, strong, fast, and mean—very mean—linebackers. It used to be that, on passing downs, a Dick Butkus would almost always blitz. About the only time he'd ever drop into pass coverage was in the late stages of a blowout. And that would be just for a laugh. Now, you have guys like Lawrence Taylor who can run, stride for stride, with a receiver and splatter him all over the field as he goes for the ball.

The thing I can never get over is watching what happens after a quarterback floats a suicide pass into the air; a receiver leaves his feet to grab it, but becomes separated from the ball by a 262-pound crowbar disguised as an outside linebacker. Invariably, the quarterback will stomp his feet and throw his hands up in disgust. Can you believe the nerve of that QB?

I've had the pleasure of playing with two of the better receivers in the league in Jerry Butler, who retired in 1988 after nine brilliant seasons, and Andre Reed, who has been on a steady climb to greatness since joining the Bills from tiny Kutztown University of Pennsylvania in 1985.

I never knew what soft hands were until the first time I saw Jerry catch a football when we were rookies in 1979. With most receivers, even some of the better ones in the game, you hear at least a small pop when ball meets flesh. With Jerry, the only sound you heard was a *poofff!* It was as if the ball landed on a bed of feathers. I can honestly say I've never heard that sound with any other pass catcher.

But don't get the idea that Butler was all grace and no guts. Nothing could be further from the truth. He was one of the toughest players I ever knew, receiver or otherwise. The guy had your typical receiver-type body, very lean and sort of gangly, yet he wouldn't hesitate to go up for every pass thrown his way, no matter how heavy the traffic. His concentration simply did not waver. And it wasn't until after he had the ball safely tucked away that he began to think about what would happen next. Jerry took some unbelievable shots.

Probably the greatest display of courage I have ever witnessed on a football field came on what proved to be the final play of Butler's career. We were playing Miami, at home, in 1986. Jerry's pattern took him down the middle, attracting, as always, two defensive backs. Jerry jumped and extended his body to catch a 25-yard pass in the end zone. The DBs jumped with him. Jerry landed face first. The DBs landed on top of him. As they did, his right leg snapped.

But amazingly, Jerry never let go of the ball. I'd have gladly given back those six points if it meant his leg's remaining in one piece.

Reed is a different kind of receiver than Butler, beginning with his build. He's much thicker and stronger on top. Really, he looks more like a defensive back than a receiver. But the additional bulk doesn't make him any slower. Andre can really motor, and there are few at the position who make sharper open-field cuts after catching the ball.

Reed's approach to the game is scrappy. It's as if, on every pattern, he's saying, "You punch me, and I'm going to punch you harder." No one can intimidate him, which was something Andre established as a rookie in training camp. Here was a guy from Kutztown, hardly one of the nation's football assembly lines, and on his very first pattern of his very first day of practice he ran across the middle. Not surprisingly, some veteran defensive back decided Andre needed to be taught an early lesson and decked him with a forearm.

What did Andre do on his next pattern? He went over the middle, of course.

Through his first few seasons, Reed was underestimated by most of our opponents. So he just kept catching pass after pass. Two years ago, he broke Elbert Dubenion's long-standing club record for single-season receptions with 71. Last year, he broke his own record with 88, and that firmly established him among the NFL's elite—right up there with Jerry Rice of San Francisco, Al Toon of the Jets, and Art Monk of the Redskins.

You would think NFL coaches would have learned their lesson about underestimating a receiver a long time ago with Steve Largent. While no one was paying attention, Largent, in fourteen seasons with Seattle, went on to become one of the all-time greats ever to play the position. Of course, watching him run, with that choppy, unorthodox stride, it was easy to sell him short. There were times when I was convinced I could cover him. That's how slow he looked.

Most defensive backs just never knew what Largent was trying to do while running his pattern. And by the time they figured it out, he was past them and wide open for the catch. I don't know if the game has ever had a more intelligent receiver. Steve didn't just break from the huddle and run a prescribed route. On each play, he analyzed the secondary, studying it every bit as closely as the quarterback. In fact, in some cases, the quarterback didn't have to make his own read. He could simply play off Largent's.

The flip side at the position, in terms of raw speed, was ex-Bengal Cris Collinsworth. But speed alone didn't take him and his English-gentleman physique to the top. He was one guy who got a ton of mileage out of his attitude. Cris just thought he could do it all. If you asked him who was the best receiver in the league, he wouldn't think twice before answering, "Me." Still, he wasn't obnoxious. Not in the least. He was very good-natured. He just believed in himself.

That also applied to his relationship with females. Collinsworth was convinced he had the looks and charm to attract the most beautiful women in the world. Maybe he could. But there was at least one instance when that attitude backfired on him. We were in the Pro Bowl together, and he received a phone call at his hotel from a woman in Dallas whom he didn't know and had never seen. She described herself as being absolutely gorgeous and told Cris she'd love to get together with him. He became so intrigued by her voice and the things she said, he arranged to have her fly to Honolulu that week.

Was he ever in for a surprise!

It turned out the woman was as large as some of the offensive linemen in the game—and not even as pretty. Cris was stuck with her for the rest of the week. And I do mean stuck. She followed him everywhere he went. (When she showed up at practice, the equipment men were almost ready to issue her a helmet and shoulder pads.) It got to the point where Collinsworth would be trying to run away from her on the beach. I hope he learned his lesson about long-distance romance.

Receivers are nuts, but the weirdest of all positions is tight end. You're talking about a guy who's a combination of two positions that couldn't have less in common—offensive tackle and receiver. You want a guy who can pound, punch, and kick the opposition one moment, then run around as if he's in a ballet company the next. It just isn't natural.

And that's why you don't see an abundance of true tight ends in the game. There are those who can block, but can't catch, and those who can catch, but can't block. The league is filled with a lot of pretenders because the genuine article is almost impossible to come by.

The closest to an authentic tight end in the game today is Mark Bavaro of the Giants. He can catch, run, and put a hurting on the largest and strongest of defenders. But he's been injured so much, the jury's still out on him.

Ozzie Newsome came pretty close in his twelve years with Cleveland—close enough, probably, to earn a spot in the Hall of Fame. But he still was a much better receiver than blocker. And despite all the success he had with the Raiders, Todd Christensen was nothing more than an oversized possession receiver. The same is true of the Jets' Mickey Shuler. You just can't call these guys true tight ends.

In eleven years, the three best and most complete players

I have ever seen at the position are former Charger Kellen Winslow, former Patriot Russ Francis, and former Raider Dave Casper. How scarce are all-around tight ends? The Patriots had to coax Francis back out of retirement, that's how desperate they were for one.

I'll never forget a conversation I had about Francis with former Bills linebacker Phil Villapiano, who, when he was with the Raiders, played against Francis when both were in their prime. In his early days with the Patriots, Francis could run a 4.5-second forty-yard dash. I knew Phil, even with a strong wind behind him, could barely break 5.0. So I asked him, "How did you ever cover Francis on a pass?"

Phil gave a typical Raider response: "Well, he didn't run too fast with me holding on to his facemask and punching him in the stomach. But you know what, Fred? The guy never let up. He took that pounding, and kept on going. You won't find a better tight end to ever play the game than Russ Francis."

But you can make a pretty strong case for Winslow. Everyone talked about him revolutionizing the position. What he really did, though, was frustrate a lot of teams that went looking for a tight end who could give them all of the things he gave San Diego.

The first time I saw Winslow was when we were participants in the 1979 Senior Bowl. I had noticed him playing chess in a bar, and when I found out he was a tight end from Missouri, I nearly spit out my beer. I was certain, with his size, he had to be an offensive tackle.

"No way could he be a tight end," I insisted, picturing him lumbering out for a pass and having the ball clang off his fingertips.

The next day in practice, a few of us stood and watched him, expecting to get a good chuckle in passing drills. Instead, our mouths dropped as we saw him leave scorch marks all over the grass and catch everything in sight. Take away his knee problems, and Winslow would probably still be devouring the NFL record book.

Casper drank every day of his life, yet he managed to drag

himself onto the field, game after game, and pummel defenders and make the most difficult catches imaginable. You had to be careful around him at the Pro Bowl, though. Occasionally, after getting drunk as a skunk, he liked to throw furniture all over the place. At the first meeting of the AFC squad one year, he walked in late. A chair was in his way, and without saying a word, Casper picked it up, smashed it to pieces against a wall, and sat in another chair.

I guess he didn't like the way the first one was upholstered.

Putting aside my natural animosity toward offensive linemen for a moment, I'll tell you that there's a lot more involved to what those hogs do on the field than meets the eye.

People think cornerbacks lead the loneliest existence in the game, but an offensive tackle is pretty lonely out there, too. He's left to take on a defensive end or outside linebacker just waiting to explode from the starting blocks like a world-class sprinter, coming at you from an angle. So the best at the position must first have the ability to cover a lot of ground. Some tackles can make up the ground with raw athletic talent, like All-Pros Chris Hinton of Atlanta and Anthony Munoz. Because of their skills, they can simply shuffle, almost without effort, to where they have to be to get in front of that screaming pass rusher. And even if they make a bad step, they have enough quickness to recover in time.

On the other hand, a guy who isn't quite as gifted physically, such as Tunch Ilkin of the Steelers, relies much more on mechanics to make his blocks. Thanks to his careful study of each opponent, he knows precisely how deep to set up after the snap to cut off the pass rusher's angle. He anticipates every single move the end or outside linebacker is going to make and adjusts accordingly, while also keeping an eye out for someone coming at him from the inside on a stunt.

Everyone thinks a tackle's just a big, burly beast who mauls people for his paycheck. In reality, he's probably doing as much thinking as anybody on the field.

People still talk about Munoz as being the game's best at

the position. I think he *was* the best at one time and will most certainly make it to the Hall of Fame. But he has lost a good deal of the strength and quickness that put him so far above the rest of the tackles in the NFL.

For my money, there isn't a better one around than Hinton. He is, by far, one of the more physically gifted offensive linemen you'll ever see. Even in his younger days, I don't know if Munoz had Hinton's athletic ability. Chris has power, he has speed. And he's very intelligent. Northwestern graduates are almost as bright as those of us from Boston College.

At the other end of the talent spectrum is Green Bay's Tony Mandarich. He had a horrendous rookie season in 1989, which, under normal circumstances, wouldn't be unusual for an offensive tackle. It's one of the more difficult positions to master, and young guys who play there experience a lot of growing pains.

But these aren't normal circumstances.

Mandarich was the second overall pick of last year's draft. Based on everything said and written about him while he was at Michigan State—especially all of the boasting he did—any team that drafted him would instantly have the best offensive line in the NFL. In fact, it wouldn't need any other linemen; the 6'5", 315-pound Mandarich could play all five positions by himself.

But once he finally started playing in the league, reality set in. He couldn't do a thing, even on field-goal protection. For all his "incredible" strength and "spectacular" athletic ability, the guy has looked like nothing more than a big goon. He's stiff. He's uncoordinated. He doesn't have any idea how to play his position.

In college, he could overpower just about every defensive lineman he faced. In the NFL, he's going against guys who not only are far superior athletically to those he saw in college, but who also know all kinds of little tricks to get past offensive linemen. If Mandarich tries to beat them with power, they're going to make his head spin with finesse. And they don't work with "gurus of weight lifting" like he does. They don't eat 15,000 calories a day like he does. They prepare themselves to be football players. Mandarich has prepared himself to be a weight lifter. And that's why he has all of the flexibility of a statue and no technique whatsoever.

With his size and potential, maybe—and I stress, maybe—he'll wind up being a quality player someday. He'll wind up actually doing a few of the magnificent things that, so far, he has conned the world into believing he can do. Meanwhile, the Packers look pretty stupid paying him a million dollars a year. They're giving him so much money, he's become the Bank of Mandarich.

Until he proves otherwise, I'd say Tony's on shakier ground than any of the nation's savings and loan institutions.

The most diversified of the offensive linemen are the guards. In addition to having enough size and strength to tango with the likes of yours truly, they must also be fast. Not fast for offensive linemen, but fast for fullbacks. Fast enough to be the lead blocker on a lot of runs and sweep plays. Fast enough, against a three-man front, to cut off an inside linebacker who has the advantage of being four or five yards off the ball and, in many cases, is far from being a slowpoke himself. Against a four-man front, guards rely on their strength to jam a defensive tackle lined up in their face. Usually, they'll see both fronts in a game, so even if the plays are the same, reads and responsibilities can change dramatically on just about every snap.

I can identify a great guard just by looking at his stance. A great one will never tip off the upcoming play with the way his feet are positioned. What can you see in a guard's stance? Plenty. For instance, if he's going to pull to his right on a run, he'll have his right foot up a little farther than normal, with the toes twisted to the outside ever so slightly. He'll also be leaning forward a little bit. If a pass is coming, he'll be sitting square, with the brunt of his weight on his heels.

A guard's eyes can give good clues, too. Often, the first defender he looks at as he comes to the line is an indication of where the play is headed. Not always, but often.

To keep you guessing on a series of passing downs, a guard might jam you in the facemask with his first move, then step back. On the next snap, you're expecting him to jam you again, but instead, he takes two steps back. Finally, once he knows you're good and ready for him to step back, he steps forward, grabs your shoulder pads, and locks you out.

It takes exceptional discipline for a guard not to give anything away with his stance and his eyes. On top of all of the other things filling his mind, he has to remember to keep his feet and eyes as neutral as possible. And the more tired he gets, the lazier he gets. The lazier he gets, the less discipline he's going to have when it comes to the little things.

One of the best in the NFL at never tipping off a play was Jim Ritcher. Having gone against him in practice for ten years, I know of what I speak.

Jim and Joe Devlin have been two of the more underrated offensive linemen in the game's history. Despite a combined twenty-three years of experience, there isn't a single Pro Bowl appearance between them. And that's a sin. I'd always heard guys around the league talk about what a tough and talented player Devlin was. He consistently did a great job on former Jets defensive end Mark Gastineau, and Gastineau consistently told reporters Devlin was the best he ever faced. In fact, Gastineau's sudden retirement in 1988 came after he was shut out by Joe on *Monday Night Football*. I guess the embarrassment was too much for him.

Defenders around the league have also been singing Ritcher's praises over the years. When San Francisco linebacker Matt Millen was with the Raiders, he told me he hated going against Ritcher more than any other guard he ever faced.

"He just kills people," Millen said.

"So why don't you vote for him for the Pro Bowl?" I asked.

"I do," Millen said. "I can't understand why nobody else does."

As offensive linemen go, Jimmy isn't huge at 6'2" and 265 pounds. But there isn't a guy at his position who's stronger, quicker . . . or hairier. And there isn't a more humble athlete alive.

Ritcher came into the league as a center, and in his rookie year, he went against legendary nose tackle Curley Culp, who was playing for Houston at the time. When he was with the Chiefs, Curley set the standards by which all nose tackles are judged. On this day, however, Ritcher was devouring him. I watched from the sidelines and thanked God it wasn't me out there with the derricks on my helmet.

But Ritcher refused to believe he could dominate Culp simply with his own strength and ability. When our offense came off the field, he walked over to me and said, "I think Curley's going easy on me because I'm a rookie."

"No, Jim," I said. "You're beating him because you're a good player, believe me."

We had a similar conversation the following year, during a game against Miami. Ritcher was annihilating their nose man at the time, Bob Baumhower, knocking him back five to ten yards every play, just abusing the guy. And he came up to me on the sidelines and said, "You know, Fred, I think there's something wrong with Baumhower."

"What makes you say that?"

"I keep blowing him off the ball."

"So?"

"So he must be sick or something."

"You're the one who's sick, Jim. You still don't realize how good you are, do you?"

Then, in a game against Denver, he was pancaking their former great defensive end, Rulon Jones, on practically every play. Most offensive linemen in Ritcher's cleats would be crowing at the top of their lungs, "I'm owning this guy! I'm killing him! He doesn't have a chance against me!"

Not Ritcher.

"I don't know what's wrong with him, Fred. He keeps coming to the line and I keep throwing him to the ground."

"Jim, did you ever consider it might have something to

do with the fact you can bench-press six hundred pounds and rip a door off its hinges with one hand? Maybe, just maybe, it's because you're a lot better than him."

"Oh, I don't know about that. He's a good player. He's probably just having a bad day."

But you shouldn't make the mistake of assuming Ritcher is some sort of marshmallow. That's what Don Smith, an ex-Bills defensive lineman, did during a 1986 practice. We were working on our pass rush, and Don, who was about 6'5" and 270 pounds, thought he could beat Jimmy through intimidation. He kept punching him and punching him, and Ritcher kept getting angrier and angrier. Finally, Smith threw one punch too many. With one hand, Ritcher grabbed him by the facemask, pulled him forward, and yelled, "You wanna play?" Then, he gave the facemask a hard twist, pulling Smith's feet off the ground and slamming him down, helmet first.

Practice stopped. Our eyes opened wide. Our mouths dropped.

"You still wanna play?" Ritcher said.

Neither Smith nor anyone else wanted to be part of Jim's little "fun period." If he *played* that way as a schoolboy, there must have been quite a long line outside the nurse's office.

It is no coincidence the first year I made the Pro Bowl, in 1980, was Ritcher's rookie season. I was one of his playthings on a number of occasions during two-a-day practices in training camp. He made me a better nose tackle because I knew that if I was to have any kind of chance against him, I had to be at the top of my game constantly.

Once the regular season began, I'd go into games wearing a party hat and tooting a noisemaker because I figured there wasn't anyone I would face who could make life as miserable for me on the field as Jim. In fact, after the Pro Bowl selections were announced that year, Willie Zapalac, our defensive line coach at the time, came up to me and said, "You'd better go thank Jim Ritcher for this."

I did. I still do.

One offensive lineman who has gotten far more credit than he deserves is Falcons guard Bill Fralic. Everyone talks about him like he's the greatest thing since ice cream, but as far as I'm concerned, he shouldn't even be allowed to play the game. He cheap-shots on every play. You see him punching, holding, kicking, you name it.

I blame the referees for allowing him to get away with that stuff. As long as they continue to look the other way, teams are going to seek their own form of justice. During the '89 season, I was looking at videotape of a Falcons game against Phoenix, and on one play, the Cardinals' defensive linemen were out to give Fralic some of his own cheap-shotting medicine. One of their tackles jammed him and stepped inside while an end came down and just smashed his ribs. Just killed him. And Fralic deserved every bit of it because he tries to hurt people.

The reason he has to resort to dirty tactics is he's just not that good of a player. He's strong, but very slow. He can't pull that well at all. Yet you keep hearing about how great he is, how well he can block for the run. Then you play against him and watch him on video, and you say to yourself, "That's the guy they're talking about?"

Washington guard Russ Grimm made a name for himself by beating Dallas defensive tackle Randy White a few times on *Monday Night Football*. He just had White's number, and sometimes that's all it takes to gain recognition. Come up with a few good games against big-name players when the whole country is watching, and you build a reputation as someone who does that every week—even if you don't.

The Patriots' Sean Farrell hasn't gotten nearly the recognition of some guards, yet is a top-notch player. Other highly underrated guards are Randall McDaniel of Minnesota, who's very quick and has outstanding technique, and Dan Alexander of the Jets, who retired after the '89 season.

As far as centers go, Randy Grimes of Tampa Bay is about as underrated as you can get. He's among the best at his position, yet the closest he has ever come to making the Pro

Bowl is being picked as an alternate. At 6'4" and 275 pounds, Randy's built like a mountain. I saw him get in his stance once and I said to myself, why is he wearing a ring on his toe? But what I was seeing was his hand; the guy's arms are the size of some people's legs. He's also as quick as a cat.

A center from the same division who tends to get a little too much attention is Jay Hilgenberg of the Bears. At 6'2" and 260 pounds, he's pretty small for an offensive lineman and his strength is average, at best. Yet he has managed to receive a lot of publicity, and I don't know why. He's a good center, but a long way from great. I wouldn't put him in the same category of Kent Hull, or any of the other truly outstanding centers, past and present, from the AFC East— Dwight Stephenson, Joe Fields, Pete Brock, Ray Donaldson. Hilgenberg's not even close.

The same goes for Washington's center, Jeff Bostic. He's just another little guy—6'2" and 260, if you really push it— with very average talent. But like most of the Redskins' offensive linemen, he has benefited from their blocking scheme. On running plays, they use a lot of jab-counter, where the tackles block down and Bostic blocks away from the flow of the play and therefore doesn't have to take anybody head-on. He can just cut defenders off along the way.

Schemes can make players look a lot better than they really are.

So can gimmicks individual players do to draw attention to themselves. A lot of guys on my side of the ball resented Mark Gastineau for becoming a household name largely because of his postsack dancing and fist-pumping, and general flamboyance on and off the field. They thought he gave all defensive linemen a bad name.

I don't look at it that way. Granted, he was a hard guy to like and, maybe, respect. But I think we should all be thankful for Mark, because he did loads to raise the status—not to mention the salaries—of our position. Before he came along, there were the Fearsome Foursome and Purple People Eaters, but few individuals could really claim their own identity. Mark changed all of that. He brought more fan and media interest to the defensive line than it had ever seen before.

The first time I met Gastineau, we were roommates at the Senior Bowl. Actually, my assigned roommate was Mike Stensrud, a defensive lineman from Iowa (who wound up playing for the Oilers). I was the first one in the hotel room, and a short while later, I heard a knock at the door. I opened it to this tall, skinny country-looking guy with furry, knee-high boots and a Beatles haircut.

"Are you Stensrud?" I asked.

"No, I'm Mark Gastineau, from East Central Oklahoma. Stensrud pulled out of the game, so I made it as an alternate."

At the time, he weighed no more than 240 pounds. (He would, by some miracle, tip the scale at 280 a couple of years later with the Jets.) But even then, he knew how to draw attention to himself. When the rest of us made tackles, we walked quietly back to the huddle. When Gastineau made them, he jumped all over the place like a madman.

Gastineau wound up getting Player of the Game. Much more recognition would follow over the next nine and a half seasons.

At the top of his game, Gastineau made the most out of his incredible speed. He was so fast most offensive tackles, desperate to get themselves in position to block him, would lean backward just before the snap. Most of the time when Gastineau saw that, he was able to take off the instant the ball was snapped, blow past the tackle, and make the sack. That was all he was really concerned with—making sacks and doing his dance, which made each sack seem like a national holiday. Especially in New York.

For all of his showboating, though, we managed to get along pretty well through our first couple of seasons in the NFL. We hung out together at the Pro Bowl, we had a lot of laughs. We even lassoed a steer. Well, Mark did the lassoing; I watched. We were sitting in a restaurant in Hawaii when, all of a sudden, we saw a steer charging down the street after it had broken loose from the docks. Being from Arizona,

Gastineau knew a thing or two about steer-roping. He grabbed a rope from someone who was trying to capture the animal, swung it over his head a few times, threw the loop around the steer's neck, pulled it to the ground, and tied it up.

Being from Boston, I never knew cattle took a larger and more aggressive form than steak and hamburger. So I climbed on the roof of a car and watched from a safe distance while Mark played John Wayne.

When he started getting a lot of notoriety, as the leading member of the New York Sack Exchange, a change came over Gastineau. We weren't quite as close anymore. After a game, he'd come up and say, "Hey, Fred, how are you doing? I haven't seen you for a while." I'd start talking with him as we walked off the field, but when we got close to the fans, he'd suddenly turn away from me and forget I was even there. Not only did his personality change, but so did his appearance. He had a different hairstyle. His nose seemed to get narrower. He lost the gap between his front teeth. He just didn't look anything like that tall, skinny country kid I had met at the Senior Bowl.

While he walked up and down the beach during Pro Bowl week one year, trying to impress the women by flexing his oil-covered muscles, I saw he didn't have any hair on his chest, arms, or legs. I distinctly remembered seeing hair on the guy before.

Joe Klecko, the Jets' other former defensive-line standout, later informed me Gastineau shaved it off—*all* of it.

"Next time you see Mark," Klecko said with a smile, "ask him why he doesn't take a shower after practice and games anymore."

He couldn't stand Gastineau. And I found out why when the three of us were part of the AFC's Pro Bowl defensive line one year—Klecko and I were the tackles, Gastineau and Doug Betters of Miami were the ends. From the start of the game, Joe and I were beating the guards off the ball and forcing the NFC quarterback, Joe Thiesmann, out of the pocket. So I told Gastineau to keep rushing from the outside and contain Theismann, who was a good runner.

Sure enough, on the very next play, Gastineau came crashing inside, hit the back of my legs, and knocked me down. Klecko was furious.

"You see the shit I have to put up with, Fred?" he said after the play. "You tell him to stay outside, and the son of a bitch comes inside."

Then, Klecko grabbed Gastineau by the jersey and said, "Next time, you stay outside, or I'm going to kick your goddamn ass."

And he would have. You didn't screw with Joe. He had a mean streak a mile long; he drove eighteen-wheelers and he could box. Just a rough, tough guy—the kind who, when he laughs, everyone around him laughs, too, even if they aren't quite sure of the reason. (He would always lose in our ugliest-player matchups, but we never told him.)

Although the timing seemed a little weird, I understood what Gastineau had in mind by retiring after Devlin shut him out in our '88 Monday night victory over the Jets. Having entered the game with a league-leading seven sacks, he was trying to get out while he was still on top. He knew, deep down, his skills were slipping, and he didn't want to go through a stretch of games where everyone was rocking him the way Joe did that night.

That same year, Klecko called it quits after chronic knee problems caused him to have a nonproductive season with Indianapolis. He retired as a nose tackle, but Klecko was the best defensive end I have ever seen play the game. He could beat you with speed, strength, and finesse. And if none of those worked, he'd use a tire iron. I saw him take apart Munoz when both were in their heyday without any problem at all. Gastineau was good, but he relied almost exclusively on speed. Klecko had those extra dimensions that just put him so far above the rest.

Ironically, he is the one who did the most to turn Gastineau into a superstar. Opponents were so determined to run away from Klecko, they put themselves right into Mark's hands on the other side.

Joe also ranks high on my list of great nose tackles from the eighties. (Even if he didn't, I sure as hell wouldn't tell him that, either.) But I can't say the same for Bob Golic of the Raiders. He had a couple good years with Cleveland, attracted a lot of media attention, and landed in the Pro Bowl a few times. But Golic isn't a true nose tackle. I consider him a linebacker, which is where he spent most of his first four seasons in the league. He even plays more like a linebacker than a true nose man. First of all, he lines up a yard or two off the ball. Then, after the snap, he reads the center and guards and flows to the play, rather than penetrating the way most of us do. One more thing that bothers me about Golic: he wears too much hairspray on that big, bushy 'do of his. His hair is so stiff, he doesn't even need a helmet.

Another guy who has prospered greatly from media hype is Bill Maas of Kansas City. He's strong, tough, and uses his hands well. But I've never been impressed with his quickness, which is critical for a nose tackle. His overall game just doesn't floor me the way it has a lot of other players, coaches, and sportswriters. He's good; he's just not unbelievable.

Cincinnati's Tim Krumrie had clearly established himself as one of the better players at the position before his leg snapped during Super Bowl XXIII. He showed remarkable courage in coming back and playing in 1989, although his game wasn't anywhere close to the level it had reached in '88 or even '87. Still, he has everything you need psychologically to play nose tackle. He's just a rugged, nasty guy— someone who would have fit right in during the early years of pro football. If Krumrie had a choice, he'd probably play without a facemask; he's that tough. He had the same personality as a wrestler in college and high school. Golic wrestled, too, but mostly because he liked to wear tights.

There isn't a more self-made nose tackle than my 49er teammate Jim Burt. I watched him play when he first joined the Giants in 1981, out of the University of Miami, and it was absolutely the worst thing I had seen in my life. He was pitiful. Then, he began to go to work on himself, getting bigger and stronger and developing techniques. All of a sudden, he wasn't getting pushed around anymore. He looked as if he knew what he was doing. He was showing good hand-quickness and footwork and becoming a real force.

The Giants gave him the chance to improve, sticking with him when it looked as if he were history, and Burt made them look smart. So smart, in fact, that after back problems put him on the street, the 49ers gave him a chance to win a second Super Bowl ring.

Besides myself, BC's other contribution to the NFL's nose-tackle collection is Joe Nash of Seattle. We're good friends and work out together during the off-season, which we both spend in our native New England. Joe's playing style is a little more lateral than mine. He tries to make tackles up and down the line, whereas I'm looking to penetrate and force the play to go left or right.

Because of his low-keyed approach and the fact he is twenty-nine, his younger teammates call him Uncle Joe, as in the star of the old TV series *Petticoat Junction*. They sing the theme song to him all the time: "And there's Uncle Joe, he's a movin' kind of slow at the Junction . . ."

Joe received some unfortunate national publicity when he kept going down with what was obviously a fake knee injury during the Seahawks' 1988 playoff game against Cincinnati. The idea was to stop the clock and slow down the Bengals' hurry-up offense so the Seahawks could make defensive substitutions and catch their breath. It worked, even though the Bengals won. It also made Joe look bad and he wasn't too happy about that.

But it was pretty naive for anyone to think he took it upon himself to fake the injury. You knew he was only following orders.

"Hey, I've got a family to feed," he told me afterward.

We had the same brainstorm for our AFC Championship Game against Cincinnati, which was a week later. Fortunately, we didn't follow through with it because I'd likely have been the one embarrassing myself on national TV.

Before he became one of the NFL's top defensive linemen with the Bears, Steve McMichael played nose tackle for the Patriots. You might say he was a nose that was out of place. Because after one season in New England, the Bears picked him up as a free agent in 1981 and placed him at one of the two tackle spots in their four-man front. Two years later, he became a starter at left tackle and proceeded to make a name for himself.

I heard some pretty outrageous stories about McMichael from his former teammates on the Patriots, whom he had joined as a third-round draft pick from Texas. They called him Stinky McNasty because of his tendency to get down and very, very dirty—off the field as well as on. He was a pretty good practice player for the Pats, holding his own against the likes of Brock and John Hannah. But every so often, he would lose control. He'd just suddenly freak out and think he was back at Texas, in the middle of a big game against Arkansas. He'd even operate out of Texas's defensive scheme.

I've had moments when I thought I was back at BC, but only after taking a severe blow to the head. Apparently, the mere stress of the NFL was enough to cause McMichael to experience post-Longhorn flashbacks.

I always had a lot of respect for Dan Hampton, the defensive tackle who, until his retirement in '89, lined up next to McMichael. He'll go down as one of the more dominant defensive players of the eighties. And he'll be missed by the Bears. I don't think their decline and his being out with the knee injury that forced him to retire was just a coincidence.

Hampton wasn't shy about his athletic prowess. Typical of his style was a remark he made during our 1988 loss to the Bears. On his way back to the huddle after a play in which he beat Leonard Burton, our left tackle, Hampton looked down at his own arms and in a real cocky voice said,

"Four twenty-five, sets of five." That was his way of telling Burton he overpowered him because he could lift 425 pounds in three sets of five. Big deal. Jim Ritcher does that in his sleep—with one arm.

Hampton stands 6'5" and for whatever reason likes to wear his pants way up high, almost to his shoulders. The first time I noticed this was at the 1980 Pro Bowl. He must have been wearing size-70 shorts. They were so high, he had to pull down his zipper to scratch his chest.

No player in league history has gotten more mileage out of a few carries and a nickname than Bears defensive tackle William (Refrigerator) Perry. I have the distinction of being the first person to cause the Fridge to fumble. It happened in a 1986 exhibition game at South Bend, Indiana, the summer after the Bears won Super Bowl XX. I saw the fat guy coming my way, and the ball looked like a pea in his hands. I buried my head in his belly button—which hit me long before the rest of him got there—and I guess the ball just popped loose on impact. I couldn't say for certain, because it wasn't until five minutes later that I saw daylight again. And it took a good hour before I removed the final piece of belly-button hair from my mouth.

Linebackers are like the fish that learned to walk on land. They're evolutionary defensive linemen. We operate out of a three-point stance. They're upright, on two feet. We do our jobs in a small, overcrowded area, often moving only inches at a time. They have all kinds of room—to blitz, drop into pass coverage, and most of all, chase running backs. They're the designated antibodies for running backs.

It's a position that demands tremendous athletic ability and something special upstairs. A linebacker needs instant field recognition. This is especially true with an inside linebacker. He's the defensive field general. When the offense breaks its huddle, he has to, without hesitation, call out the set, the formations, the shifts, the stunts, the coverages. Down in our stances, those of us on the defensive line can't see what he sees. He's our eyes. He and the quarterback are up there, trying to outthink each other, and the linemen are down below, waiting to kill each other.

Great linebackers are also able to think on the run. One of the brightest was former Patriot Steve Nelson. I remember, during one game against New England, Ritcher came to the sideline and in complete frustration said, "Nelson's calling all of our plays before we run them."

Mike Singletary of the Bears is another inside linebacker who maintains his composure and by keeping his eyes as wide open as possible sees every single thing happening on offense. That's the kind of guy I want behind me. Even if he isn't the world's best athlete, he can compensate for that by making sure we've made all of the proper defensive adjustments.

One mistake in recognition and we all can look like a bunch of idiots.

No player in the league offers more aggressiveness than John Offerdahl, Miami's Pro Bowl inside linebacker. He's just a rock-head with absolutely no regard for his body—a real give-it-up guy. He can take on a guard, buckle him, then run outside and tackle the halfback, which is rare for someone his size (6'3", 237 pounds). Plus, he's decent in pass coverage. Not long ago, Offerdahl *was* the Dolphins' defense.

Matt Millen may play for the 49ers, but he'll always be an old-time Raider at heart. Other San Francisco players, such as linebacker Bill Romanowski, were a little taken aback when they saw Millen in action after he joined the team in 1989. He began screaming at opposing players, challenging them to fights, pushing them after the whistle. And that just isn't 49er-type conduct. His new teammates were looking at Matt as if he were an escapee from a mental institution.

An inside linebacker who offers next to nothing, in any respect, is Brian Bosworth. I know it won't make any difference, but I just hope NFL teams will remind themselves about him before falling in love with college players who have been hyped to death. There aren't enough pages in this book to list all of the league's first-round flops through the years. In Buffalo, alone, you've had Walt Patulski, Tom Ruud, Terry Miller, Tom Cousineau, Perry Tuttle, and Tony Hunter.

But in terms of the hype and the finances involved, there hasn't been a bigger bust to emerge from the college ranks than The Boz. His shoulder and knee problems don't change the fact that he never has been nor will ever be the incredibly dominant player who had the whole country excited before he joined Seattle in 1987.

I mean, we're talking about an inside linebacker who can't take on blocks. When you break it down, he's really nothing more than a glorified safety with painted hair. He runs well, but for the position he plays, he's small (6'1" and 230 pounds, if he's lucky) and not that strong. The inside linebacker the Bills have from the same draft, Shane Conlan, is so much better, it's an insult to Shane to mention them in the same paragraph. For that matter, I probably could find a more talented player on the high school level.

But The Boz is having the last laugh on us all. His great job of self-promotion made him a legend at Oklahoma. The Seahawks, by being selected to have the first pick in a supplemental draft, won the opportunity to shower him with millions of dollars. And for what, a haircut?

At the Pro Bowl—something I doubt The Boz will ever see in person unless he buys a ticket—you have an entire week, between low-intensity practices, to talk and drink. Some guys do a lot more drinking than talking. The Raiders, of course, had a bunch, starting with one of their former outside linebackers, Ted Hendricks.

I didn't know quite what to make of old Ted. I still don't. Night after night, he'd sit in a bar and drink his way through conversations with himself.

But on the field, The Stork was all business. He was very serious about practicing and playing the all-star game, even though it pretty much amounted to nothing more than a glorified exhibition.

Ditto for his invisible friend.

Jack Lambert was another linebacker who was a major-league drinker, as I discovered at the Pro Bowl. I've never seen anything like it. He drank as if he were going to the electric chair. He would actually bring a giant cooler filled with a couple of cases of beer to practice each day and invite a few guys to help him empty it when the workout was over.

Once you got to know Jack, he was a great guy. The problem was getting to know him. That same leather toughness he showed on the field, while playing inside linebacker for the Steelers, was part of his off-field personality as well.

One day at practice, Lambert was throwing a football around with some kids. Gastineau watched for a couple of minutes, then decided it was a good opportunity for him to become pals with Lambert. So he asked one of the kids for the ball and turning toward Lambert, said, "Here, Jack, catch."

Lambert never lifted his arms. He just let the ball bounce at his feet.

"Fuck you, Gastineau," he said before walking away.

After another Pro Bowl practice, Jack invited me to have a beer from his cooler. We ended up knocking off a case, drank some more at a bar, passed out, woke up, and from that point on, I was his friend.

In eleven years, I've seen my share, good, bad . . . and ugly.

And for anyone else, I suppose I'll just have to keep judging them on the basis of their game-program mugs.

CHAPTER

FIVE

FROM HARD KNOX TO HARVARD

You won't find four individuals as different from each other as the head coaches I had with the Bills.

Chuck Knox was the first. He was a larger-than-life character who not only walked with a swagger, but talked with one, too.

Then there was Kay Stephenson. Until I heard him speak one day, I was convinced he was a mannequin.

Then there was Hank Bullough. He had his own language—but even he couldn't understand it.

And finally, there was Marv Levy. You could understand what he said—provided you carried an unabridged dictionary along with your playbook.

Knox is my all-time favorite head coach. And the thing I liked the most about playing for him, from 1979 until he left for Seattle in 1983, was his straightforward approach. Chuck was a bottom-line guy. He let his players play and his coaches coach.

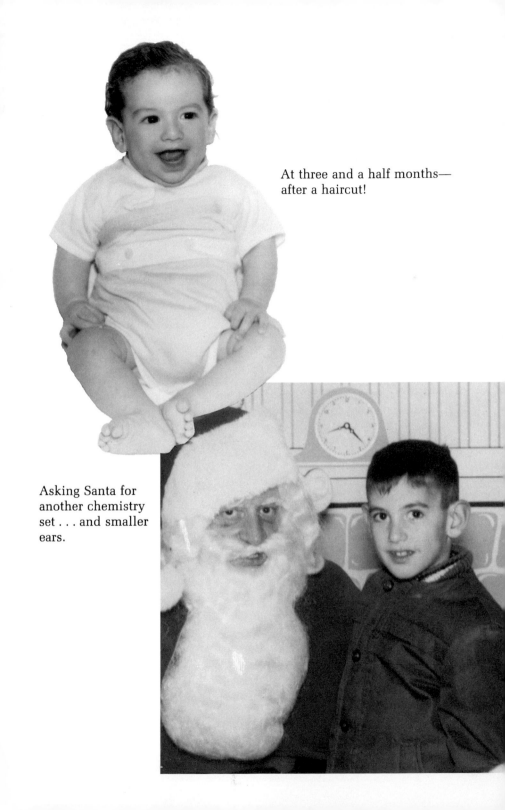

At three and a half months—
after a haircut!

Asking Santa for
another chemistry
set . . . and smaller
ears.

That's me, number 71, burying a defender on a touchdown run while playing offensive tackle at Waltham High.

This scene followed all sixty of my wrestling matches as a junior and senior in high school.

Mom and Dad cheering me up after yet another loss in my 0–11 senior year at Boston College.

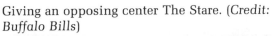

Giving an opposing center The Stare. (*Credit: Buffalo Bills*)

Closing in on a legend, Terry Bradshaw. (*Credit: Robert L. Smith*)

Celebrating a victory with my all-time favorite head coach, Chuck Knox. (*Credit: Buffalo Bills*)

Sharing a rare serious moment with my partner in crime, Jim Haslett. (*Credit: Buffalo Bills*)

A loaded spring waits for the snap. (*Credit: Robert L. Smith*)

Causing the ball to pop loose while hitting San Francisco's Roger Craig. (*Credit: Robert L. Smith*)

With the brilliant form displayed on fumble recoveries such as this, it's a wonder I've never played running back in the NFL. (*Credit: Robert L. Smith*)

Trying to butter up Jim Kelly for a small loan.

"Hanging loose" with teammates John Kidd and Kent Hull.

Getting Boomer Esiason to cooperate for the photographer with fellow nose men Bob Golic (center) and Jim Burt at the Goofy Games.

With Kris, the one who brought direction to my life. (*Credit: Yanka and Yolanda Van Der Kolk*)

California, here I come!

All you had to do for him was win.

He liked to project an image of being really tough, and he could intimidate you when he felt it was necessary. But above all, he treated you like a man. He wasn't concerned with a lot of the trivial things, like other head coaches who need to make themselves feel important and remind the players who's in charge.

Chuck felt important. The players knew he was in charge.

With Chuck, there was no dress code for road trips. No suit jackets. No ties. As long as you didn't get on the plane naked and whatever you wore wasn't ripped or dirty, he wouldn't hassle you. That was perfect for a guy like me, who believes the only code for dress should be c-o-m-f-o-r-t. He also never made a big fuss over training-camp meals, the way some coaches do. You wouldn't be fined for missing breakfast, lunch, or dinner. If you didn't know enough to eat when you were supposed to, you weren't going to last very long on Chuck's team anyway.

Before every season, he would lay down the following ground rules: "I don't care who you fuck, who you fuck with, what you wear, what you eat, what you drink . . . I don't care what you do, as long as you win. Play good, or you're out of here. It's that simple."

Well, maybe it wasn't *that* simple. He would warn us against being involved in criminal activity . . . that is, the kind that takes place away from the football field. And that kind of warning was particularly necessary with the type of team he put together in Buffalo. Consider some of the wackos he acquired through drafting, trading, and the free-agent market: Jim Haslett, Conrad Dobler, Phil Villapiano, Isiah Robertson, Lawrence McCutcheon, Ron Jessie. And of course, yours truly.

Knox would always stick behind his players, especially when it came to dealing with our hard-assed general manager, Stew Barber, who wasn't one of his favorite people. On the day, late in the 1980 season, that I learned I had been voted to the Pro Bowl for the first time, Chuck came up to me and said, "Just keep playing like you're playing. Then, you take all of those awards you're going to get, put them in a wheelbarrow, roll it up to the GM's office, dump them right on his floor, and say, 'Give me some goddamn money!' And I'll be right there behind you."

If a player did get into serious off-field trouble, Chuck was willing to help out.

"Just don't come to me with a traffic ticket or a jaywalking ticket or any little crap like that," he'd tell us. "You can take care of the little crap yourselves. The favors I've saved up are only for big things. And I mean big things."

I never heard of Chuck's helping anybody beat a murder rap, but who ever really knows about stuff like that? Chuck did have his connections. And the way he carried himself reminded me of another blue-eyed, larger-than-life character. In fact, he came up to me one day and said, "Do you know who Ol' Blue Eyes is, Fred?"

"Sure, Frank Sinatra."

"Nope, it ain't Sinatra."

"Who is it then?"

"Me. I'm the original Ol' Blue Eyes."

"Right, Chuck."

A lot of coaches couldn't joke around with players like that. They'd be too afraid they might actually show a human side. They'd rather operate as if their thoughts and emotions come from a computer chip.

Not Chuck. Hell, I used to have slap-fights with the guy. How many NFL players can say they've ever had a slap-fight with their head coach? I remember one that started after Chuck swaggered into the locker room and waved a thick wad of hundred-dollar bills in my face.

"Need some money?" he said, looking as cocky as always. "This is the kind of dough an NFL head coach makes."

I grabbed for it, and he pulled it away and started jabbing me with his other hand. I jabbed back, and before you knew it, we were slap-fighting, like a couple of kids. Chuck always felt secure enough with his authority to do something like that. He didn't worry that it might cost him some respect, which it never did. Besides, most of us were smart enough to realize there was a limit to how much horseplay there could be with the head coach. And Chuck knew how far to push a hairy, 300-pound guy getting paid to be violent.

One night I called Chuck's radio show in Buffalo, and, disguising my voice, I said, "Don't you think Fred Smerlas is the greatest player you have ever seen?" Chuck cleared his throat, and said, "Well, he is a pretty good football player . . ." Then I said, "And don't you think he is one of the best-looking guys on the team, too?" After a long pause, Knox said, "Well, uh, that's really not for me to say." And I hung up.

When I mentioned the call to him the next day, he insisted he knew it was me all along. But judging from the way he hesitated on that second question, I think I had him at least partially fooled.

I always looked forward to Chuck's meetings because, for the most part, they were pretty relaxed. Haz and I would be lying on the floor in the front row, with our feet facing Knox and our heads resting against upside-down chairs. He'd look down at us and say, "Now there's a pair that could beat a full house." Our posture was perfectly fine with him, provided we paid attention and kept our mouths shut. Which wasn't too difficult because, for one thing, his meetings never lasted very long. For another, you usually wanted to hear what Chuck had to say. He'd be chomping on that cigar of his, really grinding on it, and giving us all of his chichés— Knoxisms, as they were called. He had a million of them, such as:

"Don't write a check with your mouth that your body can't cash."

"Don't overload your ass with your mouth."

"What you do speaks so well, no need to hear what you say."

"A faint heart never won a fair maiden."

"Peace at home; war on the outside."

"You play the hand that's dealt you."

He also knew the right things to say, and how to say them, to get us motivated. During our meeting the night before we were going to face the Steelers, Chuck said, "Listen, I don't want you to take any shit from these guys. If Dwight White opens his mouth, fuck him where he breathes. Just jump their asses and pull their fucking hearts out. I want to see their shit on the ground."

I jumped out of my chair, along with everyone else in the room, and started yelling and screaming, "Yeah, Chuck! Let's go! Bring 'em on!" Then, I stopped for a second and thought to myself, fuck him where he breathes?

But Chuck's tough-guy image wasn't an act. He grew up poor in a town called Sewickley, Pennsylvania. He had to fight his way to the top. Even after having established himself as one of the more successful head coaches in the NFL, he never lost the edge that provided the staircase for his climb. He never stopped being a fighter.

There was one morning he walked into the locker room with a scratched-up face and two black eyes. It was obvious they weren't souvenirs from a playful slap-fight—they were from a barroom brawl the night before.

"Looks like you got your ass kicked, Chuck," I said.

"Yeah," he said. "But you should see the six other guys."

Chuck maintained the strong friendships from his old neighborhood. His Sewickley buddies were always around the team, even on game day. They were some of the strangest characters you've ever seen. Like "Big D." He weighed about 500 pounds and would run up and down our sidelines, putting whammies on players from the other team. Sometimes, Big D didn't watch where he was going as he ran, and that could prove very painful to anyone in his path. Now, that's a real *whammy.*

Chuck could swing with both sides of the fence. He could be Hard Knox, drinking beers and shots and throwing punches with the best of them. Or he could be Mr. Sophisticated, putting on a tux and mingling at a cocktail party with the upper class. Whatever the situation called for, Chuck would adapt.

He was extremely well organized. He put together a great staff of assistants, including Tom Catlin, still the best defensive coordinator in the game, and he trusted them to do most of the work while he acted like a CEO. Some head coaches can't function that way. They think they have to be involved in every single facet of the squad, no matter how small, and all they wind up doing is making it harder on everybody—especially themselves.

Because Chuck knew exactly what he wanted to accomplish and wasn't afraid to delegate responsibility, his practices were always short and crisp. You were in, you worked, and you were out. The sessions never dragged on to where players' minds drifted and they'd start screwing around. He knew he wasn't dealing with the longest attention spans in the world. And if things ever did get a little too loose, he could tighten them up in a hurry just by staring holes through somebody or telling whoever needed to be told to "get in the fucking practice." He only had to say it once.

Chuck demanded respect from his players, but he also wanted to be liked. And he knew how to enhance his popularity without becoming a pushover. For instance, during our 1980 training camp at Niagara University, he threw an impromptu beer party for us. It had been a long, hot summer of two-a-day practices, and after we came out for our afternoon session one day, Chuck called us together in the middle of the field.

"You guys have been working your asses off," he said. "So I want you to take it back inside for the rest of the day. Four kegs of beer are waiting for you . . . on me."

We let out a big cheer and went charging back into the locker room. For the next several hours, we drank, laughed, sang, told war stories, and poured beer on each other's head. We were like a bunch of kindergarteners whose teacher had given them a surprise snack. It really helped bring the team closer together. From that day forward, you found yourself working just a little bit harder in practice because there was always that possibility Chuck might give us another foamy treat.

Not that every minute around him was a picnic. The day after a Thursday night loss to Philadelphia in 1981, Chuck came up to me in practice and he didn't look too happy. In fact, he was downright pissed off and wanted to chew some ass.

"You made Guy Morriss look like an All-Pro," he said, referring to the Eagles' center. "There were about six or seven plays that you could have made last night just by diving over him. Don't you know how to dive?"

Figuring this wasn't a give-and-take discussion, I didn't bother to respond.

"This is how you dive, Smerlas," Knox said.

With this, he ran, jumped, and landed flat on his stomach.

"See that? Dive!"

He got up and did it again.

"Dive!"

And again.

"Dive!"

Here was a forty-nine-year-old NFL head coach doing belly flops all over the field.

Chuck, I thought to myself, maybe the stress of the job is finally getting to you.

Most of the time, though, he was very calculating in everything he did. And that included berating officials. Although we held a 24–10 lead, Knox didn't like a couple of calls against us in the first half of our 1981 wild-card playoff game against the Jets at Shea Stadium. He wanted to leave the officials with a little something to think about for the final thirty minutes. So, as we started toward the locker room at halftime, he grabbed me by the arm and said, "Come with me." I had no idea what he was up to and I didn't ask any questions. I just stayed right behind him as he jogged toward the officials. When he caught up with the referee, he tapped him with his clipboard, and all of sudden, Chuck started going out of his mind.

"What the fuck kind of calls are you making out there?" he screamed. "Tell me! What the hell are you guys looking at today?"

Then, out of the corner of his eye, he gave me a quick wink. As he started to charge the ref, as if he were going to kill him, I wrapped my arms around Chuck and pulled him back—just as he had wanted me to. The officials pretended to ignore him as they headed off the field, but you knew he had made his point. And maybe, just maybe, that worked to our advantage on the way to our 31–27 victory.

When Chuck resigned to take the Seahawks' job after the 1982 season, I was crushed. I wanted to cry. As I said, the guy is my all-time favorite head coach. I had always assumed I was going to play for him the rest of my career. But toward the end of the '82 season, rumors were floating around that he was getting out of Buffalo. The Monday after our final game, as we cleaned out our lockers for the off-season, I walked up to him and said, "Chuck, don't leave me. You brought me into this league, and I don't think I could play for another coach. Take me with you, Chuck. I don't care where you go, just take me with you."

At first, I really thought it was that simple—Chuck could just tell the Bills, "Hey, Smerlas is my nose tackle; he's coming with me," and we'd be off on our merry way. I didn't stop to consider the compensation his new team would have to give the Bills for me or any other player it acquired from them. My stuff is still packed, with stickers on the boxes that say, "Chuck or bust."

Joe Devlin, who up to that point in his life had barely cleared his throat, let alone spoken to another human being, also approached Knox that day. "As you know, Chuck, I'm a man of few words," Joe said. "But I just wanted to let you know I appreciate and thank you for the way that you treated us. You treated us like men."

Chuck had a tear in his eye.

I hated it, but I understood his decision to get out. For one thing, he had a major problem with Barber. They didn't see eye to eye on anything. Chuck had never forgiven him for losing linebacker Tom Cousineau, whom the Bills had made the No. 1 overall pick of the '79 draft, to the Canadian Football League. When that happened, his blue eyes turned red.

Chuck was looking to build his team around defense, which was obvious when you considered that six of the first eight choices we made that year were Cousineau, me, Haslett, defensive end Ken Johnson, free safety Jeff Nixon, and strong safety Rod Kush. Chuck got the rest of us, but he saw the loss of Cousineau as a backward step. It really soured him on the organization, as did the Bills' refusal to build an indoor practice facility (which they now have), turbulent contract negotiations with key veteran players, and his own contract talks with Ralph Wilson, which, finally, led him to seek a better deal elsewhere.

Still, it hurt when Chuck took off for Seattle. To me, he'll always be the guy who raised me from a pup—from a little nose to a big nose.

I was in Hawaii, for my third Pro Bowl appearance, when someone from Buffalo called to tell me Kay Stephenson had been hired as our new head coach.

"Kay?" I said. "That's my mother's name."

Then I received a call from my mother. Stephenson had called her in Waltham, looking to get in touch with me.

"Fred, isn't it wonderful?" she said.

"What's that?"

"Your new head coach has the same name as me."

"Yeah, Ma. Wonderful."

"And he sounds like such a nice man."

"I wouldn't know. I've never heard him speak."

And I hadn't, even though he'd spent the last five seasons as an assistant to Knox, in charge of our quarterbacks. Kay was even more of a sphinx than Devlin. When he stood still, with his thick head of hair that never moved and clothes that never wrinkled, you wondered if he had fallen off a truck carrying mannequins to a department store. The only way you could tell Kay was alive was the occasional puff of smoke from his ever-present cigarette. (He was very slick; you never saw his hand touch the cigarette between drags.)

After we finally spoke on the phone, I liked what I heard.

He didn't have the most inspiring voice in the world, but he sounded confident. He sounded as if he knew what he was talking about. So I decided to give him the benefit of the doubt. After all, he had spent six seasons on Chuck's staff, counting one with the Rams. He was one of Chuck's protégés. It only made sense that he'd do things Chuck's way. Right?

I couldn't have been more wrong.

Before I explain why, let me say that I liked Kay a lot. He was a great person. If you had a son, you'd probably want him to grow up to be just like Kay (although you might lose him in department stores because he'd want to stand next to every mannequin he saw). I just didn't agree with his coaching philosophy. I'm sure some of it had to do with my feelings toward Chuck, but I also think Kay went overboard in trying to remove the free-spirited atmosphere Knox created.

Once he took over, we stopped feeling like men and started feeling like children.

The first sign that things would be different came in training camp, when he established all sorts of new rules, beginning with our meals. If you missed breakfast, lunch, or dinner, you were fined. Again, Chuck never bothered with that. He figured the eventual loss of your job, when poor eating habits caused your performance to suffer, was punishment enough. Besides, what good was it to make sure a player ate his meals in training camp when he'd only go right back to missing them once the regular season started and he was on his own?

Then there were Kay's practices. They were marathons. And after each one, he'd have us run like marathoners—with our pads and helmets on. It wasn't long before our legs felt like rubber. From head to toe, we were like giant rags.

So, I went up to him and said, "Kay, you're killing us. The team needs a break."

"Oh, Fred, we have so much stuff to cover," he said. "We're going to need at least two more weeks of double sessions to get it done."

I pulled another clump of hair out of my head and went back to work.

With Chuck, everything was crisp, everyone was laughing, everyone was lively. With Kay, we were drained from the moment we climbed out of bed in the morning until the moment we collapsed onto our pillows at night. Chuck would give us an occasional day off from practice or a night off from meetings, just so we could recharge physically and mentally. Kay would never hear of it. He had it set in his mind that more was better—that the only reason a team lost was because it didn't work hard enough. That is one of the great misconceptions of football. Working a player too hard can be every bit as damaging as not working him enough. He doesn't develop a stronger body, he develops fatigue. You need a happy medium, where you gain and maintain good conditioning but still feel fresh on Sunday, when it counts the most.

You also have to know your team. What Kay inherited from Chuck was a bunch of freewheeling individuals. There were a lot of characters who needed room to be themselves. Kay didn't want that. He tried to dictate the personality of his players with mandatory meals, dress codes for road trips, and all of the other little things Knox wouldn't allow to get between us and the bottom line, which was winning. Even after he weeded out some of the guys he felt couldn't or wouldn't do things his way, Kay had a hard time selling that approach. I know it was one of my tougher purchases.

Another of Kay's ideas that didn't make a whole lot of sense to me was borrowing training methods from every other team in the league. Our running program was from Dallas. Our isometrics program was from Washington. Our lifting program was from Pittsburgh.

The only thing we could call our own was mediocrity. We went 8-8 in 1983, 2-14 in 1984, and were off to an 0-4 start when Kay lost his job in 1985. We reached a point in '84 when, in the midst of losing our first eleven games of the season, Kay would congratulate us for good practices. He'd say, "Men, we can take a good practice and put it right in the bank." The question I always had was, when were we going to make a withdrawal?

I'll admit that, overall, Kay didn't have the greatest talent in the world. After the '83 season, with the Joe Ferguson Era coming to an end, we had a major hole at quarterback. We had problems at a lot of key positions, but Kay also didn't receive much help from his coaching staff. When Chuck left for Seattle, Tom Catlin and some other topflight assistants followed. Kay wound up hiring some real beauties, especially on defense. During an '83 game against the Rams, we stayed in the same defense for about thirty-one plays in a row. Meanwhile, the Rams moved the ball up and down the field as if we weren't even there. I became so frustrated, I smashed my helmet on a table on the sidelines, knocking cups of water all over the place.

"Hey, Coach, don't you think they've figured out what we're doing by now?" I yelled to Stephenson. It didn't do any good. The Rams pounded us, 41–17.

With Catlin, we did things to try to keep opponents off-balance. We slanted, we stunted, we blitzed. After he left, we just played straight defense. And opponents just shoved the ball straight down our throat.

Through all of the losing—and even after the occasional victory—you never saw any emotion from Kay. He did absolutely nothing to try to motivate us. During meetings, Haslett and I sat in chairs. Kay didn't want us on the floor anymore, and it was a good thing because we'd probably have fallen asleep. Kay would speak for fifteen to twenty minutes, about ten to fifteen minutes longer than the average Knox address, but you couldn't remember a word he said. He'd speak in that constant monotone, and it would automatically shut off your brain.

Kay left the job as quietly as he took it. The morning Ralph Wilson told him he was fired, Kay didn't mention it to anyone in the office, including his personal secretary. I guess he didn't want to upset her. So, just before he departed for good, he told her he was only stepping out for a few minutes to go to the bank.

I can picture her sitting there thinking, "Gee, that must be one heck of a long line Kay's standing in."

When Hank Bullough became our defensive coordinator before the '85 season, I thought things were turning in the right direction. His nickname was Doctor of Defense, and I figured he could perform the necessary surgery to bring our ailing unit back to health. I was just so happy that, once and for all, Kay had hired a legitimate, knowledgeable guy.

I couldn't wait for the season to start. I couldn't wait for Hank to get to Buffalo. I even tried to call him in Cincinnati, where he had helped the Bengals reach Super Bowl XVI, to welcome him aboard. He wasn't home, so I spoke with Mrs. Doctor of Defense.

"I just want you to know how excited I am that your husband is joining us," I told her.

It wasn't until the week before our spring minicamp that I finally had a chance to see Hank in person. I was expecting someone fairly intelligent. Well groomed. Well dressed. Maybe wearing a stethoscope.

I was expecting anyone except the person I saw the moment the elevator doors opened to the third floor of the administration building at Rich Stadium—a grungy-looking, gruff-sounding guy in purple polyester slacks and white plastic shoes. When our eyes met, my heart dropped to the first floor.

It all came back to me.

January 1979. I was on a plane headed for Mobile, Alabama, where I would be playing in the Senior Bowl. I sat in the back, and, during the entire flight, I kept hearing this loud, obnoxious voice belonging to a male passenger in the front of the plane. The rest of us would look at each other and roll our eyes; that's how annoying the guy was. But we all minded our own business—that is, until the plane landed and he started harassing a stewardess. So I walked up to him and said, "Why don't you just leave the stewardess alone, okay?"

I didn't know him, but he recognized me.

"Goddamn, Smerlas," he said. "Can't even dress right to get on a plane."

I'll admit, I wasn't going to win any fashion awards that day. I wore a flannel shirt, with cutoff sleeves, and jeans. But what of it? His attire wasn't exactly best-dressed material, either. Then, I noticed a Patriots emblem on his shirt. I figured he was someone from their organization scouting the Senior Bowl and he knew me from Boston College. Still, that didn't give him the right to harass a stewardess or anyone else on the plane, I told him so, and that was the end of it.

I was the No. 1 rated defensive tackle in the '79 NFL draft, and everyone in the world expected the Patriots, who were desperate for help at the position, to select me, a hometown product, with the twenty-fifth overall choice. Instead, they picked a safety from South Carolina named Rick Sanford. In the next day's *Boston Globe*, there was a story on the Patriots' draft, and it quoted their defensive coordinator, Hank Bullough, on the reason they passed on me: "Smerlas didn't run athletically."

I never connected the name with a face.

But as soon as those elevator doors opened, everything began to swirl around in my mind—the incident on the plane, the quote in the *Globe*. It was a nightmare come true, one of the worst moments of my life. I didn't even bother to get off the elevator. Without either of us saying a word, I pressed the button for the first floor, where our locker room was located. I knew it was only a matter of time before the man in the purple polyester pants and white plastic shoes ran me off the team, so I decided to start packing.

Then, while sitting on a stool in front of my locker, I began to think things over. Even after our 2-14 finish in 1984, the prospect of going to another team didn't appeal to me. I had invested six seasons with the Bills. I had represented them in four Pro Bowls. I liked Buffalo. I wanted to finish my career there. So, I just said, screw it. If this guy wants to get rid of me, he's going to have to get rid of me at my best.

Of course, I knew I was about to face one of the greatest challenges of my life. I knew I couldn't make a mistake, because the second I did, old Hankie Pie would be jumping down my throat. My ass was on the line. Hank was going to try to kick it to oblivion.

Sure enough, when I showed up for the first day of practice at training camp that summer, I noticed about fifteen short, fat guys stretching with the defensive linemen. I didn't have to ask what position they played. Hank had combed the earth, looking for every unemployed nose tackle he could find. After a while, I wasn't worried about who was behind me on the depth chart; I was worried about who was going to parachute in the next day.

If I didn't give Hank ammunition to convince Stephenson to ship me out, he was determined to find it. That was obvious from the instructions he gave me before our first workout—I was only supposed to play two-gap, which means pushing the center a yard into the backfield and playing the gaps between him and each guard. Hank didn't want me coming off the center under any circumstances. In other words, he was seeing to it that I'd be swallowed up in the middle of the line and look like a complete dildo.

During one drill, I hit the center, but instead of pushing him back a yard, I threw him to one side and tackled the ballcarrier for a loss. It was the kind of play most defensive coordinators would love their nose tackle to make, but Hank had a fit.

"Dammit, Smerlas!" he screamed. "I told you I don't want you coming off that center."

It was a horror show. I was being forced to do things I knew wouldn't work—things that a four-time Pro Bowl nose tackle just doesn't do unless he's in the advanced stages of brain damage, which I wasn't at the time. With me always two-gapping, teams never had to guess where I was going to be, so they could do just about anything they wanted. Centers actually would come to the line and start giggling, "Ha! Ha! I know you're going to be two-gapping on this play, Fred, so I'm going to jump around you and go after the linebacker." And *whoosh*, they'd be gone.

To make my life even more miserable, Hank started taking me out on passing downs and putting in Don Smith, whom he had picked up from Atlanta. Don couldn't even get off the line of scrimmage. I was rushing the quarterback ten times better. But because I wasn't in there, I started to see newspaper articles that said: "Fred Smerlas can't pass-rush anymore. He's over the hill. He's washed up."

After we lost the first couple of games of the regular season, Don, no Bullough fan himself, said to me, "You know, Fred, if they fire Kay, things could get worse around here."

"What do you mean?"

"Hank could wind up being the head coach."

"No way. They'd never promote Hank. Not in a million years."

After our fourth loss, Kay was fired. Things got worse.

"I told you so," Don said.

The day it was announced Hank would replace Stephenson, I was at Jim Haslett's ranch in Lockport, New York. I slumped down on a bench and just stared into space.

"This is it, Haz," I said. "It's finally, completely over for me. I made it this far with Hank as the defensive coordinator. No way am I going to last with him as head coach. This boy is history."

I started looking around the ranch to see if there were any chores I could do. Maybe Haz would hire me to clean the horses' stalls. I was already knee-deep in manure in my current job.

But again, I decided to stick it out. I decided to face the challenge.

And the first obstacle was sitting through one of Hank's meetings. They were even longer and deadlier than Kay's.

Not to mention a whole lot dumber.

To say Hank fractured the English language would be a gross understatement. He pulverized it. He would talk about our "work ethnic" and the importance of being able to make decisions "on the spare of the moment." After a loss to the Jets late in the '85 season, he said a long pass from Ken O'Brien to Wesley Walker "really took the sails right out of our wind."

Pretty soon, Hankisms began showing up in newspapers throughout the country. Unfortunately, they were accompanied by equally embarrassing Bills-related items, such as our won-loss record and the scores of our games.

Some samples from the Worst of Bullough:

"We keep beating ourselves, but we're getting better at it."

"I don't believe in morale victories."

"I haven't exactly been divulged with phone calls." (after being asked about the poor response to an opening on his coaching staff)

"I don't wish to indulge that information." (after being asked about the length of his contract with the Bills)

"Well, you've got that Jackson kid at Auburn and the Napolean Bonaparte kid at Navy." (after being asked to assess the talent of the 1987 draft, which featured Bo Jackson and Napoleon McCallum)

"You mean Lords of London?" (after being asked about the Bills' insurance policy on Jim Kelly's contract)

One of the more frightening things that ever happened to me was thinking, after one of Hank's meetings, that some of his remarks almost made sense. Then, I said to myself, Oh, my God! I must be developing brown spots on my brain. This guy is actually beginning to sound normal.

Most of Hank's discussions centered around money. He'd constantly bring up our contracts, saying how much he hated incentive clauses for statistical accomplishments and post-season honors. He didn't believe in paying for production, which always seemed reasonable to me. And his idea of motivating us was to write "$100,000 to $0" on the chalkboard, then explain how difficult it would be to make payments on a Mercedes or a Cadillac without a job—when your income went from $100,000 to $0. I guess the many players who didn't drive luxury cars had to find another means of getting psyched.

When we lost, which was often, Hank never made any attempt to build us back up. Instead, he'd yell and scream and call us "a bunch of low-lives." In the middle of games, he would pull the starting defense off the field, get us together on the sidelines, and say things like, "You no good pieces of shit. You're playing like crap. You're letting me down." After we took a 49–17 beating at Indianapolis, Hank really tore into Bruce Smith, in his first season after the Bills made him the No. 1 overall pick of the draft, in front of the whole team. He told him he wasn't ever going to amount to anything as a player. Three Pro Bowls later, Bruce appears to be having the last laugh.

Hank was loaded with all kinds of inconsistencies.

In one speech he said, "The problem with this team is that there is too much 'my, my, my' and 'me, me, me' and 'I, I, I.' " In another speech he said, "This is *my* team. *I* waited a long time to get a team of *my* own. You guys are not going to ruin it for *me*."

In another speech he said, "Look, I don't care what happens this season—if we win, if we lose, if we tie—as long as you grade out with a plus. If you get blocked, but run to the play, that's a plus. Just get those pluses, and I'll be happy." After our sixth loss of the season he said, "The hell with the pluses; win some games. I don't care how you do it, just win."

During a meeting at our 1986 minicamp, his first as head coach, Hank announced that veteran players would no longer be given the special privilege of staying in the larger dormitory suites at our Fredonia (New York) State College training camp. There were only three such suites, and they'd be shared by the six oldest players on the team. I happened to be among the six, but it was no big deal if I didn't have one. Hank wanted to make the point there were no veterans or rookies on the squad—that we were all the same, that we would all be treated the same. For a change, I thought he was making a good point.

All of sudden, after our 1-5 start, he said to us, "Hey, you know something? This isn't my team. This is the veterans' team. You veterans are supposed to be my leaders. Where have you been this year?"

A lot of us, rookies as well as veterans, felt we had left the best part of ourselves back at training camp. Kay's practices were bad, but Hank's were unbelievable. He would just beat us into the ground. Realizing we were on the brink of burnout, the assistant coaches one day talked Hank into having us go through a low-intensity workout in shoulder pads and shorts. But halfway into it, Hank snapped, "This is horseshit! This is my team, we're going to run it my way, and I'm not going to listen to anyone else. So get your full pads on and we're going to start the practice over, right from the beginning."

With so many players bitching about him among themselves, it was inevitable that someone would finally have a showdown with Hank. That someone was Bruce Smith. As we headed into the meeting room at training camp after another long day of torturous practices, Bruce glared at Bullough and said, "Hi, Hank, you fuck stick."

Bullough was stunned. He just stared back at Bruce, without saying a word.

"Don't give me that brook-trout look, you blob of shit," Bruce said.

Sensing this might turn into a fight—and probably a very short one considering Bruce's overwhelming physical advantages—some guys shouted encouragement for their teammate. No one seemed interested in coming to Hank's defense. But it never went any further than Hank's just standing there looking like, well, a brook trout.

Before another training-camp meeting, Bruce played a not-so-friendly prank on Bullough when he hid his golf cart behind a building. Hank, who acted like a general as he drove the thing around campus, went crazy trying to find it. Finally, he stormed into the meeting room and said, "We are not leaving here until someone tells me where my golf cart is."

No one told him. We left anyway.

I think one of the more telling examples of how the players felt about Hank came later that summer. As I was driving past a 7-Eleven store in Fredonia, I noticed a long line of my teammates standing outside. I stopped and found out they were buying tickets for the New York State Lottery, whose jackpot had reached something like $56 million.

"If I win," one guy said, "I'll hit the motherfucker in the face and gladly pay the damages."

After about a half second of contemplation, I said, "Move over, boys. I think today's my lucky day."

Actually, the luckiest day for us all came November 2, 1986. We were playing the Buccaneers at Tampa Stadium. We had lost six of our previous eight games. Everyone had a feeling that if the Bucs, who were even more pathetic than we were, beat us, Hank would be gone.

As we gathered for the first defensive huddle of the game, Bruce looked at us and said, "If anyone makes a tackle today, I'm going to beat the shit out of him."

Maybe it was only coincidence, but we wound up losing, 34–28. The next day, Hank was out; Marv Levy was in.

At first, the best thing Marv had going for him was that he wasn't Hank Bullough. Almost anyone would have made us feel like a person tasting that first drop of cold water after being lost in a blazing desert. That is, anyone who spoke English.

Marv's credentials seemed a little suspect. He was out of football. He hadn't been very successful in his only other NFL head-coaching stint, with Kansas City. Most of us assumed the only reason he got the job was because his good friend Bill Polian was our general manager.

After winning the first of back-to-back division championships in 1988, we discovered Marv had a little bit more going for him.

But even before we started to win again, we were already giving him the respect none of us could ever bring ourselves to give Hank. For one thing, he not only spoke English, he could speak it more articulately than anyone we'd heard since the last time we were changing channels and paused briefly on PBS. For another, he was a gentleman. Maybe too much of a gentleman for the NFL (Marv's the one you see, on that clip from NFL Films, calling the ref an "overofficious jerk"). But when you've been exposed to the other extreme, you realize there isn't a whole lot of room to complain.

He also didn't wear purple polyester pants and white plastic shoes.

Marv looked and acted like a professor. In fact, some of his football friends call him The Professor. But, unlike Hank, there was credence to his nickname. If Hank was the Doctor of Defense, he should have been sued for malpractice. Marv has a master's degree in English history from Harvard. His master's thesis was on twentieth-century English diplomacy.

Not exactly your typical background for a business filled with so many homicidal maniacs.

After Marv's first few meetings, I found myself writing down several words I hadn't heard before. I'd go home and Kris and I would look them up in the dictionary. I tried to do the same with some of Hank's gems, but I could never find any definitions because the words didn't exist.

For the most part, Marv knew the limits of our intelligence. But there were occasions when he'd forget he was in an NFL meeting room and not a Harvard classroom. He'd use a word like *felicitous,* see all of the blank stares, and then come back to earth. I told him once, "Marv, your practices aren't too bad. But with some of those words you use, those meetings really stress me out."

The only other time you dreaded being in one of Marv's meetings was when in training camp he went over certain portions of our playbook. We called them Big Book meetings, because he'd pull out that monstrosity, plop it on the podium, and say, "Okay, men, let's open to page fifty-seven, rule number two thousand eight hundred and one. It states, 'Do not wear your socks above your calves.' Now, turn to page three hundred. I know I've read this for the past three years, but let's read it again, the section entitled 'How to Protect Yourself in Case of a Hotel Fire.' . . ."

When Marv pulled out the Big Book, the rest of us in the room pulled out big chunks of our hair and sweat began to pour down our faces.

In all seriousness, though, the atmosphere was a thousand times more relaxed than when Hank was in charge. Before Marv's arrival, we were like a hand that had had its circulation cut off. As long as it wasn't cut off too long and you could get the blood flowing again, the hand would come back to life. All we asked was for a head coach to treat us like human beings. When Marv showed us he would, we came back to life, too. He allowed us to be ourselves, both as players and people. It wasn't as wide open a situation as we had with Knox, but close enough.

Oh, he would scream and yell with the best of them. He could get right in your face when he felt it was necessary. But usually, he'd go up to a player afterward and apologize, just to make sure there were no hard feelings. With Hank, hard feelings were a way of life.

Marv's first step was for us to work at recapturing our confidence. Between back-to-back 2-14 seasons and Hank's browbeating, there was none left. The second step was for us to recapture an understanding of the game, beginning with penalty-avoidance. Hank never bothered to talk about that, and we had tons of penalties. We were helter-skelter. Marv stressed the importance of not picking up the stupid penalties. His motto: "Don't be dumb and don't be dirty."

Perhaps the most critical thing Marv did in his first couple of seasons was keep everything on an even keel. He wouldn't panic after a loss. He wouldn't get carried away with a win. He just kept us moving steadily, but swiftly, toward a series of goals. For the first time since the Knox years, I felt the team had some real direction.

Then something changed. And I think it all started when Marv was named 1988 NFL Coach of the Year by *The Sporting News*. He committed the cardinal sin of pro football: he believed he was as good as his accolades.

I first noticed the difference in Marv right before our 1989 training camp. We were scheduled to open the preseason against Washington in the Hall of Fame Game, giving us an extra exhibition contest and starting the preseason a week earlier than normal. The only problem was, we were due to report to Fredonia two and a half weeks before facing the Redskins. That meant nearly eight weeks of practicing and playing before our regular-season opener (making it the longest camp in club history). And that meant we'd be burned out by the time we started playing for keeps. I mean, there are only so many times you can study and execute the same stuff before you turn into a vegetable.

As one of the team's elder statesmen, I felt it was my job to talk to Levy and see if he would reconsider the extra-early start of camp.

"Marv, you've always been open and wanted us to come to you whenever we had a problem with something," I said.

"What's the problem, Fred?"

"I think coming to camp this early, while having to play that extra preseason game, is a mistake. It's going to make us stale."

"We don't think so, Fred. We've researched it thoroughly, and some of the top athletic minds in Russia feel this is the best way to train."

"Yeah, but Marv, how many Russians play in the NFL?"

He wasn't interested in hearing any more. We reported to Fredonia two and a half weeks before the Hall of Fame Game (the Redskins showed up a week and a half before it). We were as flat as pancakes when we began the regular season.

I wasn't the only one Marv refused to listen to.

All of a sudden, he was tuning everyone out, including some of his assistants. More and more of the decision making began and ended with him, and a lot of us were liking it less and less.

After all, Marv was the Coach of the Year. The rest of us were merely assistant coaches and players.

SIX

THE TREE THAT
BECAME A NOSE

I WAS A VERY HAIRY CHILD. When I was born, on April 8, 1957, I had hair down to my shoulders. No kidding. My hair was so long my mother twice had to get permission from the priest to cut it before my baptism. Most babies cry as they enter the world. I came out in black leather and riding a Harley.

My great-great-uncle was George Smerlas, who, according to legend, was a heroic giant known as The Tree. He was a Paul Bunyan–like character who stood seven feet tall, weighed 350 pounds, and lived in the hills of Greece at the turn of the century. And as the legend goes, he cleared the land by uprooting trees with his bare hands. One time, on his way home after a long day of leveling a forest, The Tree was attacked by a mountain lion. They wrestled a little bit before The Tree grabbed the lion's tail and yanked it right off. The lion ran away, never to be seen again.

I was ten pounds at birth, which made me larger than any other baby born in the family in quite some time. And the bigger I got, the closer the resemblance my relatives saw between me and The Tree. Years later, they showed me photographs of the guy, and I could see what they were talking about—very large, very hairy. The Tree's genes skipped two generations and took root in me.

At four and a half months, I was walking. Nobody believes it, but my parents will tell you the story. My crib was in their bedroom, and my mother awoke early one morning to find me walking back and forth in the crib. At four and a half months!

"Peter, wake up!" my mother yelled to my father. "It's Fred. He's walking. Wake up, Peter, you've got to see this."

"Go back to sleep, Kay," my father grumbled. "You're just having a dream."

"I'm telling you, Peter, he's walking. Look for yourself."

Finally, my father squinted up from his pillow. He almost died when he saw me standing in the crib, looking down at the two of them with a big smile on my face. My mom said I was always smiling, especially when it was time to eat.

I suppose whatever athletic ability I have came from my father. He was an all-American basketball player in high school. He also played baseball, football, and boxed. He went on to play guard on the University of Georgia basketball team, although I didn't find out about that until I was twenty-eight years old.

"Gee, Dad, why didn't you tell me sooner?" I asked.

"I don't know," he said. "I guess I didn't want to brag."

"For twenty-eight years?"

But that's my father—just a laidback, mellow kind of guy. Tough as nails, but very easygoing. He grew up in the projects of Cambridge, Massachusetts. My mother's from Somerville, Massachusetts. They were introduced by one of my mother's brothers, got married, moved to Waltham, and had three sons. Pete's the oldest, I came along two years later, and Chuck was born three years after that.

Until his retirement in 1987, my father helped run Smerlas and Sons, a family-owned grocery store, for thirty-five years.

We lived in a ranch-style house on a hill, in your typical *Leave It to Beaver* neighborhood. It was nice, except there were a lot of wild kids running around, most of whom were older than me. I never cried, so they let me hang out with them.

Having Pete for an older brother helped toughen me up to face the rest of the neighborhood kids. When I was a baby, he would push me around in a carriage. How I survived that, I'll never know, because one of Pete's favorite tricks was to push me to the highest point of the front lawn, let go of the carriage, and laugh as it rolled all the way down—right into traffic.

If Pete didn't put me in danger, I'd always find a way to get there myself. Once, when I was about a year old, I managed to escape from the house and walk onto the top of a stone wall at the base of our front yard. Naturally, I fell about four feet to the ground before my mother, screaming hysterically, came to the rescue. I took another fall shortly thereafter, all the way down the basement stairs, and landed headfirst on the concrete floor.

If any single incident prepared me for a career as a nose tackle, that was it.

I certainly was destined to be heavy enough for the position because I never wanted to leave the kitchen table. I would eat an entire jar of Greek olives in one sitting. And that was just for an appetizer.

Anyone who knows me today wouldn't have been able to recognize me when I was in grammar school. Back then, I was quiet and very sedentary. I had no interest in sports whatsoever. Most of my fun came from things I could do alone, such as playing with my chemistry set. I was like a little mad scientist, mixing all sorts of chemicals . . . until I caused an explosion. On almost any given day, you could find either of my brothers outside, taking part in some form of athletic competition, and me in the cellar, trying to blow up the house.

Pete was the true jock among us. He was a great basketball player and had enough baseball talent to attract pro scouts when he was in ninth grade. But he didn't pursue it any further and went on to earn a master's degree in psychology from the University of Massachusetts. He thought it would help him figure me out.

If forty-seven kids from the neighborhood showed up for a sandlot baseball game, I was the forty-eighth picked. The captains would choose the bases before they got around to deciding which team would be stuck with me. In fact, there were times when I served as a base. I may have been an early walker, but in my grammar school years, I was terribly uncoordinated. I just couldn't run. I'd go five feet and fall on my face. The only way I could get around was if the wind caught my big, floppy ears just right and lifted me off the ground.

While the other kids dreamed about playing for the Celtics or the Red Sox, I dreamed about being a dentist, just like Herbie, the misfit elf from *Rudolph the Rednose Reindeer*. When I wasn't dreaming of that, I was at the controls of the "flying saucer" in the woods behind our house. I'd sit on a pile of rocks, with two sticks protruding from opposite sides like antennas, and for hours at a time, my imagination took me on action-packed journeys through the galaxy. The only thing that could pull me back to earth was the smell of food.

My childhood heroes were Aqua Boy and Billy Mumy, who played the part of Will on the TV series *Lost in Space*. I would pretend that I ate aqua gum and swam under water, just like Aqua Boy. Sometimes, I'd pretend Billy Mumy ate some aqua gum, too, and the three of us would hang out together, exploring the depths of the Atlantic Ocean.

All of this should help explain the culture shock I faced on day one at Central Junior High School in Waltham. Suddenly, my nice, innocent daydreams were replaced by nightmares that were real. I got sucker-punched while walking down the aisle in my first class, a girl got raped, and a kid OD'd on drugs and jumped out a window. I figured, if this is day one, I don't want to be around for day two.

But I was. And it got worse. Just about every class was disrupted by kids rolling apples and pennies down the aisles. One kid threw a knife and it stuck in the wall, right next to a teacher's head.

I'd go home and look in the mirror. What I'd see was a chubby, goofy-looking creature with big ears, a pocket pencil-holder, checkered pants, and penny loafers. I'd say to myself, "Man, I've got to do something to survive." So I started to get physical. I lifted weights, hit a speed bag (I was always quick with my hands), and ran—with combat boots on. Gradually, my body began to change. I became bigger, harder, stronger.

I would go on to Waltham High School and become a two-time all-American in football, an all-American and two-time state and New England heavyweight wrestling champion, and an all-state shot-putter.

But before all that, some kid jacked me up against a wall one day in seventh grade and stole a quarter from me. I never forgot that. Seven years later, when I was at Boston College, I saw that same kid downtown, sitting in his Volkswagen Beetle. I ran over, and without saying a word, I just started smashing his car with my fists, denting it everywhere.

"What the hell are you doing?" he screamed. "Are you nuts or something?"

"Remember me?" I said, still crushing his Bug. "I'm the guy you stole a quarter from seven years ago. You shouldn't have done it. Now, it's coming back to haunt you."

I have Michael (Tiny) Martin to thank for launching my athletic career. Tiny and I have been friends since third grade, and whatever he did, I did. When he got into sports, I got into sports. And we always picked the positions or events that would keep us as close together as possible. In baseball, I was the pitcher, he was the catcher. In track, I was the shot-putter, he was the discus thrower. In football, I played halfback, offensive tackle, and defensive end; Tiny played fullback, offensive guard, and linebacker. In wrestling, I was a heavyweight; he was in the next class down at 188 pounds.

My first exposure to organized football came when I was in sixth grade. I weighed 140 pounds, which made me too heavy to play Pop Warner. So I wound up in another youth league, just in time for the final game of the season. I was used as a kickoff returner. And on the first kick that came to me, I barreled over everyone in my path—including a few teammates—and went all the way for a touchdown. Everyone was screaming and yelling and slapping me on the back. I thought, hey, this is a lot of fun! The coach wanted to put me on his all-star team, but couldn't because I had played in only one game. No big deal. I just went home, ate some brownies, played with my Matchbox cars, and didn't give football a second thought.

The next time I suited up for an organized football game was in the ninth grade. I played halfback, Tiny played fullback. At that point, I was still trying to differentiate between offense and defense. So, before every snap, I'd be asking Tiny, "Who gets the ball on this play? Which way is this play going?" At 6'2" and 185 pounds, I had enough size and strength to compensate for whatever knowledge I lacked. Also, since I ran a 6.2 forty, I spent most of the season at offensive tackle, a position that, on the freshman level, didn't require a whole lot of thinking.

In my sophomore year, I became a defensive end on the varsity squad. With each practice and game, I began to feel more comfortable with what I was doing. And after an all-star-of-the-week performance in our season-opener against Malden (the coach loved the films so much, he had a special screening for the school's booster club), I was convinced I knew all there was to know about football.

Was I ever in for a rude awakening.

Our third opponent, Arlington, exposed me to something I had never seen before—trap blocking. There I was, on the first play of the game, running through what I thought was a wide-open doorway to the backfield. All of a sudden, I looked down and noticed a helmet being planted into my crotch. I walked back to the huddle with my knees rubbing and my voice an octave higher. The same thing happened on the next play and throughout the game.

Arlington ran right through us for a lopsided victory. I sang soprano all the way home and had to sleep standing up.

I had another humbling experience later that season against Brockton. Those guys were bigger, stronger, and meaner than anyone on our team. They all had thick, dark facial hair—not peach fuzz, but full-fledged beards. And they smelled like whiskey. Our defensive line, including yours truly, served as a blocking sled for their offensive line as they mauled us by something like 28 points.

We wound up having a horrible season, but I felt myself growing as a football player and a man. Of course, thanks to my ever-increasing appetite, the family grocery store nearly went out of business.

Most of the fun I had that year came after a bunch of us formed a gang called Freddy's Army. It was good for a few laughs and occasional fights with other gangs, but we never did anything criminal. We were just a bunch of fifteen- and sixteen-year-old punks who liked to go around acting tough. We even wore trench coats.

The rest of the army included the Martin brothers, Tiny and George; Rockhead McCarthy (we called him that because, during one fight he was in, the other guy used a rock to open a 150-stitch cut in his head); Muncher Dalaney (we called him that because he liked to bite people); and Tommy Hernandez, who had two nicknames. One was Rican because, even though he was of Spanish descent, he looked Puerto Rican and wasn't offended by the nickname. The other was Tommy the Pimp because, even though he was only sixteen, he looked twenty-five and dressed like a pimp. So much so that a teacher at our school asked if Tommy could fix him up with a girl. Rican even drove a big, green Cadillac his father gave him.

Wherever Tommy's Pimp-mobile was parked, that's where you'd find Freddy's Army.

By my junior year, I was carrying 230 pounds, bench-pressing 400, and running a 4.9 forty. Puberty had really kicked in—to the point where I began to shave with a hatchet instead of a razor. And I started developing a mean streak. I wasn't the one getting clobbered in the balls anymore; I was hunting the balls down. I averaged 12 tackles per game that season, and in the course of bringing each ballcarrier to the ground, I left my own little calling card—two forearm chops to the helmet. It was just my way of saying, "The name's Smerlas, and if I were you, I wouldn't run this way again."

Because of those chops, my teammates nicknamed me High Karate. The rest of my performance in our 8-1 season earned me all-American honors, which I would also receive as a senior, when we were 9-1 and burying just about every team we played.

My other big sport in high school was wrestling. My record as a junior and senior was 60-0. All but two of my victories came on pins, and fifty of the pins came in the first period. For whatever reason, wrestling was very natural for me. I only had to see a move once and I'd know it cold.

I liked wrestling as a sophomore and loved it as a junior, when I started to develop a pretty strong following. We'd have two thousand people in the gym, and most were there to see me. Not only fans, but college scouts and even some people from the U.S. Olympic wrestling team. I was probably better known as a wrestler than a football player.

But while it was nice to have the support of a large crowd, there was a lot of pressure to perform at a higher level than everyone else. I wasn't too crazy about that. In my senior year, if I didn't pin my opponent in the first minute, it was considered a bad day. The match would start, and everyone would actually be on their feet chanting, "PIN! PIN! PIN!" And if it didn't happen before those first sixty seconds expired, the next thing you'd hear was a groan. It was like I had lost. In fact, in my junior year, there was a kid from Newton South who actually jumped for joy after becoming the first opponent in sixteen matches to survive the first minute without being pinned. Talk about your moral victories.

Mothers would come up to me before matches, and in some cases with tears in their eyes, and say, "Whatever you do, please don't hurt my son." I'd always tell them, "I'm not going to hurt him. I'm just going to pin him."

Some big-time colleges, such as Notre Dame and Iowa State, offered me scholarships for wrestling. But I wasn't interested. I just couldn't see myself going from college to a career as a professional wrestler. Football seemed to hold a better future, but like most high school seniors, I wasn't entirely sure what I wanted to do with the rest of my life.

Having fun still occupied the top spot on my list of priorities.

When word got out that I wanted to play football, I was suddenly bombarded with letters and telephone calls from practically every major-college program in America: Maryland, Michigan, Penn State, Pittsburgh, North Carolina, USC, Oklahoma, Nebraska, Tulane, Syracuse. It was a far cry from Fat Freddy, the guy nobody wanted on his sandlot team.

The letters would show up at school, as well as my house. I had boxes of them. And the phone never stopped ringing. A Maryland recruiter would call every night just to say, "I hope you're eating right and taking care of yourself, Fred. Now, get a good night's sleep and we'll talk to you tomorrow." Some guys would show up at the school cafeteria during lunch, hand me a football schedule from their college, and say, "Put this under your pillow and dream about us." It was ridiculous.

And the most annoying thing was when the recruiters started showing up at the house. Night after night, they'd set up their projectors in the living room and show my parents and me a highlight film of what would always be "the finest institution in the land." It didn't take long for those films to get old. After a while, when the recruiters came over, I'd hide in my bedroom and let them bore my parents to tears.

But the experience did have its entertaining moments. The most exotic inducements came from a recruiter for a college in Virginia who said, "Come down here, Fred, and we'll get you the nicest piece of ass you could ever want—all of the time. Hell, we'll even throw in a car."

Tulane flew me and our quarterback, David (Fat) Poirier, down for what resulted in nothing more than a couple of high school kids' getting three fun-filled days in New Orleans. We stayed at one of the nicer hotels in town and were given tickets to one of the worst Super Bowls ever played, Pittsburgh vs. Minnesota.

Our southern-fried host was a piece of work. He brought us over to his house, fed us some red beans and rice, turned off the lights, and turned on a projector. After only one play of a Waltham game flashed on the screen, he shut off the projector, turned on the lights, and said, "You guys run great. Boy, would we love to have you down here playing for us."

I thought to myself, this guy has got to be kidding. But he wasn't. His recruiting pitch stopped right there. So did our interest in attending Tulane.

During the course of our stay, which was prolonged an extra twenty-four hours because our flight was canceled, we decided to have a charge-a-thon. We bought everything in sight—food, booze, souvenirs, girlie magazines, more food—and just charged it to the room that Tulane was paying for. When our host got the bill, his eyes widened, and he said, "For what this trip is going to cost us, you guys had better go to school down here."

"Thanks," we said. "But no thanks." And we took off for the airport as fast as we could.

When I visited Maryland, one of the recruiters was Randy White, who had just finished a great career there as a defensive tackle and linebacker, and would soon be drafted by the Cowboys.

"What do you plan to study when you come down here?" he asked.

"I don't know," I said. "What are you studying?"

"I'm studying to be a general."

"They have a curriculum like that here?"

"Sure. General Studies."

Randy thought he was a real comedian. Of course, who was going to tell him otherwise?

I knew Syracuse wasn't the place for me when the head coach, Frank Maloney, told me that for every point the opponent scored we would have to run a 40-yard dash. In the previous season, SU had given up something like 45 points in one game.

"You're never going to get me to come here and run forty-five forties in one practice," I said. "See you later."

Fat Poirier's father, Cliff, was our head coach at Waltham. He was a Boston College graduate, so he did all he could to steer me in that direction. Naturally, his son was headed for BC, even though he was going to be switched from quarterback to linebacker. Back then, the program didn't have the size or the money of most of the other schools trying to attract me. By the same token, there was less chance of my getting lost in the shuffle, which often happens at bigger schools.

My preference all along was to stay in the East, and when I considered the campus was six miles from my mother's kitchen, Boston College sounded like the right place for me. I spent the next four years as a defensive tackle and end, with occasional appearances at middle guard when we went to a five-man front—while majoring in education.

The rest of BC's freshman football class of 1975 was loaded with street-tough kids, including a few whose yearbook photos were taken from the side, as well as the front. At our first team meeting, one guy showed up with a bottle of beer in his hand. Another guy, a big monster with no neck and hands the size of catcher's mitts, cut in front of me as I stood on line for the water cooler.

"Hey, the line starts back there," I said.

"Fuck you," he replied.

After some pushing and shoving, we were pulled apart.

It was quite a litter of sick puppies.

We had a twenty-four-year-old linebacker named Mike Siegel, who enrolled as a freshman after serving in Vietnam and racking up several registered kills. We had another line-backer, Mike Tyler, who shaved his head and spent a lot of time sitting in the corner of his dormitory room drinking tequila. He told me about how, after a friend of his passed away, he placed a joint and a can of beer in the casket so the guy could "stay high, even in death."

After one semester break, Tyler returned with a broken arm, broken nose, stitches in his head, and a missing tooth.

"What the hell happened to you?" I asked.

"Oh, I was just fighting with a friend of mine," he said with a shrug.

"Over what?"

"Nothing. We just wanted to see who could win the fight."

"I take it your friend won?"

"Nope. I did."

Then there was Charlie Morris, a 6'5", 255-pound defensive end with long, shaggy hair and a Fu Manchu. We called him Choo Choo Charlie. He was a real biker, complete with a black-leather vest, tattoos, and a knack for finding trouble—if it didn't find him first. Believe it or not, he was an elementary-education major.

We had another defensive end, Steve Anzalone, who looked and sounded exactly like Luca Brasi, Don Corleone's longtime "associate" in The Godfather. And that wasn't all they had in common. After someone threatened to tell the dean of students that Anzalone was involved in breaking some windows on campus, Steve relieved himself in a box and sent it to the would-be snitch, along with a note that said, "If you talk, you'll end up like this stuff."

Even our quarterback, Kenny Smith, was a maniac. He had great physical talent, one of the finest throwing arms I've ever seen. But mentally, he was fried. Two days before a late-season game against Syracuse, Kenny, who had been having a good year up to that point, showed up for practice drunk. I mean, he was reeking of peppermint schnapps. The

first time the center snapped him the ball, Kenny fell down
and passed out. Most of us thought it was kind of funny, but
not the head coach, Joe Yukica. He suspended Kenny, who,
after college, wound up serving a prison term.

"Enter at Your Own Risk" was painted over the entrance
of each of the three dormitory buildings in which I resided
at BC. To say we didn't have much regard for the rules would
be an understatement. We did everything imaginable . . .
plus a few things that weren't. We'd have pig roasts out back,
turn the hallway into a golf-driving range, set off smoke
bombs at all hours of the day and night, hold demolition
derbies in the student parking lot, and throw countless drink-
and-drown parties. In one semester, we went through three
resident advisers.

I must have been thrown out of the dorm a half dozen
times, but I was always reinstated. And for the most part,
my behavior wasn't nearly as insane as some of my psychotic
roommates, such as Fat Poirier. His idea of fun was pulver-
izing doors with his bare head. The kid had a skull like
concrete, and he enjoyed performing for the crowds that
would gather whenever he got into a door-crunching frenzy.
During one game, he lost his helmet while hitting a guy, so
he smashed another guy without it. I'll never forget the time
Poirier looked at me, pointed to his forehead, and said, "Go
ahead, Freddy, give it your best shot."

I did. I ended up with a broken knuckle.

We had another psycho who shot a television set to pieces.
Hawaii Five-O was on. You know, at the end, when Mc-
Garrett says, "Book 'em, Dano"? Well, my friend said, "Shoot
'em, Dano." And he pulled out a gun and shot the TV.

Of course, there were times when our reputation made it
difficult for us to do the most innocent of things, such as
sing Christmas carols. 'Twas the season in my freshman year,
and to help put everyone on campus in the proper mood,
we put some Christmas tunes on the stereo, hung a couple
of speakers outside our windows, and had one big sing-along.
Then, the campus police showed up, made us turn off the

music, and sent everyone home. The dean of students had seen to it the school wasn't going to be overtaken by a bunch of *vicious* carolers. Okay, so maybe we did have to tie the RA to a chair so he wouldn't stop us. But we meant well.

Compared to my style of play, the things I did off the field made me seem like the choirboy I had attempted to impersonate that day. I had no technique in college. My approach to every game was simple—kill the guy in front of me. My goal was to get him to quit in four plays or less. I'd grab him by the earholes of his helmet, hit him in the throat, really unload on him. Hell, I'd chase someone fifty yards just to deliver one good shot.

I was out of control. I'd be spitting and screaming and grabbing facemasks. I'd yell at the other team's huddle, trying to get them so ripped that they'd all want to come after me. I didn't care. There were times when I wouldn't even bother to go to our defensive huddle; I'd just stand at the line, yelling at the other team. That tended to make some of our players a bit uncomfortable because they didn't want the opponents any more inspired than they already were.

On the first play against Pitt in my senior year, they tried to run the ball right at me, with Matt Carroll, an all-American offensive tackle, leading the way. I was really pissed off about that. They weren't showing me the respect I thought I deserved. So I just picked up Carroll and threw him into the backfield. Then I started screaming at him, "What are you, nuts or something? You're trying to run at me? Well, go ahead. Try again!"

They didn't.

After a game against the Air Force Academy, one of their players actually came up to me and asked for my autograph. He said I was the craziest guy he'd ever seen.

We went 7-4 when I was a freshman, 8-3 in my sophomore year. The highlight of that second season—not to mention my college career—was beating No. 1 ranked Texas, 14-13, in our home opener. Russell Erxleben, the Longhorns' celebrated kicker, just missed a 53-yard field goal as time ex-

pired. And Earl Campbell, their great running back, finished
with only 23 yards, one of his lowest rushing totals as a
collegian.

Before the game, Choo Choo Charlie shaved a message into
his ultrahairy chest: "Beat Texas." While watching films the
next day, everyone burst out laughing when, right after Erxleben's miss, they saw a 280-pound lunatic doing cartwheels
up and down our sidelines.

It was yours truly.

We were 6-5 in my junior year, and that's when the reality
began to sink in that I was good enough to earn a living as
a football player. NFL scouts started pointing at me as a top
prospect for the 1979 draft. I had visions of being a first-
round pick.

But before that day came along, we suffered through the
humiliation of an 0-11 finish in my senior season. I learned
that year that there was a definite correlation between individual honors and team success. For instance, I made
twenty-eight tackles in our 19-8 loss to Navy and I didn't
even get ECAC Defensive Player of the Week—in New England. It went to a kid from Holy Cross, who had made four
tackles and a fumble recovery in a winning effort.

Even while averaging fifteen tackles per game, I didn't
receive any form of weekly recognition. I was pounding the
hell out of highly regarded offensive linemen such as Carroll
and Texas A&M's Cody Risien, who wound up with Cleveland. Just about everybody we played ran away from me.
Opponents would double- and triple-team me and call audibles at the line when they saw where I was.

I figured by the end of the season I'd at least be chosen
first-team all-East, maybe second team all-American. But
there was nothing, except the high praise of my coaches and
NFL scouts.

Ed Chlebek, the head coach in my senior year, called me
the greatest defensive lineman in the school's history. I found
that extremely flattering because among those who played
the position before me at BC are former Colt Art (Fatso)

Donovan and ex-Steeler Ernie Stautner. Their busts are in the Pro Football Hall of Fame.

"I've never seen a guy play better on a bad team," Norm Pollom, the Bills' chief scout at the time said about me. "Boston College would be losing hopelessly in the last quarter, and Fred would still be coming on every play. When a guy plays like that on a poor team, you've got someone you know is going to be there all the time."

I was invited to the Senior Bowl, then to one of the NFL's scouting combines in Philadelphia. I weighed 286 pounds and was benching 450, which made me bigger and stronger than anyone else at my position. I was the No. 1 rated defensive tackle in the country. And when the agents caught wind of that, another kind of recruiting game—even worse than the one played when I was at Waltham High—began.

To them, I wasn't Fred Smerlas. I was Fred Signing Bonus. That was all they wanted from me and everyone else who figured to be a high-round draft pick—a share of those big bucks we would receive up front. The guaranteed cash. They were ready to grab future earnings, too, but there was a chance that money would never be seen if we got hurt or flopped. And as soon as the money vanished, so would they.

I heard from just about every major sports agent in the country, as well as lawyers from my hometown who wanted me to become the first pro athlete for whom they'd ever negotiated a contract. Even some of my uncles, who were neither lawyers nor agents, offered to represent me.

The big-timers from out of town would show up at the house looking to buy everyone they saw. But my parents weren't poor. They were upper-middle class and knew a thing or two about business. It was going to take more than flashing wads of cash to win their trust. Meanwhile, I'd let those guys take me and my buddies out for dinner and drinks, then say, "Thank you very much. Now, don't call us, we'll call you."

I ended up signing with Bob Woolf, partly because he was

a prominent agent from Boston and a BC graduate, but mainly because he won my parents over. He had an impressive list of clients that included Carl Yastrzemski. I think my parents made up their minds about Woolf when he took them to meet Yaz. For many New Englanders, that's like meeting God.

On draft day, '79, I got together with a bunch of friends at BC and did what every other college prospect in the country was doing—I waited by the telephone. I waited all the way through the first round, and it never rang. The Patriots, whom everyone had assumed would make me their top choice, passed me over for Rick Sanford.

Then, as the second round began, I received a call from a representative of the Tampa Bay Buccaneers.

"Fred, we can't believe you're still out there and we're getting ready to draft you," the man said, sounding as friendly as could be. "We didn't have a pick in the first round, but we have one in the second, thirty-third overall. And I promise that we'll treat you just like a first-rounder. Now, just stay on the line until we make the selection."

My first thought was, who are the Tampa Bay Buccaneers? My second thought was that I'd be going to Florida and roasting like a peanut.

When I told everyone where I was headed, there was one big groan.

"It's Buffalo's turn right now," the man from the Buccaneers said. "We're expecting them to take Greg Roberts [an offensive guard from Oklahoma], and we're going to take you with the next pick. Now, when we get you down here, we're going to have a real nice parade for you and . . . wait a minute."

"What's wrong?" I said. "Hello? Hello? Is anybody there?"

After a few more seconds, the man from the Buccaneers got back on the phone and in a voice that wasn't nearly as pleasant as before, said, "Buffalo just drafted you."

Click. He was gone.

Actually, the Bills weren't considering Roberts, whom

Tampa Bay wound up drafting thirty-third. It was down to Mark Gastineau and me, and from what I would find out later, their original plans were to take Gastineau. They even made arrangements to fly him to Buffalo from someplace called East Central Oklahoma.

But at the last minute they reconsidered, deciding I was more physically mature and could make a bigger impact right away at nose tackle than Gastineau could at defensive end.

I didn't know all that much about the Bills. The only thing I knew about Buffalo was that it was the hometown of Mike Siegel, one of my not-so-stable teammates at BC. I thought to myself, if that vegetable is any example of a typical Buffalonian, I'm in big trouble.

The phone rang again. It was Chuck Knox.

"How ya doin', Coach?" I said, trying to come off as bright and chipper as possible.

"I hear you're a tough motherfucker," Knox growled. "Are you ready to come here and kick some ass?"

I couldn't believe my ears. Having spent the past four years at a Jesuit school, I wasn't used to a coach's using that sort of language. I was used to Joe Yukica, the head man for my first three years at BC, walking around in *Father Knows Best* suits and beginning every sentence with a polite, "Okay, gentlemen . . ."

I was going from Dr. Doolittle to Dr. Detroit.

CHAPTER
SEVEN

FRICK AND FRACK

I FIRST VISITED Buffalo when the Bills flew me and one of their two first-round draft choices, wide receiver Jerry Butler, to town for a Quarterback Club luncheon. It was a chance for the Bills to show us off to the local bigwigs in the group, as well as the large media turnout. Coming from an 0-11 college team, I saw more TV cameras and microphones in one hour than I had seen in a year. In fact, having forgotten what a microphone looked like, I thought, with that little red ball on top, I was being offered an ice-cream cone. I nearly electrocuted myself.

Chuck Knox handled the introductions from the podium. When he got to me, he said, "We thought this guy should have been a first-rounder, and luckily, we were able to get him in the second round." I thought, Jeez, Chuck, if you thought I should have been a first-rounder, why the hell didn't you draft me in the first round?

But as I returned to my seat after telling the audience how glad I was to be there, Knox punched me in the leg, gave me a little wink, and said, "We're glad to have you here, too."

That meant a lot to me.

Little did I know at the time that those would be the last kind words I'd hear from the man for quite a long time.

My next trip to Buffalo was a month later, for mini-camp. I brought a girlfriend from Boston to spend a couple of days with me. As we walked through the hotel where the Bills had all of their rookies and other out-of-town players staying, we ran into Jim Haslett. The Bills had also drafted him in the second round that year, nineteen picks after yours truly, from little Indiana University of Pennsylvania. Haslett reminded me of a bird, with his teeny head, long, skinny nose, wide shoulders, and high-pitched voice. It didn't take long to discover he was of the cuckoo species.

When I saw him later, by myself, the first thing he said was, "Hey, your girlfriend has nice tits." It wasn't the kind of thing a 230-pound guy normally says to a 280-pound guy he doesn't know very well.

Which was why we instantly hit it off.

Haz didn't have his car at camp and I had my Corvette, so I asked if he wanted to go for a ride to get some tacos.

"Sure," Haz said, although he learned, from that day forward, not to be so quick to accept an invitation from me.

As we flew along a highway at 110 mph, he was so terrified, he nearly bit off a piece of the dashboard.

"Jesus Christ! I'm going to die!" Haz said, no longer acting like Mr. Tough Guy. "I'm only twenty-two and I'm going to die."

Slowing down for a traffic signal, I noticed the flashing lights of a police car in my rearview mirror. I knew it would only be a matter of time before my first encounter with one of Western New York's finest.

"I had you clocked at seventy miles per hour," the cop said. "Then I lost you."

"If I told you how fast I was going, you'd throw me in jail," I said.

"Don't say that," Haslett interrupted, poking me in the ribs. "Or he will put us in jail."

The cop recognized us as two of the "saviors" the Bills had drafted after their third consecutive losing season, which might explain why he let me off with only a warning.

Later in that minicamp, I discovered how awful the Bills really were defensively. We spent a few hours watching film from the previous season with Willie Zapalac, our position coach, and it was a horror show. To call him blunt in criticizing holdovers such as Phil Dokes, an end whom the Bills had made a first-round draft pick in 1977, would be putting it mildly.

"I'll tell you what, Phil, you must have given them someone else's college films when they drafted you in the first round," Zapalac said. "You're really sorry."

After the Bills allowed an NFL-worst 200-plus yards per game on the ground in 1978, Knox was determined to plug the middle of his defense. Step one was to switch from a 4-3 to a 3-4 scheme. Step two was to find the right players for it, which was where Haz, an inside linebacker, and I came in. Step three was to make it work.

That, of course, would be the hardest step of all.

I didn't know the first thing about playing nose tackle. I had been an even-front tackle and end in college. And my occasional appearances at middle guard, where I anchored a five-man line in a four-point stance, gave me no feel for what it would be like to anchor a three-man line in a three-point stance. Having always worked with 4-3 schemes, Zapalac and the other coaches weren't all that familiar with nose tackle, either.

But I was the guy they picked to fill the position and I was expected to take charge of it—immediately. I had received only a nose hair's worth of briefing at minicamp. The crash course would begin two months later, at our Niagara University training camp.

My weight lifting made me something of a curiosity among a lot of the older players. Back then, there weren't many serious lifters on the team. The weight room was slightly larger than a closet and consisted only of two barbells, a bench press, and a rack with pins on it. When I started doing repetitions with 400 pounds, everyone looked at me as if I had three heads. They had never seen another player bench more than 300 before.

For some of the veterans, it was just another reason to resent my arrival. All the publicity the rookies were attracting, starting with the No. 1 overall choice, Tom Cousineau (who would never sign with the Bills), was beginning to get on their nerves. Their job security dangled by a thread and we were giving the final tug that would make it snap.

Not that that was any cause for me to take a passive approach. Quite the contrary. For instance, in minicamp drills, which were supposed to be only padless walk-throughs, I went full bore. I hit every guy across from me, including respected veteran guards Reggie McKenzie and Joe De-Lamielleure, as hard as I could. Consequently, I wound up in a shoving match on almost every play.

The first guy I actually fought was Will Grant, in his second season as a backup center. I had heard that he was really lewd and crude and couldn't get along with anybody. But other than the fact that he rode a three-wheel chopper and needed a shave, I didn't notice anything about him that was particularly offensive. He seemed friendly enough. He was articulate and had a deep voice that made him sound almost downright sophisticated. And he was from my home state of Massachusetts, so I figured on that basis alone, I'd give him the benefit of the doubt.

The first hint that something wasn't quite right with Will came when instead of running inside to use the bathroom, he urinated on the artificial turf in Rich Stadium, almost hitting the shoes of those of us around him. Then, before our first encounter on the field, he gave me a pleasant smile. As I smiled back, thinking maybe he's not such a bad guy after all, I felt his fist smashing me in the balls. Once I regained my vision, I returned the favor and we mixed it up.

The more time I spent around Grant, the more I realized he didn't place a high priority on personal hygiene. That was one of the reasons for his nickname, Hooker. He was originally called that because he did a lot of holding, but veteran tackle Ken Jones said it was also because Will smelled like the Hooker Chemical plant in Niagara Falls.

Fortunately, I didn't have to room with the guy. Haslett was my roommate for that and every summer until he left the team after the 1987 preseason. We were a couple of flakes, so it made perfect sense for us to hang out together.

But we were far from a perfect match. In many ways, we were like Felix Unger and Oscar Madison. Haz's clothes would always be neatly hung in the closet or neatly folded in drawers. My idea of being neat was when my dirty socks landed in the same spot on the floor. It drove him crazy.

Like any newcomer to Buffalo, I was introduced to the local delicacy—chicken wings. It was love at first bite. I'd order them nightly at camp, as many as two hundred at a time, and toss the bones in a corner on my side of the room. It didn't take long for the pile to become a small mountain. And it didn't take long for the mountain to attract bugs. Not that there was anything left for them to nibble. I also loved sunflower seeds and pistachio nuts. I'd always eat sunflower seeds when I had trouble sleeping. Haslett would be on the other side of the room, snoring away, and I'd be spitting the shells on him. He'd wake up covered with the remnants of my sunflower-seed binges.

"That's what you get for being able to sleep when I can't," I'd tell him.

On most teams, veterans pull pranks on rookies as a way of welcoming them to the NFL. But from that very first camp, Haz and I established ourselves as the Bills' leading pranksters. None of the returning players had taken command in this area—probably because they were too worried about staying employed to think about anything else—so we fig-

ured it might as well be us. We went after a few rookies, but
since most of them were in the same boat as us, our primary
targets were veterans.

We quickly became known as Frick and Frack, Tom and
Jerry, Tweedle Dee and Tweedle Dum, Pete and Repeat, and
a few other names I don't care to mention. We were young,
and because Knox's practices weren't killers, we had plenty
of energy to carry out our "missions." Even after a night of
drinking beer and playing pinball at the Old San Juan, our
favorite training-camp hangout, we were ready to strike.

Haz kept a "hit list" of guys who either had done something to us, on or off the field, that demanded retaliation, or
whose personalities just rubbed us the wrong way. We began
with Marvin Switzer, a second-year defensive back who had
once referred to us as "nothing but rookie crap." Early one
morning, before practice, Haz and I filled a fifty-gallon barrel
with water and leaned it against Marvin's door. We tied
athletic tape around the outside doorknob and ran it to a
fire-extinguisher box in the hall, so that Marvin would only
be able to open the door far enough for the barrel to fall but
not far enough for him to escape.

Sure enough, when he turned the knob and pulled, he was
greeted with a massive flood. It was so bad, Switzer couldn't
get out of his room and was late for practice.

Another daylight prank was ransacking rooms. While Haz
hid, I'd use the pay phone at one end of the hall to dial the
one at the other end. Someone would answer, and disguising
my voice, I'd ask for a certain player. If, while taking the
call, that player was dumb enough to leave his door un-
locked, Haz would sneak inside, grab all of his personal
belongings, and move them into a vacant room down the
hall. Sometimes, he'd put pickles and shoes under the guy's
pillow, or cover his bed with ice. Or if time allowed, he'd
steal the mattress.

Some guys caught on quickly and refused to take any calls,
even legitimate ones, while others were careful to lock their
doors anytime they were summoned to the phone. Still oth-

ers, such as Phil Dokes, fell for the prank once, sometimes twice, a week.

We had an entirely different repertoire for our evening maneuvers. We'd jump guys, wrap them like mummies with tape, and leave them until someone came to their aid in the morning. (Switzer was found that way a couple of times.) We'd take an empty record-album jacket, fill it with shaving cream, put the open end under someone's door, knock, and as soon as he was about to answer, we'd stomp on the jacket and splatter our victim from head to toe. Or we'd get him with a shaving-cream bomb. We'd shake up the can, punch a tiny hole in it, knock on the door, and when it opened, toss the can inside. It would fly around the floor like a wild rat, spraying everything in its path, until it was empty.

We'd light firecrackers and roll them under doors. We'd make crank calls to players' rooms at two and three in the morning. We'd do something to somebody every day and every night.

Even assistant coaches who handled nightly bed checks had to be on their toes. One night, when we heard Steve Moore leaving the room next door, we shut off our lights and hid—me in the closet, Haz under his bed. As Steve opened our door and fumbled around in the dark, I flicked on the light and we emerged from our hiding places with the loudest of screams. Poor Steve almost jumped through the ceiling.

We did terrible things to Knox, too—from a distance. Remember the Mr. Bill skit from *Saturday Night Live?* Haz and I took some clay and made a Mr. Chuck doll. Except that ours was anatomically correct. And for each thing he did that we didn't like, we yanked off a part of the doll's body. Finally, Haz bit the head off and whipped the rest of Mr. Chuck against a wall.

We were a splinter in everyone's side, but it wasn't long before the splinter grew into a harpoon. After a few weeks, Haz and I were numero uno on everyone's hit list.

One of the more impressive individual retaliations came

from our placekicker, Tom Dempsey. Haz was mouthing off
to him as the three of us, after returning from a night on the
town, rode up the elevator in the dormitory building. Having
had enough, Dempsey, who was a wrestler in high school,
got Haz in a headlock and started jabbing him in the stomach
with the nub he had for a right hand. That thing could really
hurt. I eventually pulled Dempsey off after Haslett tried in
vain to punch himself loose.

For the most part, Haz and I stuck together as rookies. We
had to; our allies were so few. But being compulsive pranksters, there were times we couldn't resist going after each
other. Like the night Haz was out of the room and I pulled
the covers off his bed, drenched it with a gallon of wine,
sprinkled Rice Krispies and Raisin Bran over the wine, and
put the covers back on. Haz wasn't the smartest guy in the
world, but even he knew his bed shouldn't smell like a vine-
yard. So he refused to climb into it.

Frustrated by his lack of cooperation, I pulled the mattress
off the bed and tried to throw it out the window. Haz put
up a fight, we stumbled into the hall, and he wound up under
the mattress . . . and me. The commotion drew about twenty
guys into the hall. Noticing Haz's predicament, they seized
a perfect opportunity for revenge by jumping on the mattress.
Haz was flat as a pancake when we let him up.

Near the end of camp, a bunch of veterans finally gave
both of us an overdose of our own medicine. First, they taped
our door shut so we couldn't get out—unless we wanted to
jump out of our seventh-floor window. Then, they attacked
us with firecrackers, shaving cream, water, the works. We
tried stuffing towels under the door to keep the barrage from
getting in, but they kept poking them out with coat hangers
and continued the assault.

We knew we had it coming. All we could do was take it.

Unfortunately, I was much better at pulling pranks than
playing nose tackle at that point.

"Just get down there and play," Zapalac kept telling me
in practice.

I wish it could have been that easy.

I had decent quickness and really good strength, but something wasn't clicking. I always felt as if I were trailing the play. For the first time since my early days of high school, I was the one getting mauled. I wasn't in command of anything I did on the field. I just wasn't comfortable.

Because I had virtually no technique, no idea what to do with my feet or hands, I resorted to thuggery. I would push, punch, kick, anything. If I couldn't beat my opponent, I was going to beat the hell out of him. And that led to daily fights with Grant and the starting center, Willie Parker.

I realized most of the things I did in practice would have drawn yellow flags during a game. But I didn't know what else to do. I had no model from whom to learn. I had no one to teach me. I felt as if I were running on a treadmill. And losing ground. Fast.

As I stretched before practice one morning, Knox walked up to me, looking as disgusted as ever.

"Big, strong Greek, huh?" he grumbled. "Supposed to be a real tough-ass, huh? Well, you ain't shit. You should be killing people, and you're not doing a thing. I just hope I didn't waste a draft pick on you."

Then he turned and walked away.

I was devastated. I began to wonder what I was going to do at the end of the week, when I received my plane ticket back to Boston. I second-guessed myself for not studying harder in school—for putting all of my eggs into a football helmet rather than spreading them around so I'd have something to fall back on.

But the ax never fell. In fact, I was made a starter for our first preseason game, at home against Pittsburgh.

The night before, I drove to the airport to meet my girlfriend, who was flying in from Boston. Haslett, who would also start against the Steelers, followed me because we were going to leave her his car, then he and I had to return to Niagara, which was forty-five minutes away.

It was ten-twenty when we left. Bed check was at eleven.

We knew if we were late, we'd both be spending the game on the bench.

I knew, with me behind the wheel of my trusty Vet, we had a chance to make it.

Once again, I had the needle of the speedometer buried. Once again, Haz was convinced he would end up the same way.

"My first pro game, my parents are in town from Pittsburgh to watch me, and I'm not going to live to play in it," he said, whimpering.

By the time we hit the Grand Island Bridge, I was doing 135 and Haz was gripping his seat for dear life. I'm not sure, to this day, whether the wheels actually touched the bridge or if the car just flew across the Niagara River. Anyway, we skidded into the parking lot of the campus at eleven on the dot. Then we sprinted into the dormitory building, ran up seven flights of stairs, and dove into our beds—only seconds before Elijah Pitts, our running-back coach, who was making bed-check rounds, opened the door.

Noticing our heavy breathing and profuse sweating, he asked, "What's wrong with you guys?"

"Oh, nothing," I said. "Just a little hot in here, that's all."

I spent most of the rest of the night with my eyes wide open thinking about facing Mike Webster in my rookie debut. There I was, a big mound of feta cheese with no idea of what I was doing, and I'd be lined up against one of the best centers in the NFL. I just put my head over a bucket and let whatever sweat remained in my body pour out.

In the end, though, it wasn't nearly as bad as I expected. I pretty much held my own on sheer power and aggressiveness. And that would be good enough to get me through our remaining three preseason games.

Knox didn't like starting rookies, but he saw enough of an improvement to give me the nod for our regular-season opener against Miami. His only other choice was Mike Kadish, who, despite having seven more years of NFL experience, had also never played an official down at nose tackle. Kadish's physical attributes were totally different from mine. He was pretty strong and had good leverage, whereas, in addition to having great strength, I was really quick and had more explosiveness.

The thought of being a starter in my first regular-season game was exciting. Now, I'd be playing for keeps in front of 80,000 fans at Rich Stadium. And I'd begin to collect from my $55,000 base salary, which, combined with my $65,000 signing bonus, made me feel as if I were set for life.

I was fairly pleased with my performance in our 9–7 loss to the Dolphins. But the next day, Haz still found me crying.

"Hey, it's all right, Fred," he said. "We'll win the next game. Don't worry. You'll get better, we'll all get better."

"Fuck that," I said. "Look at how much they took out of my paycheck in taxes. Can you believe it?"

The following week, we waxed Cincinnati, 51–24. I had an okay game, but on a few plays, I allowed myself to get scoop-blocked. That's when the center avoids me to block the backside linebacker, and I get cut off by the backside guard while attempting to put myself between the center and backside linebacker. In Knox's eyes, I had committed a mortal sin. I was never to allow the center to come free like that. I was to control him right in front of me. And I was to never, ever, let him beat me physically one-on-one.

After the Bengals game, Knox said, "Next time, Smerlas, grab the center. Whatever you do, don't let him go."

"Okay, Chuck," I said. "I'll grab the center."

Our third opponent was San Diego. The first time the center tried to slip away from me and block the backside linebacker, I not only grabbed him, I got on his back and tried to tackle him. Naturally, flags flew all over the place and I was called for holding.

When I returned to the sidelines, Knox glared at me and said, "What the fuck are you doing? You look like an idiot out there."

"Chuck, you told me not to let the center get out on the

'backer," I said with my palms turned up. "You told me to grab him."

"Yeah, yeah. But I meant for you to get in front of him, not on top of him!"

"You didn't tell me how to grab him; you just said to grab him."

"Oh, what's the use? You know, I did waste a draft pick on you. I should have taken Gastineau when I had the chance."

Things didn't get much better the rest of the game, which we lost, 27–19. To make matters worse, Haslett had a good game and reporters were all around him. No one wanted to talk to me. They were looking to interview football players, not clowns.

The following day, Knox informed me that Kadish, who had been nursing a broken hand, was going to take my place as a starter in our next game, against the Jets.

"I have to play a guy with a broken hand, that's how bad you are," was how Knox informed me of the switch.

I walked into our dressing room, but no one could see me because I was standing about an inch tall. I crawled up onto the stool in front of my locker and sat there, with tears streaming down my face. Now, I thought, I will get that ticket back to Boston. I'm finished as a football player. It's time for this boy to think about another career.

"Fred, don't let this get you down," Zapalac said. "I've seen guys overcome setbacks like this before."

But again, I was spared the ax. Kadish would start the final thirteen games, while I relieved him periodically. Of course, I was hurt by Knox's decision to bench me, but I knew it was the right thing to do at the time. I wasn't playing well. I wasn't ready to be a starter.

Once the regular-season began, Haz moved into an apartment with his wife and I moved in with another rookie, defensive end Kevin Baker.

But we still kept the Frick and Frack Show alive on road trips. For instance, we couldn't help but notice that an employment agency rented space at our hotel in San Diego to take applications for airline stewardess jobs. Within an hour after we arrived, Haz and I were sitting at the table, helping the agency people "interview" prospective stewardesses. We gave our decision with either thumbs-up or thumbs-down, depending on their looks.

We'd walk into out-of-town restaurants, with no more than a dollar between us, and walk out with big meals in our bellies. I'd pass myself off as Budd Thalman, the Bills' public-relations director at the time, and we wouldn't have to pay a cent. Not as long as I had my supply of little cards with our schedule on them.

"Here's a copy of our schedule," I'd say to the maître d'. "Stop by and see us play when you get a chance. Just give me a call, and I'll set you up with as many tickets as you need."

I also established myself as a no-frills traveler that first year. Several of my teammates would board the plane carrying their fancy designer bags—Gucci, Mucci, all the big names—and I'd walk on with a brown paper bag that contained a change of underwear, a tube of toothpaste, and a toothbrush. I wrote "travel" on it in Magic Marker. I even drew straps.

My turning point as a player came in week six of that year as we prepared to face Chicago. Knox and his assistants were becoming more familiar with the finer points of the 3-4 scheme. They began discovering ways to use it to exploit the opposition. Among the things they noticed about the Bears' center, Dan Neal, was that he wasn't very strong and didn't have good foot movement. Figuring this would make the Bears' offense susceptible to penetration through the middle, Knox instructed Kadish and me to get as close to Neal as possible and jam him with our hands the instant he snapped the ball.

While working on the technique in practice, I noticed, in jamming our centers, my feet would follow theirs. I was reacting and moving, whereas in previous games and practices I just sat there, waiting for the action to come to me and head-butting. All of a sudden, my hands were like a second pair of eyes. I never felt more comfortable as a pro.

Sure enough, I had my best game to date while alternating with Kadish in our 7–0 loss to the Bears. Bingo! I was on to something.

With so much improvement from a single adjustment, I took it upon myself to search for more ideas to incorporate into my game. I had made up my mind that I was going to do whatever it took to become the best nose tackle I could be. I was going to give myself every chance to prove, beyond a shadow of a doubt, I had what it took to start in the NFL. If I did, I would. If I didn't, I wasn't going to waste anybody's time, including my own.

So I began yanking films from our library of all the top nose men and regular defensive tackles in the league, watching them after practice and on our weekly day off. I'd spend as many as two hours by myself studying every single aspect of their games—how they used their hands, how they positioned their feet, whether or not they arched their backs. The first thing I noticed was how they used their hands. If the center tried to cut them off, they kept their hands on him and controlled the block. And if he tried to push them, they locked him out and used their arms to get separation from him.

I broke it all down. Bob Baumhower of Miami: made the most of everything he had, head-butted, got good leverage, arched his back nicely, kept his feet parallel, bent his knees just enough to enhance his explosion. Curley Culp of Kansas City and Houston: nothing fancy, a bull, just a straight-ahead banger who tried to kill people. Rubin Carter of Denver: made good use of the swim and arm-over technique to avoid blockers. Randy White of Dallas: mesmerized them with head fakes, did a lot of shaking and baking, and quick feet.

I began mixing it all together and came up with my own style. I would crowd the ball, get as close as I could to the center, square my stance, and get my hands into him as

quickly as possible. If I was quick enough, he'd take me
where I wanted to go. It was a case of reading on the run. I
was like the Sundance Kid—couldn't shoot straight, except
when he would draw. That was me. I could read while I was
moving, but not sitting still before the play.

With each relief appearance, I felt myself getting better
and better. I decided it was time for me to return to first-
string status. And I made Knox aware of my feelings one
morning after a meeting.

"Okay, Chuck, you benched me when I sucked," I said.
"Now, I'm kicking some ass, so I want to be back in there
starting."

"You're doing great," Knox said. "Just keep it up and
you're going to be an All-Pro someday."

"How am I going to be an All-Pro as a backup? I want to
be starting."

"You will be starting. Just keep to it, just keep working
hard. And be patient."

Patience never has been, nor will be, one of my virtues.

I had been told, before we faced New England in week
ten, I would replace Kadish from the first play of the second
half. But when the defense took the field for the first time
in the third quarter, Kadish trotted onto the field while I
remained on the sidelines.

"What's the deal, Willie?" I asked Zapalac. "I thought I
was supposed to be out there. What's going on?"

Zapalac was furious.

"Listen, you goddamn rookie, I'm the coach and I'll tell
you who's supposed to be out there and who isn't," he yelled.

I became more furious, grabbed him, and in an even louder
voice, said, "You son of a bitch! It's my turn to be out there.
Now, put me out there!"

Just as we were about to come to blows, several players
and coaches pulled us apart. A short while later, Zapalac
walked up to me and said, "You're a son of a bitch for acting
the way you did, but I love your desire."

I could probably have handled the situation a lot better.

But the point was I wanted to play some ball. I didn't want to collect a paycheck for free.

I did, however, want one of the free turkeys being offered to everyone on the team the day before Thanksgiving. At least, that was what it said on the sign-up sheet tacked to the dressing-room bulletin board. I couldn't get my signature up there fast enough. There was a space to indicate the size you wanted, from fifteen to twenty-eight pounds. Some guys put fifteen, and I thought, how stupid can they be? When you're getting a free turkey, get the biggest one there is. I went for the twenty-eight-pounder.

The catch was each player had to pick up his own bird, in person, at a butcher shop about twenty miles from the stadium. So, as soon as practice was over, I headed down there with my girlfriend and Kevin Baker.

We were greeted by a little guy behind the counter, underneath which was a glass case containing all sorts of meats.

"I'm Fred Smerlas and this is Kevin Baker," I said. "We're here for our free turkeys."

"Excuse me for a second," the little guy said.

He disappeared into the back room, then returned about a minute later and handed each of us an envelope. We opened them, and inside was the same note: "Gobble! Gobble! You're the turkey."

"What the hell is this?" I said.

"A joke," the little guy said. "There are no free turkeys. It's only a joke."

"A joke? A joke? We drove all the way down here for a joke?"

"Afraid so."

"Well, I don't see the humor in it. And if you don't give me my fucking free turkey for Thanksgiving, I'm going to kick in your case and take all of the meat."

Looking nervous, the little guy disappeared into the back room again, then came out with another guy, who owned the shop.

"What's the problem here?" he asked.

"I want my goddamn turkey," I said, getting angrier by the second. "Now, either give it to me, or I swear I'll kick in that case."

"Calm down, Fred. It's only a joke. We do it every year."

I kept yelling and screaming before I finally turned around and stormed out the door. When I showed up for practice Thanksgiving morning, I didn't say anything about the scene I'd made at the butcher shop. I was too embarrassed. Besides, I figured nothing more would come of it, anyway.

I figured wrong.

Joe Ferguson, wearing a big smile, walked up to me and hung a sign around my neck that said the same thing as the note handed me the night before: "Gobble! Gobble! You're the turkey." And that was only the beginning. As we gathered for our team meeting, defensive tackle Dee Hardison walked up to the front of the room and said, "Every year we have a player whose behavior is outstanding enough to warrant his winning the Turkey of the Year Award. And this year's winner is Fred Smerlas. Hands down."

Everyone started laughing and cheering as Hardison presented me the award—a turkey made out of a football. I had to wear the sign the rest of the day, which pleased to no end all my teammates Haz and I had terrorized all summer.

In the thirteenth week of the season, we played our second game against the Patriots, at Foxboro. The artificial turf there is notorious for causing knee injuries, and I became the victim that day. While running, my toe got caught in a seam and I felt a tear in my right knee. The immediate diagnosis was that I would be sidelined for the final three games.

I couldn't believe my bad luck. I was making such great strides, with fifty-seven tackles and a team-leading three fumble recoveries, including one for a touchdown against the Jets. And now, I wouldn't be able to play for the rest of the year. I didn't know if I'd be able to play again, period. Sitting on the bench, I could actually feel something moving around in the knee. I was so frustrated I started to cry.

"Hey, don't do that," Will Grant said, leaning over in front of me. "You're a great player, Freddy. Don't ever let 'em see you cry."

My knee was placed in a cast, and I was a spectator for the 0-3 finish that gave the Bills their fourth-straight losing season, at 7-9. Several weeks later, right after he removed the cast, Dick Weiss, our team physician, said, "Okay, bend your knee." So I bent it, assuming it would move as easily as always. But when I did, my eyes sank about three inches into my head; the pain was unbelievable. I spent the next two hours rubbing the knee and moving it slowly—very slowly—before I was able to limp out of the trainer's room.

"You're going to be fine," Weiss said.

And I was fine—until a week before my second training camp when, while playing a pickup basketball game in Waltham, I reinjured my right knee. This time, I needed arthroscopic surgery to remove damaged cartilage, sidelining me for the start of workouts. Then, I came down with gastritis, which prolonged my inactivity and made me feel as if I were going to die. For about four days, there were nonstop explosions in my stomach. I couldn't eat solid food and wound up losing about twenty pounds.

When I finally began practicing, I told Knox, "I want to start, I want to play."

"Just relax," he said. "We have faith in you and we're going to start you eventually."

I thought he was only appeasing me. But when the season began, I finally had my starting job back. And this time, I knew I was ready. I knew, if I did something wrong, I could correct it. Unlike the beginning of my rookie year, there was a base from which to work. It was an entirely different feeling.

Our No. 1 draft pick that year was Jim Ritcher, who had won the 1979 Outland Trophy as a center at North Carolina State. It's amazing we became the close friends we are today because when he was drafted, I hated the guy. I hated him before he ever set foot in Buffalo. And the reason I hated him was because I had seen him on Bob Hope's Christmas special on TV, along with the nation's other top college football seniors in '79. Jane Kennedy was also on the show, and there was a segment where Ritcher, with the cuffs of his dungarees rolled up above his Nikes and a goofy smile, came up to her and said, "Of all the things I have, the one I cherish the most is my autographed picture of you, Jane." I thought, what a nerd! How could he say something like that and keep a straight face?

The first time I saw him in person, at minicamp, all he would do was stare at me. No matter where I went, I'd turn around and there would be Ritcher, giving me this strange look. I tried my best to ignore him, but I could almost feel his eyes burning holes in my back. I later found out that Haslett had pulled him aside and, pointing at me, said, "You see that guy over there? He hates your guts. He hates all rookies, but he hates you the most. And when we go to training camp, he's going to be fighting you every single day in practice."

I hated Ritcher so much, I made him share a house with me and two other teammates—defensive end Scott Hutchinson and linebacker Chris Keating—during the regular season. It was especially cruel because the place was haunted.

I would be in my room upstairs at night, all alone, and I'd hear someone breathing. I'd turn the lights on, look around, and there would be no one in the room. Night after night, I'd lie awake hearing all sorts of strange noises—doors opening and closing, footsteps going up and down the stairs—and knowing full well that everyone else was asleep and the outside doors were bolted shut. I'd be sweating up a storm.

Then one night, having finally gotten to sleep, I woke up suddenly to find a little boy, with sandy-blond hair, walking by. I had never seen the kid before in my life. I shook my head, rubbed my eyes, and said, "What are you doing here?"

"Did you see my ball?" the boy said.

Realizing it wasn't a dream, I yelled, "Who are you?"

Keating heard me, and as he came running into the room, the boy disappeared.

"Chris, who was that little kid who was just in here?" I asked.

"What little kid?" Keating said.

"Never mind."

A short while later, Ritcher and I were playing catch in the house with a Nerf football, and one of my throws ended up bouncing into Keating's room. I went to look for the ball, and it wasn't there. Ritcher looked, we all searched every inch of the room.

We never saw the ball again.

I came home one night and found Hutch sitting in his car outside, all by himself. He had been waiting there for one of us to show up because he refused to go in the house alone. Another time, I found him sitting at the kitchen table with three of my pistols in front of him. He said he was going to kill the ghosts. Worrying that he might start putting holes in everything, including his roommates, I explained that guns didn't kill ghosts. Then I grabbed the pistols and put them away.

One afternoon, we were in the backyard, and there must have been 50 million flies covering a huge outside wall of the house. I knew a couple of the guys I lived with didn't smell too good, but this was ridiculous. So, we went inside, and when we came back out about an hour later, the flies were gone. It was the weirdest thing I had ever seen. The next time I saw that many flies on a wall was a couple of years later while watching a movie—*The Amityville Horror.*

We didn't talk to any exorcists. Not wanting to break our lease and pay a penalty to the landlord, we just put in our time and left after the season. We may have been chicken, but we were also cheap.

For a while, things were pretty strained between Ritcher and me, mainly because of how I felt about him before the draft. During one play in practice, I thought he cheap-shotted me, so on the next play, I smashed him in the helmet as hard as I could. He tried to act as if it didn't hurt, but he wound up with a slight concussion and was throwing up after he

got home. I walked in later that night and found Ritcher
sitting in front of the fireplace with a BB gun. A football card,
bearing my picture, was inside the fireplace, with about a
hundred BB holes in it. He had just sat there, firing away
at me.

"Nice going, pus brains," I said.

Keating looked at both of us and said, "Why don't you
two stop fighting and try to be friends?"

We agreed. After drinking a couple of cases of beer and
using the BB gun to shoot up the empty bottles in the fireplace, we were buddies for life.

Of course, that doesn't mean I won't harass him from time
to time. Ritcher's the only guy on the team with a hairier
body than mine. After he got married, I'd call his house, and
if his wife, Harriett, answered, I'd say, "Hello, this is Larry,
from Larry's Landscaping. Jim scheduled us for a back-
grooming today, and we just wanted to find out what time
he'd like us to come over."

"Who is this?" Harriett would say in her southern drawl.
"Is it you, Fred? Now, you quit that."

"Well, I suppose Jim's already in bed by now; I know how
important it is for him to get a good night's sleep."

"Why's that?"

"He has a big day of shaving tomorrow."

Once, I made Ritcher a back scratcher with razor blades
on it. Another time, I bought him a Chia Pet—an animal-
shaped plant that spouts furry leaves. It looked so much like
him, I couldn't resist.

You pronounce his name Rich-er, but we call him Rick-
tor. He's one of the nicer, more down-to-earth individuals
you'll ever meet. However, in his younger days, after one
drink too many, Rick-tor became a frightening character
known as Sick-tor. I remember one time, right after the trans-
formation took place, he ate a wineglass, took off for a while,
and returned with a mug of beer and a glazed look in his
eyes. After finishing the last gulp, he said, "Fred, watch
this." He proceeded to chomp on the big, thick mug, snap-
ping off a piece of glass and breaking a tooth.

Of course, that wasn't nearly as scary as what he did one day during practice when he was perfectly sober. I was lined up across from him, and before the snap, he reached over, tapped me on the shoulder, and opened his mouth. Inside were a bunch of worms, squirming all over. As if that weren't enough to nauseate me, he began chewing on them like a wild dog. Then he swallowed.

We began the 1980 regular season with a 5-0 record, and our defense was dominating as no other Bills defense had in quite some time. Halfway through the season, it became clear we had the top defensive unit in the NFL. In particular, people noticed that opponents had a hell of a time trying to run on us through the middle. Backs who got between me, Haslett, and Shane Nelson, our other inside linebacker, just seemed to disappear into thin air. Mike Dodd, a writer for *The Buffalo Evening News*, noticed that our three positions formed a triangle and wasted no time renaming us—The Bermuda Triangle.

Our fast start was followed by a 1-3 stretch, but we rebounded strongly with wins in three of our next four. Then came the highlight of the regular season—a 10–7 overtime victory against the Los Angeles Rams at Rich Stadium. It wasn't just the dramatic finish that made it such a memorable game. It was the reaction of the 77,000 fans. After Nick Mike-Mayer's winning field goal, the crowd simply refused to leave. The day was typical for December in western New York—cold, damp, miserable—yet all the fans wanted to do was stand and cheer. And cheer. And cheer.

We didn't clinch a championship, but we proved to them—and ourselves—we had arrived. We had won the type of game a top-quality team, the kind Buffalo hadn't seen since winning back-to-back AFL titles in the mid-1960s, was supposed to win.

As we celebrated in the dressing room, the fans chanted for us to come back out to the field. We said, "Hey, not only did we win, but those people out there won, too. Let's go out and share it with them. Let's go party with them."

After removing our jerseys and shoulder pads, we ran back

down the tunnel for a curtain call, NFL-style. We formed a chorus line with our cheerleaders, the Jills, and danced and high-kicked as "Talkin' Proud," Buffalo's theme song, blared over the public-address system. You don't know what entertainment is until you've seen big goons like me, Ritcher, Haslett, Ben Williams, Dee Hardison, Conrad Dobler, Phil Villapiano, Isiah Robertson, Chris Keating, and Baby Johnson imitate the Rockettes.

Everyone seemed to forget all of the bad things that had happened to the team and the area. This was a new beginning, the birth of something big and beautiful. I had never seen anything like it before. I have never seen anything like it since.

Meanwhile, I saw myself soaring to heights I had never experienced, physically and mentally, as a player. One day, a veteran cornerback named Mario Clark said to me, "You're going to make the Pro Bowl. I just know it."

"Don't tease me," I said.

"I wouldn't."

I loved hearing that, but reaching the Pro Bowl was just so hard for me to visualize. I mean, it had only been a year earlier that Knox was telling me I stunk, that he had made a terrible mistake drafting me. Now I was being told I was headed for the Pro Bowl?

That isn't to say I lacked confidence in my abilities. As a matter of fact, I walked into the office of our general manager, Stew Barber, that year and offered to bet my base salary of $62,000 that I would be a Pro Bowl selection at the end of the season. Double or nothing.

"I can't do that," Barber said. "But how about a hundred bucks?"

"You're on."

With a 10-5 record, we needed to beat the 49ers in our regular-season finale at Candlestick Park and clinch the Bills' first division championship since 1966, or miss the playoffs altogether. Because it was such a critical game—and Buffalo weather being what it is that time of year—Knox had us practice in San Francisco the week before. It was while we were out there that I learned I had been voted to my first Pro Bowl. It was one of the greatest thrills of my life.

Realizing I had that hundred dollars coming from Barber, I took Haz and a couple of other guys out for Chinese food to celebrate.

Then we celebrated again in the giant mud pit called Candlestick Park after our 18–13 victory.

But not before the 49ers, looking like anything but a 6-9 team, gave us all we could handle. And then some. We were in a do-or-die situation, yet they played us to a standstill. You wanted to say, "Hey, guys, just fall down. You aren't going anywhere. Why are you trying to ruin our day?"

Little did anyone know they were assembling the foundation of a dynasty. They were out to make a statement to the rest of the league: "Get ready, 'cause here we come!"

As a result, it was your basic blood-and-guts game. The 49ers' center, Fred Quillan, and I spent the whole day punching and tripping each other. He'd chop-block me and I'd turn around and chop his ass. I was so fired up after someone chopped Haz, I chased the guy fifty yards to return the favor.

The field was a joke. You'd get in your stance and your drive-foot would be swallowed in the turf. But it was fun to roll around in all of that mud after Joe Montana's final desperation pass fell incomplete and time expired. In the dressing room, as we peeled off large chunks of sod from our bodies, everyone sang:

I've got a feelin'
Buffalo's goin' to the Super Bowl;
Won't be the last time
Buffalo's goin' to the Super Bowl.

Our playoff game, the Bills' first since 1974, was against the Chargers at San Diego. The week before, we traveled to Vero Beach, Florida, and practiced at Dodgertown, the spring-training facility of the Los Angeles Dodgers.

Time for Frick and Frack to do their stuff.

We read in the papers that the Ku Klux Klan had a fairly strong presence in the area. So, one night, Haslett and I thought it might be fun to put white hoods over our heads and see if we could get a rise out of some of our black teammates. We kicked in the door of one room, shared by veteran wide receiver Frank Lewis and tight end Reuben Gant, and yelled, "It's all over for you guys!"

Without even flinching, Frank said, "Hi, Fred. Hi, Jim."

It was then we realized, even in disguises, everyone would immediately recognize Haz's high-pitched voice and my Boston accent. So much for that stupid prank.

Another idea surfaced when I learned that Vero Beach was loaded with armadillos. I had never seen one before, except in pictures. And the only thing I knew about them was they looked like rats covered with shells. As soon as I found out they went absolutely crazy in a confined area, tearing up everything in sight, the prank alarm went off in my head.

"Couldn't you just imagine one of those things loose in somebody's room?" I asked Haz. We got Ritcher, and the three of us went on an armadillo hunt.

It didn't take long to spot one, digging away in the dirt. The next question was, how were we going to capture it?

"Let's sneak up from the back," I said. With that, I got behind Ritcher, Haz got behind me, and we began tiptoeing.

All of a sudden, the armadillo turned around and spotted Ritcher. Threatened by the sight of the hairiest beast it had probably ever seen, the armadillo got up on its hind legs and let out sort of a bark. Ritcher and I spun around and started running. Ritcher runs a 4.6 forty; you need a sundial to time me. Yet I was passing Ritcher—that's how terrified I was.

"Hey, wait for me!" Haslett screamed

Couldn't you just picture the headlines? "Three Big, Strong Football Players Flee From Four-Inch Armadillo."

Despite all the playing around, I was certain we would beat the Chargers. Although the game was in San Diego and we both had 11-5 records, I felt we were the stronger team because of our defense. I felt we had the best team in the AFC, for that matter.

As the game progressed, I grew even more confident, because we were keeping the wraps on Dan Fouts and the Chargers' high-scoring offense. Sherman White and I worked a stunt where I would go in one direction, and coming around from his defensive end spot, he would blast through the middle. Sherm, who was tall and fast, was getting into Fouts's face all day.

Everyone was pumped up. Dobler was punching the piss out of Louie Kelcher, the Chargers' mammoth defensive tackle. I was battling hard with center Don Macek, another Boston College product. It was a war on both sides of the line.

Despite Ferguson's being hobbled by a badly sprained ankle, we built a 14–3 halftime lead on a touchdown run by Rosey Leaks and a Fergy-to-Lewis TD pass. The Chargers cut the margin to 14–10 when Fouts and Charlie Joiner connected for a third-quarter score, and a Rolf Benirschke field goal made it 14–13 in the fourth.

Then, on third and ten from the 50-yard line and with a little more than two minutes remaining, Fouts dropped back. In the face of a strong rush, he threw a 30-yard pass to Ron Smith, a receiver who had seen so little action before then, there were cobwebs between his fingers. Our safeties, Billy Simpson and Steve Freeman, had double coverage. While closing in for what figured to be a sure interception, Simpson fell, and Smith caught the ball and took off for the end zone. Our jaws dropped. Our hearts did the same.

Fergy made a desperate attempt to bring us back, but with his ankle throbbing, he managed only two completions before being picked off.

Final score: San Diego 20, Buffalo 14.

It was a long plane ride back to Buffalo. Most of us just sat in stunned silence.

The next day, I watched films of the game with Willie Zapalac. We were going over some mistakes I'd made when all of a sudden he said, "Shut off the projector, Fred, and throw the film away. You had a great season. The team did fine. Let's just enjoy what we did and not dwell on what we didn't do."

I followed his advice, climbed aboard my Harley, and drove home. With a smile.

In 1981, we moved training camp from Niagara University to Fredonia State College, creating a new stage for the Frick and Frack Show. On the first day, as we were being checked in and given our dorm-room keys, Haz caused a distraction while I stole a passkey. It couldn't have been in more dangerous hands.

After eleven-o'clock bed check, we'd stalk the hallways at one-thirty, two in the morning, carrying huge hunting knives. We'd wait until one of the rookies got up to go to the bathroom (there was one for each floor, so you had to leave your room to get to it). When that happened, Haz and I would sneak into the guy's room and hide in the closet or under the bed. After he returned, we'd wait a few minutes until he got really comfortable and relaxed. Then we'd jump out, screaming and holding the knives over our heads like a couple of psychotic killers.

Some guys would just about have a bowel movement on the spot.

Dobler and Villapiano had a different idea of training-camp fun. They would hit the local bars after the afternoon practice, skip dinner, and drink nonstop until the team meeting at night. It's a wonder they didn't pass out in their playbooks. And the amazing thing was they were still ready for more action after the skull session.

One time, a bunch of us were at a place called B. J.'s, when in walked a women's softball team for some postgame drinking. They were as sweaty and dirty as you'd expect after a hard night on the diamond, but that didn't stop Conrad from offering to suck the toes of each member of the team. Sure enough, the next thing you saw was Connie pulling off the shoes and socks of one of the players, pouring beer on her toes, and removing it—along with a lot of dirt and grime—with his mouth. I thought I was going to throw up.

Still, as we approached the regular season, we were a different team from what we were in 1980. We had gone into the previous year with modest goals, and when it was over, it was as if the team had come out of a coma. Great success after four straight seasons of failure. Pride and respect taking over for despair and ridicule.

But things were different in '81. We were viewed as a Super Bowl contender. We had to deliver. Period.

Fans who'd made preseason reservations for Detroit, site of Super Bowl XVI, looked pretty smart after our first two games. We blew out the Jets, 31–0, in the opener and dominated the Colts, 35–3, at Baltimore in week two.

Villapiano was one of our motivational leaders at the time—not to mention a certified lunatic. At just about every players-only meeting at the end of the week, he'd stand up in front of the team and get all red-faced and hyper while trying to work us into a frenzy. The day before we left for Baltimore, he made Dobler stand up and vow he was going to take Colts defensive end Mike Barnes out of the game (which he would by leg-whipping him until he left the field with a hyperextended knee). Conrad was reluctant at first, but Phil got everybody to chant, "Vow, Conrad! Vow, Conrad!" And when Connie finally gave in, Phil celebrated by throwing one chair against the wall and another through the ceiling. The rest of us followed suit, smashing a chalkboard and every other piece of furniture in the room.

I never knew getting motivated could be so messy.

Haz and I had the reputation for doing dastardly deeds, but even we had limits. I'm afraid the same couldn't be said for Dobler and Villapiano. After one of our victories, they took advantage of the chaotic scene in the dressing room to pull a prank on Ralph Wilson. There he was, the owner of the team, wearing a big smile and going from locker to locker to give everyone a congratulatory handshake. When he shook hands with Phil and Conrad, they slapped him on the back of his trench coat. They kept slapping and slapping, which Ralph thought was their way of expressing joy over the win. What they were really doing was plastering him with Bills stickers, about twenty of them.

When Ralph walked out the door, he looked like the back of a Winnebago after a cross-country trip.

He wasn't the only victim. I was set up perfectly for one prank during a players-only meeting. Fergy laid the groundwork when he started addressing the younger guys on the dos and don'ts of off-field behavior.

"Don't drink too much, don't get into fights, don't go getting laid all the time," he said. "Remember what we're here for. We're pros and we're being paid to do a job, which is to win."

I nodded on every point. It all sounded good to me, especially coming from a well-respected veteran like Joe.

All of a sudden, there was a knock at the door of the meeting room. It was a messenger, with an envelope for me. I opened it, with the whole team watching, and pulled out documents that said a paternity suit had been filed against me. It was very official looking, right down to the judge's signature.

"What's wrong?" Fergy asked.

My hands trembled as I handed him the documents. I was scared to death, wondering when, where, and with whom I had been so careless.

Fergy looked through the lawsuit for a minute, shook his head, and resumed his speech.

"This is exactly what I'm talking about," he said, holding up the papers for everyone to see. "You guys always want to go out and have a good time, but you have to remember one thing: if you don't keep it in your pants, something like this is going to happen. Now, Fred's in trouble."

I was in shock. I didn't know whether to buy cigars or cyanide. Just as I was about to call the judge whose signature appeared on the suit, the rest of the guys told me they had made up the whole thing, including Fergy's speech.

They got me good that time.

I later found out Haz had been part of the paternity scam. Considering the real run-ins with the law he had had for barroom brawling, I thought it took a lot of nerve for him to do something like that. I did the only natural thing and got him back. I knew, because of his off-field reputation for getting into trouble, Haz wasn't very popular with the Erie County district attorney. The DA wanted his butt on a platter. So one day, when I knew Haz wasn't home, I called his answering machine and, disguising my voice, left a phony message for him to call the DA. He took the bait.

"What do you want?" the DA snapped.

"What do I want?" Haz said. "You're the one who left a message for me to call you."

"I never called you. I don't know what you're talking about."

"Sorry."

Click.

Realizing instantly who had set him up, Haslett dialed me, and as I laughed uncontrollably, he called me every name under the sun, then hung up.

After our 2-0 start, we cooled off quickly, suffering back-to-back defeats to Philadelphia and Cincinnati. When we got to 6-5, hitting our lowest point in week eleven with a 24–0 loss at St. Louis (the Cardinals were on their way to a 7-9 season), all of the doubting Thomases came out of the woodwork. The attitude of the fans and media was, "Maybe these guys aren't as good as we thought they were. Maybe we're back to the same old lousy Bills."

Before, a 6-5 record would have caused banners to fly all over town. After our 11-5 finish in 1980, it was as if disaster had struck. Winning was expected; losing just wouldn't be tolerated.

But after our humiliating loss to St. Louis, we went on a four-game winning streak. The doubting Thomases grew silent. The bandwagon again became standing room only.

The streak began with a miracle. We trailed New England,

17–13, with thirty-five seconds on the clock and no time-outs. A number of fans had already left Rich Stadium, writing the game off as a third consecutive defeat.

When Ferguson and the offense took the field deep in our own territory, those of us on defense held hands along the sidelines. It was our way of showing support for each other and, perhaps, summoning a little divine intervention from the big Bills fan in the sky. We had faith in Fergy. He was cool. Contrary to popular belief, he was a true leader who was well liked and well respected by his teammates.

In shotgun formation from our 27-yard line, Fergy fired a beautiful rainbow pass 37 yards to running back Roland Hooks, who made the catch fully extended. The offense then hurried to the line, and Fergy quickly threw the ball out of bounds to stop the clock with twelve seconds remaining. We were still holding hands, yelling and screaming and praying our heads off.

There was time for one desperation pass for a touchdown or, at the very least, a pass-interference penalty. Fergy brought the team out of the huddle in "Big Ben" formation, with three receivers lined up to his right. He launched the ball toward a pack of Bills receivers, surrounded by Patriot defenders, in the end zone. All at once, you saw feet leaving the ground and hands reaching into the air. The first person to touch it was linebacker Mike Hawkins.

But the last person was Hooks, who hung on for dear life. Miraculously, we walked off the field with a 20–17 victory.

We felt, then, that destiny was on our side—that, no matter what, the ball would bounce our way.

In the next three weeks, we would beat Washington by a touchdown, San Diego by a point, and New England again to secure a playoff spot. But we blew a chance to win our second consecutive division championship by losing to Miami, 16–6, in the regular-season finale, and ended up with a 10-6 record.

Our wild-card game was against the Jets at Shea Stadium. The week before, Haz told reporters in New York that Shea was "filled with nothing but Puerto Ricans and degenerates." And worst of all, he said I shared his feelings.

After his words hit the papers, I asked Haz, "Why do you say that kind of shit? What is wrong with you?"

"I just said what I felt," he replied.

"Yeah, well, I just wish you would have left it at what you felt."

As soon as we walked onto the field the day of the game, I heard the clicks of 30,000 switchblades. That was followed by catcalls and all sorts of nasty remarks directed at us. My brothers Peter and Chuck were in the stands and were afraid to mention my name out loud. They even removed the SMER-LAS caps they were wearing.

I did my best to disassociate myself from Haslett that day. I figured, if anybody was going to get attacked first, it would be him.

With leads of 24–0 in the first half and 31–13 in the fourth quarter, it looked as if we were going to have an easy win for a change. But the Jets took us right down to the wire, with Simpson intercepting a Richard Todd pass, from our 11-yard line, with ten seconds left to preserve a 31–27 triumph.

Nevertheless, we thought we were on a pretty good roll heading into our divisional-round game at Cincinnati.

The week before, I decided to play a little joke on Jim McNally, the Bengals' offensive-line coach and a Buffalo native. We had been friends since he coached our offensive line at BC. Doing my best imitation of a gangster, I left a message on his answering machine that said, "Hello, this is Leonard from Buffalo. I've found one of the Bills playbooks and I'd be willing to let it go for a price." And I left my phone number.

A short while later, McNally called back.

"Why do you want to give us a Bills playbook, Leonard?" he asked.

"Because I'm fond of the Bengals," I said, still disguising my voice. "I'd like to put some money on the game, and I think this playbook would reassure me of coming out on top. How much would you be willing to pay for it?"

"Well . . ."

"Would you be willing to give me, say, a couple of hundred dollars for it?"

"Well . . ."

"Why you son of a bitch!" I said, returning to my normal voice. "You're willing to cheat on the goddamn game? I can't believe it."

"Oh, I knew it was you all along, Fred."

"Yeah, sure, you lying bastard."

"I did. And if I thought you really were someone trying to sell us a playbook, I'd have called the police on you."

Forrest Gregg, the Bengals' head coach at the time, was standing with McNally and got on the phone. We wished each other good luck. Then, I talked to Jim again and told him I was going to scare his center, Blair Bush, to the point where he would have "brown spots on his pants." We wished each other good luck, too.

Like I said, we thought we were on a pretty good roll at that point. But after we fell behind 14–0 in the first quarter, I wasn't so sure about that.

We did come back to make it 14–14, and we were tied again, at 21–21, before Ken Anderson threw a 16-yard touchdown pass to Cris Collinsworth to give the Bengals a 28–21 lead. Our last hope to keep our Super Bowl dreams alive came after Ferguson moved us to the Cincinnati 20 with just under three minutes left to play. On fourth and three, he threw an apparent completion to Lou Piccone for a first down, and it looked as if we were headed for overtime. But there was a yellow flag on the ground—the 30-second clock had expired before Fergy took the snap. We were penalized five yards for delay of game. Fergy then fired in the end zone for Hooks, but there would be no miracle this time. The pass was overthrown.

The next day, I dropped by Knox's office on the third floor of the administration building at Rich Stadium. He was in his film room, which is off to the right as you walk inside, having a scotch and a second look at the crushing disappointment we'd experienced less than twenty-four hours earlier. He didn't say anything at first. He just kept pushing the buttons on the remote control of the projector, moving the film back and forth, back and forth.

He was watching the delay-of-game penalty, shot from the end zone behind Ferguson. You saw the 30-second clock expiring: 3 . . . 2 . . . 1 . . . 0. Then you saw Fergy take the snap. Knox stopped it at that point and rewound to those final three seconds: 3 . . . 2 . . . 1 . . . 0 . . . snap.

"So, Chuck," I said.

But before I could say anything else, he started grumbling about Fergy, "We pay that motherfucker six hundred thousand dollars a year and you mean to tell me he can't read a goddamn clock?"

"Uh, yeah, Chuck. It sure was a tough one to lose."

He never heard me. He was too busy torturing himself. 3 . . . 2 . . . 1 . . . 0 . . . snap.

"We pay that motherfucker six hundred thousand dollars a year," he began again.

"Well, Chuck, I guess I'll be seeing you later."

And as I walked out the door, all I heard was the click of the projector: 3 . . . 2 . . . 1 . . . 0 . . . snap.

CHAPTER
EIGHT

"WHEN THINGS GET BAD . . ."

For as long as I live, I'll never forget that conversation with Ben Williams.

I don't remember the exact day, but it was shortly after our heartbreaking playoff loss to Cincinnati. Benny had been a defensive lineman for the Bills since 1976. He had been through four consecutive losing seasons—2-12, 3-11, 5-11, 7-9—before things finally turned around in 1980.

"Fred, it's great now," he said. "But just remember one thing: when you lose around here, you won't believe how bad it can get."

"No way, Benny," I said. "This team's going to be winning for the next ten years. We have Chuck, we have Fergy, Haz, you, me, all the boys. We came close this year and the year before. Next year, Benny, I know we're going all the way. I just know it."

"Man, I hope you're right. Because when things get bad around here, they get *bad*."

I wasn't buying a word of it.

And I was even more optimistic after our first two games of the 1982 regular season. We beat Kansas City, 14–9, in the opener. Then, behind three Ferguson touchdown passes, we rallied from a 19–0 deficit to edge Minnesota, 23–22.

The one sour note in those first two weeks was the loss of inside linebacker Shane Nelson to a knee injury, against the Chiefs, that marked the end of his career and the Bermuda Triangle. I thought we were going to be in big trouble, but Eugene Marve, a rookie, did well in Nelson's place that day and for the next several years. Considering he came from a place called Saginaw Valley State, Marve's ability to step right in and do the job was nothing short of incredible.

The second game, which was a nationally televised Thursday-night edition of *Monday Night Football,* was especially important because it was one of our best overall performances since my rookie year. It was a chance to show the rest of the country that, despite our early playoff exits the previous two years, we were still Super Bowl material.

The threat of a players' strike had loomed before the season began. I was hoping it would never become a reality, that Ed Garvey and Jack Donlan would get everything resolved at the bargaining table. Of course, I was dreaming. Four days after our win over the Vikings, the season came to a screeching halt.

It didn't budge again for eight weeks.

Until the strike ended, no player in the league was supposed to have any football-related contact with coaches or other team administrators. Working out at the clubs' facilities was strictly forbidden.

"Fuck that," Knox told several of us the day the strike was called. "You guys can work out here anytime you want. I want you to keep in shape because when this thing's over, we're going to come back and kick some ass."

We tried holding our own practices at the team's grass-field site across the street from the stadium. We had a pretty good turnout for the first couple, following the routine as best we could without pads, helmets, or coaches. But the numbers quickly dwindled, and the practices became touch-football games before they stopped altogether.

It was a stupid strike. Most of us didn't even know why we walked out in the first place. All we wanted to do was play and get paid.

Two months later, we finally got our wish. It felt great to put on a uniform again, even if it did require the help of a crowbar. It seemed the equipment men had used a little too much starch in the wash. Or maybe some of us had eaten a little too much baklava during the strike.

Our record might have been 2-0, but there was little resemblance between the team that started the year and the one we fielded after returning to work. Physically and mentally, we just weren't ready to play. And we demonstrated as much by losing five of the final seven games to miss the playoffs for the first time in three years.

A wild-card spot had been on the line in the regular-season finale at New England. But for some reason, that didn't seem to matter to several of our guys. From the opening kickoff, they played as if the game were an interruption, as if it were taking them from more pressing engagements. They had no spark, no concentration. As we trailed late in the fourth quarter, I stepped into the defensive huddle and yelled, "Come on, guys! We can still win this thing."

There was little, if any, response. Then, I noticed one veteran player was staring up toward the scoreboard, paying no attention at all to me or anything else on the field.

"Hey, look at that chick they're showing on the big TV screen," he said. "What a knockout!"

"We're getting our asses kicked out here, and you're looking at some chick on the screen?" I said. "What the hell's the matter with you?"

The apathy was at least partly to blame for our 30–19 loss.

Chuck was furious. He felt we had let him down after the strike. And we had.

By the same token, I think more than a few players, including yours truly, became disenchanted with the entire situation in Buffalo after word spread that Knox was about to leave the Bills.

I first heard about it from my usual source of inside information on the team—Jim Haslett. He was the undisputed gossip king of the dressing room. He never revealed where he got his information, but more often than not, it was accurate. And when he told me, a couple of weeks after the strike, he had it on good authority Chuck had been having serious talks with a few NFL clubs, I was stunned.

"You're shittin' me, Haz," I said. "This is a joke, right?"

"No joke," he said.

The look of concern on his face seemed too genuine for even him to be busting my chops.

"Well, then, I guess I'll just have to go to the man and find out for myself," I said.

I felt I had a strong enough rapport with Knox that I could approach him on just about any subject, no matter how sensitive. I also felt he would give me a straight answer. So I walked into his office, and getting right to the point, I asked, "What's the deal, Chuck? Are you leaving us or what?"

"No, I'm not leaving," he said. "I don't have plans of leaving right now. Where did you hear that?"

"Rumors," I said. "Just rumors."

But when I walked out of his office, I felt even more depressed than when I went in. I knew Chuck wasn't telling the truth. Those ol' blue eyes just didn't have their usual sparkle.

I was in a daze, thinking about the awful prospect of being abandoned by someone I viewed as my second father. This was the man who had held me by the hands as I took my first steps in the NFL. I wondered, what am I supposed to do if he leaves? How can I play for anyone else? He's got to take me with him.

I told Haz his information appeared to be good but he wasn't taking any bows. He felt the same way I did about Chuck. I'd say about 60 percent of the players loved the guy. And their reaction to the ever-increasing talk about his departure was the same as ours—shock, followed by depression. There were some other guys who didn't care one way or another who the coach was, while a few seemed ready for a change.

"I was getting tired of all of his clichés, anyway," one guy said. "I want to hear some new speeches."

Knox's problems with Stew Barber were driving him out. As far as most of us were concerned, Barber should have been the one going, not Chuck.

But that disaster against the Patriots proved to be Knox's swan song. He left for Seattle; we were left with Kay Stephenson and impending doom.

The day Chuck's resignation was announced, I told *The Buffalo News*, "I don't think the Bills will win for a long, long time . . . if they ever do again. I feel bad for the people of Buffalo. In the end, they're going to suffer because they've seen a tough, hard-nosed football team. I don't think they're going to have that anymore."

Deep down, I hoped I would be wrong.

And after our 3-1 start in the 1983 regular season, I thought I was.

We lost to Miami, 12–0, in the opener at home, but traveled to Cincinnati the following week for a 10–6 victory, which we preserved by stopping the Bengals on four cracks from inside our 5-yard line in the final three minutes. To help him celebrate his first NFL head-coaching triumph, we gave Kay a shoulder-ride off the field. He'd have preferred to walk, but who knew when—or if—there'd be a reason to do it again?

The following Sunday, Fergy threw three touchdown passes to lead us past Baltimore, 28–23. In week four, Joe Cribbs ran for 166 yards as we pounded Houston, 30–13, to end a ten-game losing streak against the Oilers.

Six days after a humiliating 34–10 loss to the Jets on *Monday Night Football*, we showed a lot more character than I thought we had when we went down to Miami and won, 38–35, in overtime. It was Buffalo's first Orange Bowl victory since 1966—the first time any of us had won a game down there as pros.

The guy I was happiest for that day was Ferguson, who, after eleven consecutive road losses to the Dolphins, had the best game of his life. He completed 38 of 55 passes for 419 yards and 5 TDs. He set six team passing records and tied two others.

I was also happy for Joe Danelo, whose 36-yard field goal decided the outcome. Joe was a lot of fun. He had a great sense of humor, which, since he owned one of the largest noses in the world, was a must. His schnozz even made mine look petit. And that was why I called him Joe Da-nel-nose.

He didn't have to use his foot to make field goals and extra points. All he had to do was get on his back, have the ball snapped into one of his giant nostrils, and when someone jumped on his stomach, the ball would just pop straight through the uprights.

If I got to the stadium early enough on Sunday, I'd grab a whole bunch of game programs, cut out the eyes and nose of Danelo's photograph in each one, and paste them over everybody else's pictures. I'd create an entire team of Joe Da-nel-noses.

After the Miracle in Miami, we won three of our next five, with both losses coming against New England. Although our playoff chances were thriving, injuries began to take a heavy toll on our lineup. The heaviest was wide receiver Jerry Butler, our most potent offensive weapon and one of the classier players on the team. He tore up his left knee in the ninth week of the season and wouldn't play again until 1985. We just didn't have the depth to cope with his and other absences from the starting twenty-two. As a result, we suffered a collapse, losing all but one of our final five games.

It was merely a preview of the real horror shows to come.

Honest to God, I had my first bad feeling about what lay ahead when it was announced that, beginning with the 1984 season, we were going to switch from white to red helmets. I was against it all the way. White helmets had been part of the Bills since their birth in 1960. To me, they were a symbol of strength. I associated red with failure, such as a business's operating in the red. It just seemed like such a wimpy color. In fact, when a reporter asked me for my reaction to the switch, I said, "Maybe the next thing they'll do is make us wear little flowers on our jerseys, up around the shoulder pads. And then we can have Big Bird on the sides of our pants to make the kids happy."

Sure enough, we lost our first eleven games of '84. The only other time in my life I'd been on an 0-11 team was my senior year at Boston College. I didn't like it then, although I was comforted somewhat by the thought of being a high-round draft pick in the NFL. In '84, it seemed the only thing I had to look forward to was more losing.

I became so frustrated, I wound up coming to blows with Ben Williams, one of my best friends on the team, in front of 60,000 fans during our 31–28 loss at Seattle. We were in the huddle, and I was hot, tired, and pissed off. Dave Krieg, the Seahawks' quarterback, had just thrown a pass into the chest of our free safety, Donald Wilson, who allowed what should have been a sure interception to fall to the ground. Wilson, a nice kid, was already feeling low when he returned to the huddle.

In the mood I was in, I decided he should feel lower.

"Next time, you'd better catch the goddamn ball," I snapped, "or I'm gonna beat the fuck out of you."

"Shut up, Fred," Williams said. "He's trying to do the best he can. Leave him alone."

I turned to Benny, and all of a sudden, I didn't see one of my best friends on the team anymore. I saw someone challenging me in front of everybody else in the huddle. I wasn't going to back down.

"You shut up or I'm going to beat the fuck out of you, too," I yelled.

Benny wasn't going to back down, either.

"Fuck you," he said.

And we started to pound on each other. We really slugged

it out for about thirty seconds before being separated by our teammates.

"What the hell are you guys doing?" cornerback Charley Romes said, dumbfounded. "Save it for the damn Seahawks."

After cooling off, we exchanged apologies and never spoke a cross word to each other from that day forward.

It was poetic justice that the losing streak finally ended in week twelve, with a 14–3 home victory over Dallas. At the time, the Cowboys were experiencing a decline of their own; the loss to us would help knock them out of the playoffs for the second time in nineteen seasons. But they still were America's Team and had a huge following in Upstate New York. In fact, the game drew our biggest crowd of the year—74,000—and most of the people were there to see the Cowboys slaughter the hopeless, hapless Bills.

We were more than happy to spoil their day.

Before the game, a bunch of us got together and formed a Fuck You Fund. We all pitched in some money for the big party we'd have after we "fucked" the Cowboys by handing them an embarrassing upset. And what a party it was! Monte Kiffin, our linebacker coach, got so drunk he didn't show up to work for two days.

Everyone on and off the team treated it like the biggest accomplishment in Bills history. Which, of course, it wasn't. But when you've reached the point where your only thrill has come from winning a coin toss, getting that first taste of true success is very satisfying. The talk around the team was, "See, we can do it. We could have been doing it in every game before this one. We just have to put our minds to it."

That was the gist of the advice we were receiving from practically everybody. It was all mental, the "experts" insisted. Stephenson would even fly in guys like Villapiano, who retired after the '83 season, and Dobler, who retired after the '81 campaign, to give us inspirational speeches—and break up whatever furniture survived the players-only meetings we had had when they were on the team.

Unfortunately, it wasn't that simple. Our problems ran much deeper than our minds. They included coaching, scheme, talent, and chemistry. We were a mess all the way around.

As I said earlier, the disparity between Knox and Stephenson, in terms of coaching talent, was gigantic. And there was no comparing their assistants, either. Knox's staff was, and still is, one of the NFL's best. Stephenson's was horrible. We had no scheme to speak of, offensively or defensively. To compare it to a video game, there comes a point when you've played one so often, you don't even have to think to beat it anymore. That was how opponents approached us. We were going to do exactly what they thought we were going to do. We were going to be exactly where they thought we were going to be.

We were just a very basic, very predictable team.

And we didn't have enough talent to make up for whatever we lacked in trickery. Butler was still out with his knee injury, and the rest of the receiving corps just didn't provide us with any big plays or even a steady supply of small ones. We also lost our best running back, Joe Cribbs, to Birmingham of the USFL. None of us really begrudged him for doing that. Like a lot of top NFL players, he was offered a ton of money to make the jump to the USFL, so he did.

But it was really sad to see him go. For one thing, Joe was popular among his teammates; he was a great guy. For another, he was one of the few running backs in the league who made cuts upfield rather than sideline to sideline. When other backs cut, they look like they're dodging people. When Joe cut, he was still moving straight ahead.

Still, it is possible to have a team whose talent is borderline yet manages to come up with enough wins to make the playoffs. And that's where chemistry comes in. As long as you have leaders, guys who know how to bring everyone together, you can win some games you aren't supposed to win just by being inspired enough to play over your head. We didn't have that. Our chemistry was pitiful, mainly because

Stephenson didn't go after the kind of guys who could create sparks—the kind of guys Knox always had around, such as Dobler, Villapiano, Jessie, McCutcheon. They may not have had a whole lot left in terms of skills, but their offbeat personalities kept everyone loose and they still had enough crustiness to see to it no one got too far out of line. You can have all of the gunpowder in the world, but if you don't have anything to ignite it, it's just going to sit there.

Cohesiveness is critical to the success of any football team. At the time, we had fifty different lockers instead of one Bills' locker room. I know that sounds corny, but it's something you can feel as a player. And believe me, it makes a difference.

Those of us who had been around for a while heard most of the booing and criticism because ours were the most familiar faces on the squad. When I jumped offsides, it wasn't an "aggressive" mistake anymore; it was just a mistake. Just another reason for the fans to boo. I was singled out for being paid too much and producing too little.

I understood why the fans and media became so negative. We deserved to be crucified. The thing that bothered me, though, was the presumption of a lot of outsiders that we were in poor condition, that we weren't working hard enough. That just wasn't true. If anything, Stephenson's practice pace was too rigorous—to the point where we were severely fatigued on game day. But what was I supposed to do? Complain to the press? That would have just sounded like sour grapes and compounded an already dreadful situation.

Of course, it wasn't my first encounter with criticism in the NFL. I have never been more devastated than when Knox told me I was so bad as a rookie, he had to replace me with someone with a broken hand. The difference was, as a rookie, I could ask myself, what do I have to do to overcome this? In the throes of those dog days, I wondered, what do I have to do to cope with this?

The answer was to take the "two-by-two" approach. That's

two yards by two yards, as in the patch of ground immediately in front of me at nose tackle. I concentrated on limiting all that I saw and all that I heard to that little, tiny piece of turf. My turf. Every Sunday, I had to remove myself from the overall game and focus on the personal showdown between myself and the offensive lineman across from me. As far as I was concerned, the winner of that battle was the winner of the game. Because if I just went by the team's wins and losses, if I rose and fell with each final score, I'd have spent a lot of time flat on my facemask. I'd have been mentally shot.

My only salvation came in the film room. I could sit there and watch myself and know exactly how I played, good or bad. Regardless of what the scoreboard said, I had to maintain consistency. I had to keep myself on an even keel. Just as I couldn't allow all of the lofty praise I'd received earlier in my career to put my head in the clouds, I couldn't allow the negative comments I heard and read take me into the toilet.

What was the atmosphere like in the locker room? Remember Saigon in 1975, with everyone trying to get out by helicopter? The only friends you had were inside those four walls. That is, the ones who weren't cut before you could get to know them. The first thing everyone did after coming to work in the morning was check the top of his dressing cubicle to see if the nameplate was still there.

It was a horrible situation for all of us, but no one received more abuse from the outside than Ferguson.

He was probably the most misunderstood player I've ever known. Depending on how the wind was blowing off Lake Erie, he had the complete support or loathing of fans and media in town. When he was on, it was, "Way to go, Joe! Way to throw, Joe!" When things were bad, he was public enemy No. 1.

I always thought of Fergy as an offensive lineman in a quarterback's body. His idea of fun was hunting and fishing. His idea of risqué behavior was staying up to watch *Late Night With David Letterman*. Despite being paid much more than anyone else on the team back then, Fergy hardly showed it. His clothes were the type you'd see in *Field & Stream*, not *GQ*. During the season, he lived in a small, two-bedroom apartment, and he leased a Jeep—just until the end of the year.

He did all he could to avoid the spotlight, especially when everything was going well. And when he tried to maintain that same low profile during the lean times, people accused him of not facing the music. He was just being consistent.

Interceptions and incompletions drove Fergy crazy. His typical reaction was to unbuckle his chin strap with a fierce tug and stomp off the field, shaking his head all the way to the sidelines. To most outsiders, he was perceived as having a loser's mentality.

But Joe was such a great competitor, he couldn't stand anything less than perfect execution. That went for himself, as well as those around him. In his final few years with the Bills, quite a bit of his dissatisfaction stemmed from the incompetence of his supporting cast. Some of the players we had on offense were downright awful. So was the coaching. Receivers constantly ran wrong patterns; the few times they'd run right ones, passes were dropped.

But Joe never tried to put the blame anyplace but where it sat—squarely on his shoulders. He never went to the media and said, "This receiver should have been running a fifteen-yard hook pattern when he was running a twenty-yard fly." Or, "That receiver is always dropping the damn ball."

Meanwhile, Fergy moved closer and closer to becoming an ex-Bill. With Joe Dufek, a kid we had picked up on waivers from Seattle the year before, making five starts in 1984, Fergy's fate was sealed. He would be traded to Detroit during the 1985 draft.

Our only other victory in '84 came against the Colts, who weren't a whole lot better than us. Two weeks later, we closed the season by getting our asses kicked at Cincinnati, 52–21. The Bengals did anything they wanted, and we just sat there, in a straight defense, and took it.

The coaches didn't make a single defensive adjustment

the entire game. I guess it was their way of leaving us with something to think about for the following season—as if a 2-14 record weren't enough.

After the Ferguson era ended, we went through a period of some of the worst quarterbacking in the history of the franchise.

Not coincidentally, we kept losing.

Our No. 1 man at the start of the 1985 season was Vince Ferragamo, whom we acquired in a trade with the Rams. At first, I thought, hey, this is a guy who took a team to the Super Bowl. Maybe he's got something left for us?

I became even more encouraged during our regular-season opener at home against San Diego, when he completed 31 of 46 passes for 377 yards, while being intercepted only once. We lost, 14–9, but Vinny looked as if he were going to be pretty good, if not great.

Nevertheless, it wasn't hard to notice shortcomings in our offense as a whole. I mean, it's pretty embarrassing to score only 9 points against a team that had been allowing about 100 per game—a team whose philosophy is, "No matter how many points you get, we'll get at least one more."

And I blame most of our offensive ineptitude that day on the coaches. The Chargers just stayed in zone coverage, giving us all kinds of short passes, until we got to or inside their 20-yard line—then, they shut everything off. Our brain-mis-trust couldn't devise a game plan or come up with the proper adjustments that allowed us to get into the end zone.

At the same time, we were feeling pretty good about ourselves on defense. I mean, we were coming off a 2-14 season. The last time we played a game that counted, Cincinnati humiliated us. We went into the San Diego game hoping to do our best, but figuring, realistically, our best would probably still result in another blowout. So our attitude was, if we can hold Dan Fouts and the mighty Chargers to a mere 14 points, maybe we can shut out a few teams with weaker offenses . . . and get some 0-0 ties.

When we started playing teams with stronger defenses than San Diego's porous unit, Vinny didn't look so hot anymore. We were trashed by the Jets, 42–3, and lost to New England and Minnesota before Stephenson was replaced by—gulp!—Hank Bullough.

Ferragamo was a very nice guy, but something was missing upstairs. The first time I noticed this was while a bunch of us were playing a card game called Boo Ray. When it was Vinny's turn to declare, he had a blank expression on his face.

"It's to you, Vinny," I reminded him.

He acted startled, as if I'd roused him from a deep sleep.

"How many guys are in?" he asked. "How much is in the pot? Who dealt? What's trump?"

This went on every time we played. I thought to myself, if he can't keep track of what's happening in a stupid card game, how in God's name is he going to keep track of what's happening on the field?

The answer came during a 14–3 loss to New England. Vinny completed only 12 of 31 passes for 114 yards. Two of his throws were intercepted (Ray Clayborn returning the second for a touchdown), while at least ten others came close to landing in Patriot hands. We were 0-6.

There was a bright spot in that game, though. After we had pounded on each other all afternoon, Pete Brock, New England's supertough center, came up to me and said, "I just want you to know that a lot of us on this team are impressed and proud of the way you're playing in the situation you're in."

He had no idea how much a comment like that meant to me at the time.

It was during the '85 season that I started dating my wife-to-be—Kris Kefalas, a former model and school teacher from Toronto. I met her through my understudy at the time, Bill Acker. A friend of Kris's had been dating Bill's brother, Jim, a pitcher for the Toronto Blue Jays. After they broke up, the friend asked Bill to fix her up with me. We went out a couple of times, and on the third date, she asked Kris to come along to offer an opinion on me, because of Kris's Greek roots.

Kris showed up prepared to hate me because she wasn't

fond of old-fashioned Greek ideals, and had no intention of
spending the rest of her life with an old-fashioned Greek.
Her father had also been a football coach, and because of all
of the disruptions his job caused in her family, she learned
to despise the game and anyone connected with it.

But when we went to dinner, with Kris checking me
out for her friend, we ended up checking each other out
and it was love at first sight. A couple of months later I
asked if I could give her a call sometime. Okay, I begged
her. She finally consented. I left a message on her answering machine, she called back, and the moment I heard
her voice at the other end of the line, I broke into a gusher
of a sweat. My hand shook as I held the receiver. Seeing how nervous I was, Sean McNanie, a defensive end I
was living with at the time, started screwing around with
me.

"Shut up, Sean," I said in a tone that made it clear I was
dead serious.

He kept it up, and grabbing the back of one of the living
room chairs, I said, "I swear to God, Sean, I'll smash this
chair over your goddamn head. I'll smash everything in this
room over your head, Sean. Now shut up!"

There would be many more phone calls, as well as dates,
over the next couple of years. I found myself needing Kris
more and more to help get me through the depression and
frustration. She was always there to give me an ear and a
kind word—the kind I needed to keep my spirits from sink-
ing out of sight.

In week ten, Ferragamo was replaced by somebody named
Bruce Mathison. Three weeks after that, Vinny was sent
packing.

Mathison was an even bigger joke than Ferragamo because
he wasn't an NFL quarterback, period. He was a guy trying
to play the part of an NFL quarterback. With the way he
dressed, he also tried to play the part of a modern-day cowboy. Instead of six guns, he carried a blow drier and a mirror.
So I called him the Dime Store Cowboy.

I found out all I needed to know about Dime Store after our second game against the Chargers that year. We had just been pounded, 40–7, and he came up to me and said, "Jeez, Fred, I think I had a pretty good game. What do you think?"

"Let's see. You had four interceptions—one was returned for a touchdown, one set up another touchdown, one led to a field goal. And we lost by thirty-three points. If you consider that a good game, Bruce, I'd sure hate to see what you consider a bad one."

Cribbs had returned to us from the USFL, but you could tell from watching him practice, he wasn't the same runner who left. He was good, but he just didn't seem like the old Joe Cribbs—the one who was filled with big plays.

We would finish 2-14. Again.

Regardless of the sport or the town, losing is awful. It hurts. It embarrasses. It frustrates. But there is nothing that compares to being part of a losing pro football team in a town like Buffalo. The same reasons that make Buffalo a paradise when you win are what make it the world's largest torture chamber when you lose.

First of all, you have to understand that the Bills aren't merely a way of passing time in Buffalo; they are a way of life. They aren't a game in town; they are the game. In other cities, fans wear the colors of the hometown team on hats, T-shirts, sweatshirts, jackets—the usual stuff. In Buffalo, they receive transfusions of red, white, and blue Bills blood.

Nowhere will you find fans with greater knowledge of every single thing that happens with its ball club. I've met people around town who had no direct contact with the Bills, yet knew things that were going on inside the organization. Way inside. Things that I didn't even know.

Hell, guys on the developmental squad are household names in Buffalo.

As a result, the fans take the outcome of each game and each season very personally. That goes for exhibition play, too. When the Bills lose, the city loses. Everywhere you look,

there are signs of gloom and despair. People walk around
with their chins scraping the sidewalk. Cabdrivers put their
antennas at half-mast. There were studies done that actually
showed worker productivity was significantly lower the
Monday after a Bills loss than after a Bills win.

When the Bills lose, winter—hardly a picnic in the best
of times—seems colder and snowier. The sky seems darker
and grayer. On the practice field, there are forty-five black
clouds, one over the head of each player. And there are
lightning bolts coming out of them.

So, when Ben Williams, that famous fat, black philoso-
pher, said, "When things get bad around here, they get *bad*,"
he knew what he was saying. The Bills' record is scrutinized
by the fans the way a kid's report card is scrutinized by his
or her parents.

If it's straight F's, all of us face the music.

My mailbox at Rich Stadium was loaded with all sorts of
friendly letters. The opening sentences usually went something like: "I hate you," "You disgust me," "How can you
be so stupid to jump offsides when the ball's right in front
of you?" "Why don't you do us all a great big favor and just
quit right now?"

Then there was the envelope that didn't smell right the
moment I picked it up. When I opened it, I discovered why—
the enclosed blank piece of paper had been wiped across
someone's, shall we say, dirty butt. That one left me feeling
pretty depressed. Not to mention nauseated.

It reached a point where the harsh feelings the fans had
toward me and everyone else associated with the Bills made
going out in public a real problem. At best, everyone I ran
into was going to ask the same question: "What's wrong with
you guys?" or offer yet another in a long line of cures for
what ailed us. At worst, some of those nasty letters I received
were going to take the form of nasty comments to my face—
especially if the person had had a little too much to drink.

I didn't want to hear the questions anymore because, for
one thing, I was sick and tired of the whole pathetic state

we were in, and for another, I ran out of answers. I also
didn't want any confrontations. I knew, if I wasn't careful,
my emotions would get the better of me and I'd probably do
something with my fists that I'd regret later.

Thank God for restaurants that delivered or had drive-
through windows. And thank God for twenty-four-hour grocery stores. Sean and I ate quite a few meals at home, and
when we pulled up to the drive-through window at Mc-
Donald's, we'd wear sunglasses. We'd do our grocery shop-
ping at two o'clock in the morning, circling the store until
we were sure the parking lot was empty.

It was life on the run.

But losing does have its advantages. No one ever calls to
bother you for tickets. You get out of the locker room faster
because there aren't any reporters around. Your hand doesn't
get tired from signing too many autographs. You can go into
a restaurant and eat an entire meal, including dessert, without any interruptions. You don't get stuck in traffic jams
leaving the stadium because no one goes to the games.

Having missed the Pro Bowl for the second consecutive
season after making it four years in a row, my career was
seen by fans and media as headed for the graveyard. In every
football magazine there were comments like: "Smerlas still
has the ability, but seems to have lost some of his zest for
the game."

At the ripe old age of twenty-eight, I was finished. Washed-
up. A has-been.

A fire started burning inside me, and every negative word
was like another log. In addition to putting myself through
one of the more intense off-seasons of physical conditioning
I ever had, I took drastic steps to improve my game, such as
the chain-link-fence drill. On one side, I had my brother
Chuck bend over a football and bark a cadence. I was on the
other side, in my usual stance, and when he snapped the
ball, I pretended I was going against a center and jammed
the fence as fast and as hard as I could with my hands. This
went on for most of the off-season.

I left a lot of bloodstains on that fence.

I gained fifteen pounds while lowering my body fat by 5 percent. I bench-pressed 275 pounds thirty-five times, twelve more times than the year before. I felt as ready to play as I had before any season of my career. Maybe more ready.

Still, I knew we were in big trouble when our 1986 training camp opened and the No. 1 quarterback on the depth chart was Dime Store Mathison. The rest of the group included Frank Reich, Brian McClure, Bryan Clark, and Art Schlichter.

At the time, Schlichter was the best known of the bunch, but for all of the wrong reasons. He had been released by the Colts early in the 1985 season and didn't take another snap until coming to camp with us as a free agent in '86. His compulsive gambling, which had caused him to be suspended for the entire 1983 season, had put his once-promising career on the ropes. He was looking for a fresh start with the Bills, but unfortunately, it never happened. He had a horrible preseason and was released.

Before Schlichter left, I got to know him a little bit and found him to be really open and good-natured about his gambling problem. The first day we met, I said, "Art, what did you gamble on?"

"You name it, I gambled on it," he said. "Water polo, field hockey, tennis, everything. No matter what it was, I gambled on it."

"Jeez, Art, all I had to do was follow you around for one year, bet the opposite of whatever you bet, and I'd have made a million bucks."

He laughed. But you could tell the disease was still very much in his system. We were on our way to an exhibition game that summer and, as always, a bunch of us played cards on the plane. Schlichter wasn't in the card game, but he watched. As he watched, he started to shake. He kept walking away and coming back, trembling and breathing heavy like a dog desperate for a treat. Finally, it became too much for him, and he went up to Haslett, handed him fifty dollars, and said, "Go ahead, gamble it for me. But don't tell me what happens. Just gamble it." He had to be in on the action, even through someone else's eyes.

Schlichter was also the subject of a skit during the annual rookie show at camp, when all first-year players perform for the veterans and coaches. It began with four guys seated around a table playing cards. One of them was losing so badly, he took off his shirt and threw it into the pot. After he lost that, he finally said, "All I have left is my credit card."

The other three froze, and the guy turned toward the audience and said, "Do you know me? I'm Art Schlichter ..."

Everybody, including Art, roared with laughter. It was hysterical.

So was our situation at quarterback.

We needed help. Desperately.

CHAPTER

NINE

WHO SAID A NOSE
CAN'T JUMP?

THE DEATH OF THE USFL meant new life for the Bills. It meant
Jim Kelly was free to sign with them, just in the nick of time.

They had made him a first-round draft pick from the University of Miami in 1983, but he chose, instead, to join the
USFL's Houston Gamblers. Losing him then was typical of
the bumbling that took place on and off the field after Buffalo's second playoff appearance of the eighties. Negotiations
with his agents were just wrapping up in the office of the
late Pat McGroder, the club's executive vice president who
briefly replaced Stew Barber as GM, when the telephone
rang. McGroder's secretary, Phyllis, then buzzed to say,
"There's a Mr. Bruce Allen from the United States Football
League on the line and he wants to talk to Jim or his agents."

Kelly dropped his pen. Greg Lustig, one of his represen-
tatives at the time, picked up the phone.

"Don't sign anything," said Allen, speaking on behalf of

the new league. "We'll match whatever they offer—and then some."

On the one hand, I suppose you have to admire Allen's guts for making such a call at such a time. On the other hand, you have to say, why in God's name was a call like that ever put through? I mean, why else did Phyllis think someone from the USFL would be looking to talk to a No. 1 choice of an NFL team?

To make a tennis date?

Kelly proceeded to spend two standout seasons as the run-and-shoot magician of the Gamblers. As I watched him play on television, I thought, this kid is not only a great passer, but he's tough, too. He has a tough-looking face; not the typical Ken-doll features most quarterbacks have. He has a tough-sounding voice. He's a take-charge guy.

I knew he'd be the perfect quarterback for the Bills. In fact, as the USFL was about to fold in the summer of '86, I offered to drive to Houston and bring Kelly back myself.

As a team, our pride had been obliterated. Buffalo and the Bills had become every comedian's favorite punch line. There were bumper stickers around town that said, "Bring Pro Football Back to Buffalo." It got to the point where the only things that showed up at Rich Stadium on Sunday were snowflakes. And even they didn't stick around for the end of the game.

The Bills' average attendance plummeted to 37,000. Three times, they drew crowds of fewer than 30,000; when they played the Oilers in '85, only 21,881 showed up. For most fans, the big decision was whether to leave at halftime or the third quarter.

Do you have any idea how empty a stadium capable of holding 80,000 people looks when 50,000–60,000 seats aren't occupied? Ralph Wilson did, and he started wondering aloud whether Buffalo was still a viable market for pro football. I started wondering whether to put my house on wheels and aim it for Phoenix (still a few years away from getting the Cardinals) or Jacksonville, Florida, or any of the other cities waiting with open arms for an NFL franchise. I figured, one of these nights, the moving vans are going to be backing up to the stadium tunnel, just as they had the year before in Baltimore when the Colts made their midnight exodus to Indianapolis.

Finally, Wilson became fed up with all of the ridicule and empty seats. He gave his new GM, a feisty little guy named Bill Polian, the okay to go out and buy some top-quality players, beginning with Kelly. Polian grabbed the checkbook, but before leaving for Houston to begin marathon negotiations with the quarterback's agents, he told a TV reporter, "Tell the people of Buffalo to light a candle for us."

When he arrived in Houston, Polian was handed a telegram. From a Catholic parish just north of Buffalo, it said: "We'll keep 2,000 candles lit for you through the duration of your trip. Stop."

Two thousand candles and $8 million later, Kelly was a Bill.

I'll never forget the day of his signing, August 18, 1986. It was like a holiday. The city literally stood still to welcome the savior of its dying football team. After arriving by private jet, which the team provided (I couldn't even get cab fare on my first trip to Buffalo), Kelly climbed into the back of a black stretch limousine that transported him to a press conference in the grand ballroom of the Buffalo Hilton. Along the route, thousands of fans stood on overpasses and hung from the windows of their cars and homes, holding signs that said, "We love you Jim Kelly!" They were cheering him on, telling him how blessed they felt that he had chosen their town to continue his brilliant career.

At the press conference, which looked a lot more like a coronation, he received personal greetings from the mayor and the county executive, and a telephone call from Governor Mario Cuomo. (Since I am a staunch Republican, all of this political hoopla was fine—except that there were too many Democrats involved.) Charlie Mancuso, a car dealer from nearby Batavia, New York, was there to hand Kelly the keys to a new Corvette convertible and a Blazer—complimentary wheels for summer and winter. Just what every young millionaire needs.

The three network affiliates in town provided live TV coverage that preempted Peter Jennings, Tom Brokaw, and Dan Rather. What could they have been saying that was more important? Unless the Soviets had launched some missiles at Kelly's throwing arm, Buffalonians didn't want to hear about it. As far as they were concerned, their war against losing football was over. And they won.

It was time to get rid of the "Welcome" mat at the doorway of the Bills' headquarters and climb out of the AFC East cellar.

The moment Kelly's signing was announced, long lines formed in front of the ticket windows at Rich. By the end of the day, a thousand season tickets were sold. By the end of the week, four thousand—or about 20 percent of the 1985 total—were purchased.

Besides a huge pile of cash, I don't think Kelly, who was twenty-six at the time, knew exactly what he had gotten himself into. I don't think he had any idea what his coming to the Bills meant to Buffalo. The city's hopes, dreams, image—all of it was riding on Jimbo.

"It is not at all stretching it to say this man has actually had an effect on the mood of the entire area," then–Erie County executive and ex-Bill Ed Rutkowski said. "It has been an incredible boost in morale. And you're talking about an area that's been through a lot. Three years ago, Bethlehem Steel and Republic Steel shut down. You're talking about fifteen or twenty thousand jobs gone.

"And now Jim Kelly comes along, and suddenly, we're getting positive press that the Chamber of Commerce couldn't buy. Suddenly, we're on the front page of *USA Today*. I get a phone call from *The New York Times* to talk about the new spirit. I told the guy from the *Times*, 'Christ, the last time you called me, it was to get me to comment on the Blizzard of '77.' "

Kelly just planned on playing football, not the role of a messiah.

"I thought only movie stars and rock singers got this kind of treatment," he told a reporter at the time.

His inaugural practice at Fredonia State training camp drew more fans and media than I had ever seen for one of our workouts. And it was at that point that a lot of us began to appreciate fully his impact on the team. I mean, fans had stopped coming to see us play, and now hundreds had turned out to watch us practice. All because of Kelly. And there were writers, photographers, and TV reporters from all over the country. We barely got local media to cover us, let alone national. Just by being Kelly's teammates, we all became instant celebrities.

Not surprisingly, Greg Bell got a little bit carried away by it all. He stuck so close to Kelly, putting himself in the viewfinder of every camera around, I thought he was going to have to be removed surgically from Jim's hip. It was 100° out, and Greg, always the show-off, was wearing a fur coat.

But I have to admit most of us shared the sentiment that there was a lot to be gained from Kelly's arrival. We were thinking more about that than the fact his salary was many times greater than everyone else's on the team. We figured, if Kelly does his job, we'll start winning again. And if we start winning again, we'll all be making a lot of money, too. I even made a few extra bucks that first day—by carrying Kelly's bags to his room; he's a good tipper. He even let me call him by his first name.

Seriously, I was really surprised with how down-to-earth Kelly was when I met him for the first time in the locker room before practice. Oh, he was the same cocky kid I had seen on TV and read about and all. But he was also approachable.

"Hi, I'm Fred Smerlas," I said, extending my hand.

"I know who you are," Kelly said. "Nice to meet you."

"With your help, I really think we can turn this thing around."

He nodded. Then, smiling, he said, "Yeah, I think we have a good shot at it."

Of course, Kelly still had to show his stuff on the field. Like everyone else at camp that day, those of us who weren't part of the passing drill stood on the sidelines, waiting to see him throw for the first time as an NFL player. The wait ended up being longer than we expected because Bullough, in his infinite wisdom, had Kelly hand off for about ten plays before allowing him to air it out.

We were all aware Kelly hadn't played for a year, but with his salary we weren't going to cut him a whole lot of slack. Nor were too many others. Everyone figured there were eight million good reasons why he deserved such scrutiny.

When he finally did get around to throwing, he let go a pass that had pretty good distance, but was a little wobbly.

"Doesn't look like an eight-million-dollar arm to me," I said.

A few guys nodded in agreement.

But on the next one, his arm's stock went right through the roof. Without so much as a windup, Kelly threw a perfect rainbow spiral, covering about seventy yards in the air, right into the receiver's hands.

"Okay," I said, smiling. "Maybe he does have some potential."

With only one pass, Kelly looked a hundred times better than any quarterback who had played for us since Furgy's peak seasons.

Afterward, as we left the field, Jim threw one of his wristbands over the fence, and twenty kids went diving headfirst for it. Then, when he threw his towel over the fence, an older guy actually pushed his way through the mob of youngsters and skied, à la Michael Jordan, to grab it. I mean, he really got up there.

How high were the expectations for Kelly? The crowd at Rich for our regular-season opener against the Jets was 79,951—our first sellout in three years and at the time a franchise attendance record. Draped over the red wall surrounding the field was a bed sheet that proclaimed: "Kelly is God."

We lost, 28–24, but his performance left us with plenty of hope: 20 completions, 33 attempts, 292 yards, 3 touchdowns, 0 interceptions. The 3 TDs were the most thrown by a Buffalo quarterback since Fergy did the same in an '83 victory over the Jets.

Beyond the numbers, Kelly displayed the kind of toughness that guys who play his position just aren't supposed to have. For instance, late in the first half, he was knocked into a state of semiconsciousness (to the point where Bell had to call a play for him in the huddle), but returned to do his best passing of the game in the final two quarters. After Mark Gastineau slammed him down hard in the third quarter and he got up wincing, Kelly came back to throw, in the face of a three-linebacker blitz, a 55-yard touchdown pass to Andre Reed.

In the fourth quarter, Kelly tripped and fell after taking the snap from Kent Hull, quickly returned to his feet, rolled right, pump-faked, and found Pete Metzelaars in the back of the end zone for a score. I rubbed my eyes to make sure I wasn't dreaming.

As both teams walked up the tunnel after the game, Gastineau shook his head and told Kelly, "We gave you our best shot . . . and you kept getting up."

To me, Kelly has never really been a quarterback. I've always seen him as a linebacker with a good arm. In fact, there were times I wondered whether he'd have been happier on the field with the defense, knocking the hell out of people, than with the offense. He truly is one of the boys.

After home games, he invites the entire team to party in the basement of his 7,500-square-foot house (every time I left that place, I felt as if I lived in a phone booth). He has a fifty-by-sixty-foot area set up like a nightclub, complete with twelve-stool bar, a dance floor, and big-screen TV. Kelly tends bar; behind him is a giant mirror that says, "Kelly's Irish Pub." And he can get as wild and crazy as anyone, especially after a win. Once, I saw him head-butting Joe Devlin across the bar. Now, besides having been one of the team's foremost intimidators, Joe stood 6'5" and weighed 290 pounds; Kelly is 6'3", 215. Joe also had one of the larger heads on the team. And it had sharp corners. Kelly's head is large, too, but only in a figurative sense.

So there they were, each taking a drink, letting out a yell, and—smash! After a few times, Kelly began to stagger around, semiconscious, with blood streaming down his forehead. Devlin didn't have a scratch.

But that's Kelly, always willing to mix it up with anybody, regardless of his size or psychological profile. In his first NFL season, he tangled on the turf with Marty Lyons, the Jets' 6'5", 270-pound defensive lineman. Lyons was on top of Kelly, shoving a fist into his facemask. Jimbo jammed him back, and I was part of a charge onto the field to protect our "investment." The situation calmed down in a hurry. However, those of us who left the sidelines during the altercation ended up making an investment of our own—to the charity of Pete Rozelle's choice. He fined just about everyone on the team, including Kelly.

I guess Rozelle thought Jim should have known better than to bang his nose off Lyons's fist.

Kelly honestly thinks he's tougher, stronger, faster, and better looking than anybody around him. He might be kidding himself sometimes—especially when it comes to his looks—but that cockiness carries over into his performance. Most of the time, he'll make a great play simply because he believes he can beat any defender with his arm or his feet, which aren't particularly fast.

True, there are times when it seems his NFL career has been one big, bold controversial headline after another—when all he has to do to stir things up is take a breath. But like it or not, the key to Kelly's success is his punklike attitude. He loves the game, he loves to play. Most of all, he loves to win.

Of course, in '86, the winning had yet to start. Other repairs were required. The biggest came after our record fell to 2-7, with a loss to Tampa Bay: Hank Bullough was replaced by Marv Levy as head coach. Ding! Dong! The Wicked Witch was dead.

Our outlook was much brighter now that one of Hank's white plastic shoes wouldn't be pressing against our throats all the time. Of course, some of us wondered if, in addition to Hank, we'd be gone, too. Even after Levy took over and seemed to have a positive influence on the team, there were doubts—doubts enhanced by our 2-5 finish. I never unpacked my bags that year.

Before the start of the 1987 season, six veteran regulars were either cut or traded. One of them was Haz, who was released at the end of training camp. It was sad to see him and the others depart. I considered all of them friends. But at the risk of sounding cold, I couldn't let it get to me to the point where it became a distraction. After a while, you become hardened to the loss of teammates, even when guys you're close to are involved. You can't do anything for them and they can't do anything for you. So you say your good-byes and you look forward to the future. And the thing I had to focus on was the fact I still had a future to look forward to with the Bills. I realized early in my career that the only thing you can truly depend on in this game is yourself. If I allowed watching those guys go out the door to take away from my performance, it wouldn't be long before I'd be making an exit of my own.

Sure, Haz and I were tight. But we were still going to be tight as ex-teammates. He had only been cut from the Bills; he didn't fall off the face of the earth. My meaningful friendships were going to continue whether the individuals were on the team or not.

The '87 season brought us another ridiculous strike, which, like the one in '82, began after the second game (we were 1-1). But there were two major differences this time around—we picketed the stadium and games continued to be played with scab players that each club pulled out of barrooms and anywhere else warm bodies could be found. Under the heaviest of security, the scabs were bused to and from practices and games. We let them know how we felt about their taking our jobs by occasionally grabbing a bunch of eggs and serving up Greyhound omelets as they crossed our line.

I wasn't in favor of striking. For one thing, I knew it would cost me and every other player in the league a ton of money. For another, I knew it wasn't going to convince the owners to give us what we, as a union, were after, which was un-fettered free agency. The owners had been preparing for this walkout ever since the last one in 1982. During one meeting, I got up in front of the team and said, "This is a powerful bunch of guys we're going up against. If we go on strike, mark my words, it's going to be a long, bitter battle. We're dealing with people who have a lot of money—a lot more than any of us have. And they're going to keep the games going, whether we're out there or not. They're not going to break too easily, if they break at all. I think the best way to handle this thing is through the courts, while we keep play-ing, but I'll honor whatever position this team is going to take."

The position we took was to strike. Being in my ninth season and playing at a spot where the average career length is a third of that, I wasn't exactly looking forward to this unpaid vacation. But I had to deal with it. We all had to deal with it. And if older veterans such as Devlin and yours truly learned nothing else from the '82 experience, it was that the teams that did well after the strike were the ones that had remained the most cohesive while it lasted. Back then, we all went our separate ways and it pulled us apart for the rest of the season. Joe and I knew that as a team we were going to sink or swim depending on what happened on the practice field during the walkout.

So we took it upon ourselves to keep everyone together and have practices at least four times a week until a settle-ment was reached. We organized the picketing and the workouts, and attendance remained fairly strong for both through the three weeks the scabs went 1-2 in games that, unfortunately, would count in our overall record. One thing that really helped was Kelly's showing up every day for practice and picket-line duty through the duration of the strike. It was one thing for a couple of grunts like Joe and me to remain dedicated. But when the highest-paid guy on the team, a guy losing about $60,000 a week, took an active role, that gave us a lot more credibility among most of the other players.

If Kelly had crossed the line, we'd have unraveled in a hurry.

As it was, two veterans—running back Robb Riddick and fullback Carl Byrum—and two rookies—defensive end Leon Seals and tight end Keith McKeller—decided to break from the ranks and join the scabs. Our approach from the beginning was, "Whatever we do, stay out or go in, we do as a team." But I couldn't blame those guys for doing what they did. They sat out for a while. They took part in everything we did. It came to a point where they had to think about their families and, especially in the case of the rookies, their futures. I understood where they were coming from. I'd have probably done the same thing in their shoes. Hell, I wanted to go in early, too, but I couldn't. I felt if we were going to have any chance to make a run for the glory, it was more important to help keep together the majority of the guys, who were still striking.

Devlin and I expected to take a pile of crap for that. And we did. We took it from the media, the fans. Everybody looked at us as union rebels and instigators, and nothing could have been further from the truth. All we were trying to do was keep some semblance of order, which was also the case after we returned to work. The first thing Joe and I did was call a players-only meeting to eliminate any lingering tension among the troops. We said, "Whatever happened, happened. It's over. Let's bury the hatchet and get going in the right direction. There aren't any more scabs on this team. We're all Buffalo Bills. The scabs are on the rest of the teams on our schedule. And we're going to make them bleed."

Just before our first poststrike game, at Miami, Joe and I got talking. We knew if we won the game, everyone would get the credit. But if we lost, it would be our fault, Joe's and mine, for keeping the team on strike. With both of us in the last year of our contracts, it wasn't going to take much of a push to send us out the door.

At halftime in Joe Robbie Stadium, we were down, 21–3. Joe and I just looked at each other. We didn't say a word. The toilet was about to flush as we sat helplessly in the Ty-D-Bol boat. It was going to take a miracle to get us out. A miracle, such as Kelly's leading us to 28 points in the next two quarters, including two touchdown passes, to tie the score, 31–31.

After Scott Norwood's 27-yard field goal in overtime, Joe and I embraced on the sidelines.

"This one," we said, "is for the old men."

We finished with a 7-8 record and missed the playoffs for the sixth year in a row. Even more frustrating than the strike was our 13–7 home loss to New England in the second-to-last game of the schedule, which cost us a playoff spot. I guess it only proved we weren't mature enough to take the next step on our climb back to respectability.

But a lot of things were coming together. At midseason, we had acquired Cornelius Bennett in a blockbuster three-way trade with the Colts—who had made the former Alabama star the No. 2 overall choice of the '87 draft—and Los Angeles Rams. It was one of the more complex deals in NFL history. First, we gave the Colts our first-round draft pick in 1988, first- and second-round picks in 1989, and Bell. Then, the Colts took all of those choices, combined them with their own first- and second-round picks in '88 and second-rounder in '89, threw in Bell and running back Owen Gill, and sent the entire package to the Rams for running back Eric Dickerson. Confused? So was I.

Coupled with Shane Conlan, our '87 first-round selection from Penn State, we had two of the better rookie linebackers the NFL had ever seen. Bennett gave us a sacker, Conlan a run-stuffer. Meanwhile, Bruce Smith was establishing himself as one of the more dominant defensive ends in the game. With Bennett coming from left outside linebacker and Smith coming from right end, teams didn't know who to block first. That helped open the middle for me.

Everyone's performance just seemed to climb a notch or two. There was a tenacity I hadn't seen in the huddle in years, a hungry look in everyone's eyes. All of a sudden, a running back would run two yards, you'd hear a big explosion, and he'd be three feet into the backfield. That pumped everybody up. It became a warning to the rest of the offense: "Watch out! Because we're not just going to put you on the ground, we're going to take your head off."

We weren't waiting for teams to make offensive mistakes; we were looking to cause them. When we got to the sidelines, there was something else I hadn't seen in quite a long time— an eagerness to get back on the field. We were actually disappointed when we stopped the opponent in three downs and had to come off. We just wanted to keep playing. We didn't even know we had an offense.

Bennett could run like a deer and hit like an elk. Conlan, with his skinny legs and huge head, was like a 35-pound helmet flying around the field and smashing everything in its path. Referees who worked our games carried flashlights to check the inside of Shane's helmet to see if it had a lead lining.

It was clear we had the makings of something special. Very special.

The off-season that year was pretty special, too. That was when I married Kris. I had dated a few girls here and there, but I knew, when I met Kris, she was the one.

I'm glad Kris felt the same about me.

Marriage gives you something to focus on, someone to share the accolades and criticisms with. And that's something I never had before. Kris brought direction to my life.

Before training camp opened in '88, we picked up another important ingredient, veteran defensive end Art Still, in a trade with Kansas City. I also picked up a new three-year contract with the Bills.

Once camp began and we started practicing, I was even more encouraged than I was at the end of the previous season. The defense moved around the field like a storm cloud. When we pursued a play, we did it in complete unison and smothered the ballcarrier. I had never been a part of anything like that before. I had never seen a defense so ready to start a season in my life. Usually, training-camp practices are for getting honed up and sharpened. But our attitude was, "Forget the preseason. We're ready to go. Now!"

We had the right mesh of everything. We had the talent. We had the intensity. Most of all, we had the camaraderie. We truly enjoyed playing together.

We knew, when we were on, no one could touch us. And we were on in training camp.

Our regular-season opener was against Minnesota, considered by many the team to beat in the NFC. Many saw us as the team to beat in the AFC. It was billed as a preview of Super Bowl XXIII.

Then, two days before the game, all hell broke loose.

We showed up for our usual light Friday workout, and everyone was in a pretty good frame of mind. As I said, we were ready. But there was just one problem: we weren't all there. Bruce Smith, our best defensive player, was missing. Soon whispers began to circulate throughout the team—whispers that Bruce had been suspended for using drugs.

Marv called us all to the middle of the field, and the whispers were confirmed: Bruce would miss the first four games while serving the suspension. As the coach spoke, I looked at Leon Seals, the second-year man who would be taking Bruce's place. Leon's eyes underwent an immediate change, from a lackadaisical look to a glare.

I didn't have to ask him if he was prepared to start.

But I also knew I'd have to step up my level of play. Even at his best, Leon wasn't going to be able to duplicate Bruce's performance. Bruce is one of the top defensive ends in the league, if not the best. Usually, my primary function is to penetrate, collapse the front of the pocket, and force the quarterback to move from one side or the other, where he'll

be greeted by a not-so-friendly end or linebacker. With Leon
lining up to my right insead of Bruce, it wouldn't be enough
for me to get pressure up the middle; I had to get some sacks
as well. Against an offensive line as big and as strong as the
Vikings', that was going to be a hell of a challenge.

I think everyone on defense had the same attitude. We all
realized we would have to give a little bit more to compensate for a major hole in our unit. As for our feelings toward
Bruce, we were unhappy about what had happened. It isn't
like a guy's not being able to play because of an injury he
suffered in a game or practice or working out on his own.
Bruce made a mistake. He got himself in trouble. In the
course of hurting himself, he also hurt the team. It's only
natural to feel you've been let down to a certain extent.

At the same time, I didn't know all of the details involved.
If a guy's got a problem, you can't help but feel for him,
whether he collects garbage or plays defensive line in the
NFL. Drug abuse is everywhere in society, and the last time
I checked, the NFL was part of society. Bruce was a teammate
and a friend, so it's hard to make harsh judgments instantly—
the kind that a lot of fans and media were making. And
frankly, there wasn't a whole lot of time to focus on anything
except the Vikings. It was forty-eight hours before our
opener. Forty-eight hours before the biggest game we might
play all year.

With or without Bruce, the ball would be kicked off, as
scheduled, on Sunday.

Even though we were playing at Rich Stadium, the Vikes
were slight favorites. That was fine with me. I was hoping
they would come in a little overconfident. You always want
your opponent feeling as if they could have faxed in the
victory and saved themselves the bother of actually playing
the game.

However, from the opening play, it was clear our 13–10
win was going to be a defensive tug of war. And it was. Using
Bruce's absence as an added bit of motivation, we played
every bit as well as I thought we would—and then some.

We wound up getting six sacks, including two by me and two by Arthur, the other old man up front. And Leon, showing great confidence and poise, played his ass off. He felt he had something to prove, and he was proving it.

Defense helped put us on the scoreboard first when an interception by Bennett set up a 27-yard Scott Norwood field goal. Thurman Thomas, in his rookie debut, made it 10–0 on a 5-yard touchdown run before the Vikings' kicker, Chuck Nelson, hit from 30 yards. After Robb Riddick recovered a mishandled punt by Bucky Scribner, Norwood kicked a 26-yard field goal to make it 13–3 in the fourth quarter. Then, we let them drive 74 yards for a touchdown to make it 13–10. With three minutes left, the Vikings took over on their own 24. They picked up 12 yards on first down, but we stopped them on three straight pass attempts, the biggest play coming when linebacker Hal Garner sacked Wade Wilson to put them out of field-goal range.

Shutting down an offense with the kind of firepower the Vikings had was a great springboard for our defense. It confirmed everything I had seen in the preseason.

So did our 9–6 victory over Miami in week two. Norwood was a one-foot show that day, accounting for all of our points with field goals of 41, 35, and 28 yards. Once again, defense came up big late in the game when, after the Dolphins drove to our 39-yard line, we stopped Dan Marino cold on four consecutive passes. Meanwhile, our offense was trying to cope with the loss of right guard Tim Vogler, who had injured his knee against Minnesota and would be out for four weeks. To compensate for his absence, our left tackle, Will Wolford, was moved to right guard and Leonard Burton, an inexperienced backup, started in Will's place.

The following Sunday, we faced our old nemesis, the Patriots, at Foxboro, Massachusetts. We hadn't beaten them since 1981, so we were merely staying true to form when we fell behind, 14–3, at halftime. But fortunately for us, Norwood stayed true to the form he had displayed through the first two games when he connected on a 44-yard field goal late in the third quarter. Then, early in the fourth, Kelly directed a 66-yard drive that ended with his 3-yard TD pass to Riddick to make it 14–13. With two minutes left, we forced the Patriots to punt, giving us the ball at our own 48. Kelly completed passes of 14 and 7 yards to move us to the New England 31. After a pair of 4-yard runs, Kelly threw the ball away to stop the clock. That set the stage for Norwood's winning 41-yard field goal with 11 seconds left.

I remember turning to Joe Devlin on the sidelines and saying, "A couple of years ago, we would have lost a game like this."

He nodded.

Turning back to the field, I said, "Maybe this really is our year."

By "our," I meant the team in general. But I couldn't help but feel a large slice of our success belonged to the defense, as well as Norwood's foot. As the defensive unit stood on the sidelines between series, we'd leave our chin straps buckled. We hoped our offense would score fast or just give the ball back to the opponents. We didn't care, just as long as we returned to the field as quickly as possible.

We were having fun. We didn't want it to end.

Two days after that New England game, we put the finishing touch on what was shaping up as perhaps the strongest defense in the league by making a deal with Phoenix for hard-hitting strong safety Leonard Smith. Despite our 3-0 record, our secondary was in dire need of something we all knew Leonard would bring—the intimidation factor.

Picture a house in a neighborhood. In that house lives a bully. Whenever you walk past that bully's house, you know he is going to beat the piss out of you. How often are you going to go near that house? And when you do, are you going to be concentrating on where you're walking or anything else besides that house?

It's the same thing with having a guy like Leonard in the secondary. After a while, a receiver will start to avoid the zones in which he knows he's going to get one of Leonard's forearms through his back. He isn't going to be concentrating on his route or the ball; he's going to be distracted by the thought of having his head taken off. He's going to develop a severe case of alligator arms. That makes our jobs easier on the line, because receivers who are intimidated by the strong safety run longer routes; they're going to stay away from those short turn-out patterns. When they run longer routes, the quarterback has to hold the ball longer. When the quarterback has to hold the ball longer, he's a lot easier for us to bring down.

Until Leonard showed up, receivers wandered through our secondary with a whole lot of fear. He's kind of a free-lance guy. Even if we're in man-to-man coverage, he may still just run around looking to crush anyone who gets near the ball.

Our 36–28 victory over Pittsburgh made us 4-0 for the first time since 1980, when we got off to a 5-0 start. The game wasn't nearly as close as the score indicated. We had put it out of reach after taking a 30–14 lead in the third quarter. Marv decided to give the starters the rest of the day off, so, with most of the backups on the field, the Steelers scored a pair of touchdowns in the final two minutes of the game. If there was any concern, it was that maybe we didn't have the greatest depth in the world. But it wasn't enough of a concern to overshadow our 4-0 record. We were feeling great.

We saw the next game, at Chicago, as an opportunity to enhance our credibility around the league. Beating the 3-1 Bears, an NFC powerhouse, on their turf would make us the team to beat in the NFL.

By no means were we overconfident, but we truly believed we could win. Bruce Smith was back. Considering how well we did with Seals in the lineup, it only figured we would be that much stronger with Bruce. There was also a certain feeling of destiny on our part. The ball just seemed to be bouncing with a Bills spin on it.

Until we got to Chicago and got waxed by the Bears, 24–3.

We fell behind, 7–3, in the first quarter, and the Bears put

us away with 17 unanswered points in the second. Jim
McMahon just had a fabulous game, hitting 20 of 27 passes
for 260 yards and 2 touchdowns—a 4-yarder to Emery
Moorehead and a 63-yarder to Ron Morris. But the real back-
breaker came shortly before halftime, when, after a Kelly
interception, Dennis Gentry took a reverse 58 yards for a TD.
Vogler's injury and the offensive-line shuffling it caused also
took a heavy toll in this game. With the likes of Dan Hampton
and Richard Dent on their defensive line, the Bears were the
wrong team against which to start a raw offensive lineman
like Burton. As a result, Kelly was sacked six times.

We were more frustrated than disappointed, because we
knew, despite the one-sided score, we were not the least bit
inferior to the Bears. We hit with them and played with them
all day. We just made some mistakes—the kind that kill you
against a quality team. In fact, walking off the field, several
Bears players came up to us and said, "You guys are the best
team we've played so far." Considering their only loss at that
point was a 31–7 ass-kicking from Minnesota, that was a
nice compliment.

But the frustration stayed with us all week. We kept kicking ourselves for blowing such a perfect chance to make a
statement to the rest of the league. We kept thinking about
that game so much, we forgot about our next opponent, Indianapolis, which we faced at home. As we wallowed in
self-pity, the Colts built a 17–7 halftime lead. As we headed
for the dressing room, a lot of disillusioned fans, figuring we
were on our way to a second straight loss, began booing us.

We were fuming at halftime. If any team was inferior this
week, it was definitely the Colts. There was just no excuse
for us to be trailing them by 10 points. We had Bruce back.
We had Vogler back at right guard, allowing Wolford to return to where he belonged, left tackle. So, in the dressing
room, a bunch of us said, "We're playing last week's game
and losing this week's. We're turning one loss into two
losses. Let's forget about Chicago. Let's forget about the mistakes. Let's wake up."

We did. We forgot about the previous week. We forgot about the previous half. We forgot about the booing. And we exploded for 27 points on the way to a 34–23 victory. After struggling in the first two quarters, Kelly went on to have what would be his best day of the season, completing 21 of 39 passes for 315 yards and 3 touchdowns. We also turned it around on defense, allowing only 79 yards in the second half after giving up 229 in the first thirty minutes.

The outcome reassured me of the kind of club we had. Good teams bounce back from lousy first halves.

In week seven, we traveled to New Jersey to face the Jets in our first *Monday Night Football* appearance since 1984. It was the first of two we would have in '88. See what happens when you win? I can't remember a game when I've had more fun than I did during that 37–14 blowout. I mean, we just took control the instant we set foot on the field. We scored the first five times we touched the ball, as Kelly came up with another big performance (16 of 27, 302 yards, 3 TDs). We could do anything we wanted to do. Bruce Smith annihilated Jeff Criswell, the Jets' left tackle, and made 2½ sacks. I was picking up center Ted Banker and just driving him into Ken O'Brien's lap. It was fantastic.

For a defensive lineman, the best part about a game like that is you don't have to play with any sort of caution. You don't have to worry about screens or draws. You're just looking to pound the quarterback because he's just going to drop back and throw. You don't feel sore or even tired after a game like that.

Which was a good thing, because we needed all of the energy we could get to dispose of the Patriots six days later. It was a typical Buffalo–New England game, with four lead changes before Norwood beat the Patriots for the second time in a row with a 33-yard field goal with thirteen seconds left. Scott has the perfect psychological makeup for a kicker. He never allows his emotions to rise or fall. He just goes out there with a blank expression on his face, lines it up, and kicks it through.

Things were even easier the following Sunday, as we trashed Green Bay, 28–0. For the first time in ten years, our defense twice was involved in the scoring. Free safety Mark Kelso picked off a Don Majkowski pass and returned it 78 yards for a touchdown to make it 21–0 early in the third quarter. Then, with less than two minutes left, Seals picked up a fumble by Paul Ott Carruth and carried it 7 yards for our final TD of the day. We also sacked Majkowski six times and had red helmets in his face all afternoon.

But as impressive as our defense was that day, its finest hour came a week later, with our 13–3 win at Seattle. Those of us who had played for Chuck Knox in Buffalo really wanted to go out there and show him how far we had come since he left us. We wanted to show him how much we had grown. The best way to do that was to beat the Seahawks, something we had not done in the regular season since he became their coach in 1983.

Of course, Chuck, with some proving of his own to do, wanted the win every bit as much—to the extent that he tried to have Bruce Smith taken out of the game. Early in the second quarter, after Bruce beat offensive tackle Ron Mattes for the second time to sack Kelly Stouffer, Seahawks guard Edwin Bailey stood Smith up while Mattes blocked down on his knee. Fortunately, Bruce wasn't hurt.

Nothing was ever officially said about it, but I know Chuck, and I seriously doubt Mattes and Bailey took it upon themselves to execute such a blatant cheap shot. Stuff like that happens all the time; it's part of the curse of being a great pass rusher who can't be stopped through conventional means. The idea, at the very least, is to give the guy something to think about besides getting to the quarterback—such as his own health. But you can also end his career, and as much as I respect Chuck, there's just no place for that in the game.

Smith still ate Mattes alive the rest of the way, and that had plenty to do with the fact we didn't allow a touchdown for the second week in a row. So did a couple of short-yardage stands we had. The first came late in the second quarter, when the Seahawks, trailing 10–3, had a third and one at their own 30-yard line. Curt Warner tried to run to his left and was stopped cold by linebacker Scott Radecic, forcing Seattle to punt away a chance to pick up at least three more points before halftime. Then, with thirty-six seconds left in the third quarter and us still leading, 10–3, the Seahawks had a fourth and inches at our 30. Stouffer tried a quarterback sneak through the middle, and I met him head-on before he could pick up anything. That was a gutsy call on Knox's part. We'd been excellent against short-yardage plays, yet he still tried to run it up the gut. Maybe he thought I was getting old or something. But the old "Welcome Wagon" was there.

With a 9-1 record and a 3½-game lead in the AFC East with only six weeks left, we were sitting pretty. Two more wins and the division title would be ours.

Time for a little R&R in south Florida.

At least, that's what our second *Monday Night* encounter of the season, against the Dolphins, felt like. We humiliated them, 31–6. The only thing that bothered me about the game was that we broke our two-game streak for not allowing a touchdown.

I'm sure ABC was thrilled we weren't going to be on any more of its prime-time games the rest of the year. Having countless TV sets turn off or to something else by the third quarter couldn't have been too healthy for the ratings. By the same token, I'll bet a lot of fans loved us for allowing them to get to bed early enough so they wouldn't be zombies at work the next morning. And we wanted to make certain our loyal followers in Buffalo were well rested for the next game—our showdown at home against the Jets with a chance to capture the division crown for the first time since 1980.

November 20, 1988. That day will forever occupy a special place in my heart. It was the day I made the biggest play of my career and one of the biggest in the history of the franchise. It was the day "fan-demonium" broke out at Rich Stadium.

Having pounded the Jets earlier in the year, everyone
thought it would be merely an extension of our previous
weekend at the beach. But the Jets were determined not to
let us do any celebrating at their expense. They let us know,
from the very start, the price for a championship would be
a lot of welts, bruises, scrapes, scratches, and much worse
if they could help it. It was just a mean, rotten, nasty game
where defense took over, and offense, as usual, was limited
to the legs of the placekickers.

Pat Leahy's 23-yard field goal gave the Jets a 3–0 halftime
lead. Norwood's 25-yarder in the third and 26-yarder in the
fourth made it 6–3. Then, Leahy hit from 40 to make it 6–
6. We would have easily gone ahead, but a 47-yard attempt
by Norwood hit the crossbar.

With twenty-five seconds left in regulation, Leahy lined
up another try from 40, and given his tremendous efficiency,
most fans were ready to head for the exits, certain we had
lost. But a split second after he made contact with the ball,
the ball made contact with my left forearm, fell to the ground,
and miraculously, we had overtime.

The Jets won the toss for the extra period, so they'd have
the first crack at putting an end to the game. But two plays
after we kicked off, cornerback Derrick Burroughs knocked
the ball out of the hands of fullback Roger Vick. Bennett
recovered at the Jets' 32-yard line. Four runs by Riddick
pushed us to the 20, from where the ball was snapped for
Norwood's trusty foot to do its stuff from 30 yards. He banged
it through to give us a 9–6 victory. And that was when "fan-
demonium" erupted, as thousands and thousands of fans
poured onto the field to tear down the goalposts. As I ran
with my teammates in an effort to avoid being trampled, a
fan, fueled by excitement and maybe a sip or two of alcohol,
came flying out of nowhere and smashed into my right thigh
hard enough to knock me to the ground.

It was one of the best hits I had taken all day.

But I did manage to get to the tunnel before the field became a complete sea of humanity. With all of that body heat

mixing with the cold November air, a cloud of steam hung, eerily, a few feet above everyone's head.

It was an unbelievable sight, an indescribable feeling.

When we lined up for what should have been Leahy's game-winner, I had a strong feeling I'd be able to break through the guard-tackle gap in front of me and make the block. I've never had a stronger feeling in my life. That was because, on Leahy's previous field goal, I came fairly close to getting a piece of the ball. I knew if only I had turned my body a little to the left, I'd have gotten it. So the second time, I came off the line low to get the greatest possible penetration, then, as I came up, I turned to my left, popped my arm out, jumped for everything I was worth, and heard the beautiful sound of the old double thud.

Okay, so maybe you could barely fit a piece of paper under my cleats. But it didn't really matter how high I jumped. All that mattered was that it was high enough.

When I arrived at our victory party afterward at Ilio Di-Paolo's Restaurant, a favorite team hangout in Blasdell, New York, I was given a standing ovation by my teammates, coaches, friends, and family. Ilio, a former pro wrestler and one of my best friends in Buffalo, met me at the door with a huge bear hug, overlapping those monster-sized hands of his, planted a kiss on my cheek, and said, "Gumba, we did it."

Later that night, as Kris and I drove home, we noticed a bunch of handmade signs along our street. They said things like, "Great job, Fred!" "We love you," "Thank you."

Kris looked at me as we headed down the street. I had tears in my eyes.

The next day, while my wife and I were having breakfast at Denny's, the waitress said, "You know, Fred, that play put you right up there in Buffalo Bills history with the Paul Maguires, Jack Kemps, and O. J. Simpsons. It immortalized you."

"Jeez," I said. "I really didn't think about it that way. But it's a nice thought."

Winning the AFC East was nice, too. But it wasn't what we were after. It was only a little pebble. We wanted the whole boulder, which was an all-expenses-paid trip to Super Bowl XXIII at Miami. And some big diamond rings for souvenirs.

Nevertheless, that didn't stop fan-demonium from continuing to spread like wildfire.

It was as if the offices at One Bills Drive had expanded to encompass all of western New York. Fans weren't merely following us; they were a part of us. Players and coaches always get their share of free advice in restaurants, barrooms, and 7-Elevens. But this was different. The fans truly believed they had a say in whatever we did. Everywhere I went, I was being handed game plans, scouting reports of the teams we were going to face, training methods, you name it. Little old ladies would draw plays on napkins and leave them on my table in a restaurant. If I ordered two eggs, the waitress would bring me four, saying, "Just want to make sure you're well fed before Sunday's game."

"Yeah," I'd say. "Look at me: I'm wasting away to nothing."

The community also had a hand in giving our defense a nickname. All good defenses have nicknames: The Steel Curtain, the Purple People Eaters, the Fearsome Foursome, the Doomsday Defense, the No-Names, the Orange Crush, the Killer Bees, the Bruise Brothers. So *The Buffalo News* held a contest in its sports pages to come up with one for us: The Blizzard Defense. Actually, what the *News* did was gather all of the entries and let us pick the winner.

There were about 4,500 from which to choose. And a lot of good ones, including a bunch that require a word of explanation: The Bill Collectors (they make you pay), the Buffalo Rebate (get a quarterback!), the Frosted Flakes (because they're grrrRRREAT!), the Bluebonic Plague (there is no cure), SDI (Strategic Defense Initiative, it even scares the Russians!), and the Virgins (you can't score on them).

We picked The Blizzard Defense because we felt it best

captured the way things are when you play football in Buffalo, and the way our defense swarmed and hit—like a blizzard.

The difference between the fan mail I received then and
the kind I was getting in '84 and '85 was remarkable. In '84
and '85, everyone was frustrated. Everyone wanted to point
fingers. Everyone had me down for the count. Now they were
saying, "Hey, Freddy, it's good to have you back."

And it wasn't only letters I received. They'd enclose pictures of their kids wearing No. 76 shirts. They'd send me
crocheted rugs with my picture on them. After practice, I'd
find homemade cookies and brownies in my Jeep. When I
got home, bottles of champagne would be sitting on my doorstep.

Chants of "Fred-dee! Fred-dee!" rang down from the
stands the second I set foot on the field on Sunday, just as
they did early in my career. The first few times I heard it in
'88, I became misty-eyed, thinking about how far I had come
in three years. How far we had all come—fans, as well
as players. We had been so frustrated and angry during the
bad times, it made the good times feel that much better.
Our relationship was not unlike the kind you have in a
family. You fight, you make up, you fight again, you make up
again.

I just felt fortunate to have the chance to be part of another
reconciliation.

The fans didn't look at the '88 team the same as they looked
at the '80 and '81 squads. Nor did we. The '80–'81 squads
were good, they were tough, they had a lot of spunk. But the
'88 team had a lot more overall talent. We were capable of
going out and dominating opponents physically. We were
the kind of team that could go the distance.

Enthusiasm was high in '80 and '81, but with a little skep-
ticism sprinkled on top. In '88, there was enthusiasm, plus
confidence. We went to the stadium expecting to win. The
fans went there expecting to see us win.

So, with four games remaining, everyone saw our clinching home-field advantage throughout the playoffs as a mere formality.

Maybe we shouldn't have been so sure of ourselves.

What was supposed to have been a stretch run turned into a crawl.

First, we traveled to Cincinnati and were beaten, 35–21. With injuries to three key defensive players and some carelessness on both sides of the ball, we were no match for a Bengal team playing at the top of its game at Cincinnati. Conlan, our leading tackler, was out with a twisted foot he suffered against the Jets. Burroughs was out with an ankle injury from the same game. To make matters worse, Darryl Talley, the steadiest of our linebackers, left the field on the first play against the Bengals with a bruised thigh. We fell behind, 21–0, in the second quarter, and never threatened the rest of the way.

It was upsetting, but when we watched it on videotape the next afternoon, we felt our mistakes were correctable. There was no doubt in our minds that if we got ourselves healthy and met the Bengals again in the playoffs—which seemed likely—we'd win.

Our next opponent was the 3-10 Buccaneers. Before leaving for the flight to Tampa Bay, I told Kris, "This game worries me." And I was keeping a straight face. In fact, there wasn't another game on our schedule that worried me more. The first thing that caught my eye on video was the way Bucs coach/drill sergeant Ray Perkins had his players fighting for their lives. The second thing was a defense that, when it rose to the challenge, was capable of being as strong as any in the NFL.

It rose to the challenge against us.

Tampa Bay controlled the ball for nearly twenty minutes in building a 10–0 halftime lead. Our attempts to rally were thwarted by two interceptions and a goal-line stand that saw Robb Riddick get stopped on three plunges. That was a bit shocking, considering Robb was Mr. Touchdown from that range and would finish the season with 12 TD runs of two yards or less. After we cut the margin to 10–5, the Buccaneers went on another long march. This time, we stopped them, with yours truly blocking his second field goal in two weeks—a 29-yarder by John Carney. (Actually, I had two blocks in the game, but one was disallowed because of a penalty.) That set the stage for a last-minute crack at pulling out a victory.

But our hopes died when Kelly was intercepted at the Bucs' 14. We lost our second in a row. We also lost Vogler, this time for good, with the knee problem that had hampered him from the opening game.

Suddenly, there was a ripple or two in the confidence everyone had that we were Super Bowl–bound.

However, on a December afternoon at Rich, with a minus-14° windchill, we put the warm-blooded Raiders into a deep freeze, 37–21. Norwood's winning field goal marked the sixth time in '88 that his foot made the difference in the outcome. I wound up injuring my left knee in that game. It happened when, while hitting a guard, the center knocked my legs out from under me and Bruce Smith fell on the knee. I heard a pop, but it wasn't until I got up and tried to take a step that I realized I was a bit more hurt than I thought. My thigh moved fine; the rest of my leg stayed on the ground. The first thing I thought was, if this causes me to miss the Super Bowl, I'm gong to be pissed.

After our trainer, Ed Abramoski, put about seventeen rolls of tape around my leg, I said, "Fuck this, I'm going back in."

"Not a chance," Abe said. "We need you for the playoffs. You go in there now, and you're going to really mess it up."

I stayed out.

The next day, Dick Weiss, our team physician, gave me his prognosis: it would take at least six weeks for the knee to recover fully, but with some rest, I'd be able to play in our divisional-round playoff game, which was three weeks away. Not only wasn't I supposed to play in our regular-season finale at Indianapolis, I wasn't even supposed to practice for it. But I couldn't stand the thought of just standing around and doing nothing. So, with the help of about a thousand miles of tape, I took part in a couple of workouts late in the week and pronounced myself ready to play.

Although I didn't get any argument from our medical people, I also didn't exactly get a ringing endorsement from them or the coaches.

"Look, we'll start you, we'll see how it feels and go from there," said Ted Cottrell, our defensive-line coach.

On the first play of the Colts' game, I locked out center Ray Donaldson, shuffled to my left, disengaged, and made the tackle. I may not have been 100 percent, but I was pretty sure I could go the distance. Then, all of a sudden, I noticed my backup, Jeff Wright, running onto the field.

"What are you doing out here?" I asked.

"They want you out," he said.

"Forget it. I'm not going anywhere."

But when I saw Ted wave me off from the sidelines, I gave in. I realized he and the other coaches were merely trying to do me a favor by keeping alive my streak of consecutive starts. After that, they wanted me out of the game so I wouldn't risk any further damage.

Arthur was also out of the game with a knee injury. I noticed him sitting on the bench, drinking distilled water and eating Granola bars. I joined him and watched as we blew a 14–3 lead on the way to a 17–14 loss.

Home-field advantage throughout the playoffs was also blown.

Nevertheless, we did finish with a 12-4 record—the most wins by a Bills team since 1964. And our Blizzard Defense finished No. 1 in the AFC.

Another bit of silver lining was being voted to the Pro Bowl for the first time since 1983. It tied me with O.J. Simpson and Joe DeLamielleure for a club-record five appearances in the NFL's annual all-star game. It also took me by surprise. I felt I had had a Pro Bowl–type season, but having one and having other players and coaches around the conference recognize that fact are two different things. Once I stopped being picked, I figured, those who still remembered my name were thinking, this guy is way past his prime.

Cincinnati's Tim Krumrie was named the AFC's starting nose tackle, while I made second team. The year before, everyone was writing that Krumrie was the best nose tackle in the game and I was dead.

It felt good to climb out of the grave.

Our first postseason appearance since January 3, 1982— aka the "30-second disaster" in Cincinnati—was against Houston at home on New Year's Day. It was twenty-two years, to the day, since Buffalo previously hosted a pro football playoff game, when the Bills faced Kansas City for the American Football League championship. The excitement was high, the town was electrified.

But you could still sense a small undercurrent of doubt, generated by our 1-3 finish, the loss to the Colts, and the absence of Conlan, who had aggravated his foot injury against the Raiders.

"We're still the Rodney Dangerfields of the NFL, no matter what we do," Talley told reporters at the time.

Despite getting almost three weeks of rest, my knee didn't feel a whole lot better than when I injured it. As I tried to take a corner while running, it felt as if someone were smashing it with a hammer. Not that that was going to stop me from playing. Like other longtime survivors in the game, I have the proper Neanderthal attitude that allows me to play regardless of how much pain I feel. Considering it was the playoffs, someone could have cut my whole leg off and I'd probably just have fastened a stick to the bottom and still played.

At the same time, I'm not totally stupid when it comes to my health. My general rule of thumb—assuming I still have a thumb—is to ask the trainer. If Abe says my playing will make an injury more severe, I won't play. If he says it won't, I'll go out there. He told me my knee would hold up against the Oilers, which it did. But not without the help of one his magical tape jobs. In the practices leading up to the game,

Abe wrapped my leg from the crotch to the calf, so I could only straighten it three-quarters of the way. Until I got used to it, I flew out of my stance a couple of times and fell. What I could never get used to, though, was the tape's pulling on my skin as I ran. It felt as if my flesh were being torn off.

The Oilers probably had the best overall talent in the NFL. They also had one of the league's dirtier teams, a style encouraged by their coach at the time, Jerry Glanville. They were notorious late-hitters, particularly on defense. So I told our offensive guys, "You see someone cheap-shot your teammate, you make him pay. Knock his ass to the ground. Chop him. Do whatever you have to do to make his life miserable. Just don't let any of our guys feel alone out there." I wasn't too concerned about our defense's taking crap from their offense, which was also known to drift occasionally from the pages of the rule book. If anyone screwed with us, all I had to do was point to Talley. As always, he'd be standing there with a psychotic look on his face, huffing and puffing and foaming at the mouth.

"You see him?" I'd say. "He knows where you live."

Before the game, I told the refs, "The only reason the Oilers have a reputation for being dirty is because you guys never throw a flag when they start pulling all that stuff. Players can't be dirty in a game unless you guys allow it. So use those flags today. Otherwise, we're going to have a free-for-all out there."

And I wasn't just talking about players. I was talking about our 80,000 bodyguards in the stands, too. Any nonsense, and the Oilers would have had to leave the stadium in an armored truck.

But it actually turned out to be a fairly clean game all the way around. Highly emotional, but clean. The offenses and defenses wound up neutralizing each other, physically as well as emotionally. That left special teams to decide the outcome, as is often the case in the playoffs.

Leonard Smith's block of a Greg Montgomery punt set up a 1-yard touchdown run by Riddick to give us a 7–0 lead in the second quarter. A 35-yard Tony Zendejas field goal made it 7–3 a little more than six minutes later. Then, twenty-six seconds before halftime, Zendejas had another try, from 38 yards, but it was blocked by Bruce Smith.

In the third quarter, we were all over Warren Moon, to the point where he couldn't complete a pass. I became so carried away with my emotions, I wasn't fully concentrating on one pass rush, and when I hit Moon, I thought I was making contact with a back or an offensive lineman trying to block me. So I just shoved him aside, even as he held the ball, and looked around for the "real" Moon. Meanwhile, we increased our lead to 11 points on a 10-yard touchdown run by Thurman Thomas.

Kelso made an interception to set up a 27-yard field goal by Norwood to make it 17–3 early in the fourth quarter. But the Oilers answered with a 1-yard TD run by Mike Rozier. With just under two minutes left, they forced us to punt. The third and final big special-teams play came when Steve Tasker forced Curtis Duncan to fumble. Ray Bentley recovered at the Houston 18, allowing us to kill off the final 1:45 and preserve our 17–10 victory.

The night before the game, Bruce DeHaven, our special-teams coach, came up with an idea to give his unit a little added incentive. He distributed a dollar bill to each of his twenty bomb-squadders. On each one, he scribbled a message: "Special teams win championships." Bruce wanted to give out more than twenty dollars, but his wife wouldn't let him.

Our late-season collapse forced us to travel to Cincinnati for the AFC title showdown. Although we knew we'd have had a much better chance of winning at Rich, we approached the game with tremendous confidence. We felt the Oilers were the only team capable of keeping us out of Super Bowl XXIII. And now they were gone. We respected the Bengals. Based on our previous visit to Riverfront Stadium, we could only view them with the highest regard.

But we knew we were better. We knew the only way we would lose to them was if we beat ourselves.

Officially, the final score read Bengals 21, Bills 10. We'll always remember it as Bills 21, Bills 10.

Our first major mistake of the day was the second of two Kelly interceptions in the first quarter. Three plays later, Boomer Esiason threw a 21-yard pass to Rodney Holman that moved the Bengals to our 5-yard line. Ickey Woods then carried to the 1, and on the next play, he went diving into the end zone. The last thing we had wanted to do was give him a reason to perform that stinking "Ickey Shuffle."

We weren't all that rattled, though. We were certain we could get right back into the game, and we did. On the very next possession, Kelly relocated his accuracy. In leading us on a 56-yard drive, he hit on four consecutive passes, the last of which was a 9-yard rollout to Andre Reed to tie the score at 7–7 early in the second quarter.

Unfortunately, that would prove to be our only sustained march of the day.

After Scott Norwood was wide left on a 43-yard field goal, the Bengals took off on a run-oriented, 11-play, 74-yard drive, which ended with Boomer throwing a 10-yard TD pass to James Brooks to make it 14–7. The next time Cincinnati had the ball, Kelso made his second interception of the playoffs, setting up a 39-yard Norwood field goal that cut the margin to 14–10 at halftime.

Our special teams' performance hardly resembled the one it gave seven days earlier. One of their more bizarre mistakes was Erroll Tucker's decision to allow a third-quarter punt by Lee Johnson to bounce past him at our 26. The ball rolled all the way down to the 1, where it was downed by the Bengals. We picked up only four yards in three plays before punting it back.

But the series that probably best captured the kind of fog-headed showing we gave that day came late in the third quarter, with Cincinnati still leading, 14–10. On fourth and four from our 33-yard line, the Bengals fooled us with a fake punt that resulted in a first down. Backup quarterback Turk Schonert moved from a blocking back in punt formation to under center, took the snap, and handed to Stanley Wilson, who ran for 6 yards.

Five plays later, on second and goal from our 5, Shane Conlan, playing for the first time since the Raiders game, burst into the Cincinnati backfield and threw Woods for a 3-yard loss. "Let's see you shuffle now!" we were yelling. However, in the end zone, Derrick Burroughs was picking up a personal foul penalty, as well as an ejection, for throwing a forearm into the jaw of wide receiver Tim McGee. They had scuffled on several earlier downs because McGee was chopping at Burroughs's knees. Finally, Derrick just lost his composure and retaliated. Worst of all, instead of the Bengals having a third down at the 8, they had first and goal from the 4. Two plays later, Woods again shuffled in from the 1 to make it 21–10.

While not highly regarded, the Bengals' defense came up big. Our offense spent most of the second half backed up against our goal line, with an output of minus 12 yards in the third quarter. Failing to convert a single first down in ten tries, we held the ball only 20:31, compared to Cincinnati's 39:29. As a defense, you can't stay on the field all day against an offense like that, or it'll chew you up. The Bengals are a ball-control team. Boomer lulls you to sleep with hand-offs and all kinds of short throws.

Then, bang! He hits for something big.

Boomer didn't have great stats that day, but he was in control. Through the entire game, he talked to his offensive teammates on the field, saying things like, "Let's take it easy, guys. Just relax, and we'll do fine today." Then he'd look down at me and say, "How ya doin', Fred. Havin' fun? Me, too." His coolness in the face of so much pressure, his ability to lead and keep his teammates loose in the tightest of settings, was every bit as critical to Cincinnati's success as any pass he threw.

The frustration of tripping and falling at the doorstep of the Super Bowl simmered in all of us as we sat in the dressing room. We knew there was no reason we shouldn't have been able to win that game. Except one: self-destruction.

Joe Devlin looked around the dressing room at all of the sour faces. He was as angry as anybody, but he thought it was wrong for us to be drowning in self-pity.

"Hey, let's bring it up!" he yelled. "Sure, we ended the season on a bad note, but let's be proud of what we did."

Then, from the other side of the lockers, came a voice that said, "We don't need that shit."

It was Erroll Tucker.

"Who said that?" Joe asked.

"I did," Tucker said.

With that, Tucker, who is all of 5'6" and weighs 170 pounds, came whipping around the corner to confront the 6'5", 290-pound Devlin. Joe started going after him. Just then, Will Wolford, who also goes 6'5", 290, went to grab Joe and caught a forearm that knocked him back two feet. Kent Hull, 6'5", 275, tried to do the same and was also knocked back, along with one of our assistant coaches.

I was sitting about fifteen feet away, took a couple of leaps, and landed on Joe's back. I wrapped my arms around his chest, and he started to swing me back and forth as if I were a tail.

"Calm down, Joe! Calm down!" I said. "The game's over. This isn't going to solve anything."

With the help of Jim Ritcher and a couple of others, I finally got Joe to regain his poise. Tucker regained his, too, and order was finally restored. But their outburst was understandable.

We had a great team. We had a great opportunity. We let it slip away.

Still, I figured, with another year of maturity, we'd become the team to beat in the AFC, if not the NFL, in 1989.

CHAPTER
TEN

THE DROP

THE APPROACH to my eleventh training camp was quite a bit different from the approach to my first. As a rookie, I had all kinds of energy to burn. I was single, fresh out of college, and torturing other football players seemed like a great way to spend a summer at Camp Knox.

But in my eleventh year, there were about a hundred places I'd have rather been than Camp Levy. Like at home, with Kris. Or on the beach, at Cape Cod. Hell, even a trip to the dentist to have my gums scraped sounded more appealing.

At this stage of my career, training camp is miserable. No fun at all. Sure, there's camaraderie and male bonding and all of that other stuff psychologists like to babble about. But after a while, the boys can get pretty testy. You can only look at the same face across the line for so long before you want to punch it.

By your eleventh season, the routine turns to drudgery. You get up, eat breakfast, get taped, put on the pads, knock each other around for a couple of hours, get sore and tired, eat lunch, sleep for an hour, get taped again, put on the pads again, knock each other around for a couple of hours more, eat dinner, relax for a half hour, go to meetings from seven P.M. to ten P.M., go to bed at eleven.

A real blast, isn't it?

The thing I find so funny now is bed check. Imagine a thirty-three-year-old man getting checked on in a dormitory room? *It's eleven o'clock; do you know where your football players are?* The primary concern is making sure the younger guys haven't snuck out to prowl the streets or snuck in any females. The fine for such offenses is five hundred dollars. Old, tired men like my roommate Jim Ritcher and I could be found, in our beds, watching the news or our eyelids. It would take a real emergency for us not to be in our suite at that hour.

As a rookie, I'd be up by quarter to seven to make sure I was at breakfast by eight o'clock sharp. In the last few years, I set the alarm for seven forty-five, and Ritcher and I would be running to the dining hall at five to eight. Just like college, you learn the ropes.

When you're a pro football player on the plus side of thirty, you have to be a little more selective about what you put inside your body than you were at twenty-two. That was why, instead of choosing from the usual breakfast menu of eggs, bacon, sausages, and pancakes, Ritcher and I brought our portable blender into the kitchen and pulled out the ingredients for the 900-calorie, zero-fat drink we had each morning and for lunch: fifteen egg whites, four eight-ounce cups of yogurt, forty ounces of skim milk, and an assortment of fruit. It was a healthy version of a "frappe"—what we Bostonians call a milk shake—that Sean McNanie had introduced me to several years ago.

It isn't a case of trying to get thin. A lineman needs all of the bulk he can get, and I've added quite a bit since my rookie year. But I have to guard against getting heavy to the point where I lose my quickness. Age is eating away at that anyway, so I have to give myself as much help as possible by maintaining good weight, not fat.

I've also reduced the payload I take with me on the field in terms of equipment. Each year, I've played with one fewer pad than the season before, all in an effort to streamline myself. When I first got into the league, I wore—in addition to my shoulder pads—pads for my hips, elbows, forearms, hands, thighs, and knees. Now, all I have left are the thigh pads. And I've even made those lighter by removing the cushion around the plastic. Is it less safe to play that way? Yes. But the way I look at it, if anyone is consistently able to smash me in the knees or thighs, that means I'm not doing my job very well, so I won't be around too long anyway.

It's sort of like a race car. When you want it to go faster, what do you do? You take off the mirrors, pull out the seats, rip out the carpeting, maybe even lose some not-so-critical engine parts.

That's me, stripped for action.

Our defense didn't exactly open the '89 season in Super Bowl form. Basically, we were a one-man show—The Jim Kelly Show. He beat Miami, 27–24, by diving for a 2-yard touchdown as time expired on a 7-play, 51-yard drive that he engineered to perfection. After a 28–14 Monday night loss to Denver the following week, Kelly was as hot as ever in victories over Houston (47–41, in overtime) and New England (31–10).

I think some of our defensive problems were due to the fact we had played five preseason games (one more than usual because of our appearance in the Hall of Fame Game against Washington), four on the road and all in the heat. So we were pretty weary by the time we made yet another road trip to yet another hot spot, Miami, for the opener. I know, I know, the offense went through the same grind. But fatigue takes less of a toll on offense than on defense. On offense, everything is diagrammed and you're almost always following a specific assignment. On defense, you're usually reacting on the run, and when you're tired, you're a little behind in your reactions. You're a little slower off the ball. You're not anticipating correctly.

I was sucking so much air during the Miami game, I almost sucked someone's shirt off. There wasn't a single insect left in Joe Robbie Stadium.

In addition to lacking stamina, our defense also didn't seem to have the great mesh of a year earlier. That was especially true in the Denver game. The hustle was there, everyone worked hard. But we just weren't clicking as a unit for some reason. The Broncos kept getting our linebackers to overpursue on cut-back runs. All of us made terrible reads the whole night.

Opponents also took advantage of our problems defending against timing patterns. With our defense having led the AFC with 46 sacks in 1988, every effort was made to avoid our front seven. With timing patterns, the quarterback is taking a shorter drop and getting rid of the ball faster, which takes away the most potent element of our defense—the pass rush—and places greater pressure on our secondary. If he tried to sit in the pocket against us, he was quickly going to find himself on the ground . . . if not a stretcher.

But that's what happens after you've had a successful season. Teams have spent the entire off-season studying every single thing you do, either to copy it or stop it. You become a target off which other clubs can build a reputation. Every opponent is going to be performing at its highest level, and you have to reestablish your turf week after week. You have to intimidate. You have to stuff them and stone them from the very start. Even if they make a play, you must pound them and chase them and make them say, "Now I know why these guys were the best in the conference last year." Otherwise, if you're just going through the motions, they're going to say, "Jeez, these guys are beatable after all."

As a defense, we just didn't reestablish our turf at the beginning of the season. And our opponents ran and passed all over it.

Injuries also took a heavy toll. Shane Conlan suffered a knee sprain in the Broncos game that would sideline him for six weeks. Then, against Houston, we lost Derrick Burroughs, who was playing the best football of his life, with a spinal condition that would end his career with the Bills.

All of us held our breath as Derrick remained on the ground, motionless, after smashing helmet-first into Curtis Duncan. For about ten minutes, he couldn't move any part of his body from the neck down. The trainers were sticking pins in his arms and legs, and he couldn't feel them. It's the kind of thing every pro football player has in the back of his mind and prays will stay there. Fortunately, the paralysis was temporary. Unfortunately for Derrick and for us, it was later discovered his spinal canal was too narrow, which posed a threat of something more severe happening if he took another such blow. Playing football became a risk the Bills felt he couldn't afford to take.

More disasters struck in week five, during our 34–17 loss to the Colts at Indianapolis. Or so it seemed. In the third quarter, Jon Hand, a 300-pound defensive end for the Colts, slammed Kelly down on his left (nonthrowing) shoulder after he released a 16-yard TD pass to Andre Reed. I had seen Jim take hard hits before and walk slowly off the field. But when I saw him head toward the bench, holding his arm in obvious pain, the first thing I thought was, this can't be good. The second thing I thought was, oh, shit, there goes the season. A short while later, we were told the shoulder was separated, and Kelly would be out for four weeks, possibly longer.

That was when I heard a giant thump—the sound of everyone jumping off our bandwagon.

It was a good news/bad news situation the next day. The good news was the separation was a bit less severe than first thought and there was a chance Kelly would miss as few as three games. The bad news was, while meeting with reporters, he fingered our right tackle, Howard Ballard, for causing the injury by missing his block on Hand.

"It should never have happened," Kelly said. "He [Hand] should have been blocked. Watching film, I don't know what

Howard was thinking. It seemed like he was looking outside to see if a guy blitzed or something . . . and not at the guy over him [Hand].

"I think four out of our five positions [on the offensive line] are very solid," Kelly went on to say. "I don't even need to tell you guys [reporters] what position they might have to make a change in. I can't stand up here and say they should do it or shouldn't do it; I don't make the decisions."

What Kelly did make, however, was headlines—the kind that can do harm to a team's morale. Howard wasn't all that upset with what Jim said, but other guys were really offended. For one thing, Howard is as likable a guy as you'll find in the dressing room. Because of his 6'6", 320-plus-pound frame, we gave him nicknames such as House and Howard Huge. For another, he was a first-year starter at an extremely difficult position. He was still experiencing a lot of growing pains and deserved to be cut a little slack.

Joe Devlin probably put it best for all of us when he told the press, "Everybody knows Jim Kelly is an intense competitor, and he doesn't like to lose and I'm sure he doesn't like getting injured. None of us on the team feels very good about him getting injured. However, I don't think it's anybody's place, myself included, to ever point the finger at any one individual, because football is a team-oriented sport. The team has to always, always come first. Everybody makes mistakes. I miss blocks. Jim Kelly misses passes, misses reads. . . . That's the nature of the game."

Media and fans were also all over Kelly's case. Instead of lamenting the fact he was out of the lineup, they were tearing him to shreds for criticizing a teammate. The whole town seemed to be upset with Kelly.

We were off the next day, but a lot of us, as always, came in for treatment or to lift or to study some video. Kelly and I were there, and we got to talking about all that had happened to him in the previous twenty-four hours.

"Fred, I just don't understand it," he said. "If I say something, no matter what it is, I get crucified. If you say the same thing, people laugh at it. What's the deal?"

"The deal is, Jim, when I say something, I know before-hand what the response is going to be, because I joke around with the media all the time," I said. "It's different with you. As the quarterback, you're more heavily scrutinized than the rest of us, and you're not seen in the same humorous vein as me or anybody else on the team. So you really have got to think before you open your mouth, because even if you mean it one way, it's going to be taken at face value. Just be sure to always say exactly what you mean."

The following morning, during our team meeting, Marv also addressed the matter. Then he paused and said, "Jim wants to say something to all of you."

With that, Kelly got up and said, "I'm sorry some of you guys took what I said the wrong way. I didn't mean to create any rift. I'm sorry if I offended anyone."

He sat back down in a hurry. Looking around the room, I saw some smirking and eye-rolling. I got the distinct impression Kelly's apology wasn't registering with everyone. There was no doubt the incident had put at least a small crack in our team unity. Especially, coming as it did, the day after a painful loss. Any little distraction at that juncture would have caused a problem.

I was just hoping the crack wouldn't turn into a black hole.

Frank Reich, who had never made an NFL start because Ironman Kelly had never missed one, was going to be our No. 1 man for a Monday night home game against the Rams. He was going to get his baptism against a team with a 5-0 record . . . and in front of the entire nation. A lot of people expected the worst, especially the fans who had written him off as a bust long ago. They saw the loss of Kelly and Reich's promotion to starter as a nightmare come true.

Those of us on the team had our questions about Frank as well. We always knew he had great character and tremen-dous intelligence. He understood our offense and how to attack defenses as well as any of our coaches, if not better. We just didn't know if he had the necessary tools to convert that knowledge into pass completions. I'm not even sure if Frank knew.

As if this game needed another subplot, Greg Bell, feeling pretty sure of himself as one in a long line of successful Ram running backs, spent the week mouthing off to the press about me, Robb Riddick, and others connected with the Bills. He said he never got along with me during our three and a half years as teammates (1984–1987), called me a "redneck," and directed all kinds of other derogatory and threatening remarks toward me, such as, "I'm going to love playing against Fred, because Fred's going to have to watch his butt the whole game. I'm going to tell [Rams center] Doug Smith and them [the rest of the offensive line] to drive him as hard as they want. You know, he's an average player who, when he's surrounded by great players, they beef up his status a lot."

I can't say I was especially fond of Greg when he was in Buffalo. I gave him the nickname Tinker Bell, partly as a joke but partly because he didn't seem to have the biggest heart in the world when it came to enduring the punishment that goes with being an NFL running back. I think his real problem was the fact we were losing and he wanted no part of the team. Greg was a great football talent. There was no denying that. But as a person, I thought he lacked a lot of character. He was empty inside, so he tried to make up for it by being flashy on the outside with all of his fur coats and jewelry. Once, Greg came up to me and said, "Look at this watch. It cost $9,000." I said, "Look at my watch. It cost $8,995 less than yours. And it keeps time."

Naturally, I wanted to ring the Bell on a few occasions during the game. So did a lot of other guys, including a few on offense. Everyone's attitude was that he wouldn't have said the things he did unless he was absolutely certain the Rams were going to kick our ass.

I made sure I ate a lot of the worst-smelling food I could find before kickoff because I intended to spend a lot of time growling in Greg's face and I wanted it to be a memorable experience for him. The first time he touched the ball, we smothered him. In the pile, I delivered a little jab to his ribs and said, "Hi, Tinker, it's me. We're going to be seeing a lot of each other tonight." Without saying a word, Bell jogged back to the huddle. In fact, he didn't say a thing to me the entire game. He was too busy trying to pick himself up off the ground.

We were swarming all over him and everyone else in a Ram uniform. For the first time all season, everyone on defense finally seemed locked on the same channel. We finally looked like the unit that had led the AFC in '88.

And it was a good thing, because Frank was having all kinds of problems throwing the ball. Through the first three quarters, he completed only 10 of 24 passes. One of his incompletions was a screen pass that hit Thomas in the feet. The crowd started booing. It looked as if Frank were about to fold up.

But for a magical fifteen minutes, he was able to get his act together. He connected on 11 of his next 13 attempts. And he was perfect on his final 7, including an 8-yard touchdown pass to Reed with sixteen seconds left to give us an incredible comeback victory, 23–20. Frank was so excited after the TD, he just started running around in circles on the field. I mean, the kid didn't know what to do; he had never been in that position before. He ran toward the sideline, where I greeted him with the biggest of bear hugs. Then, he dropped to his right knee, buried his head in his left hand, and started to cry.

It'll go down as one of the more unforgettable nights of my life.

Besides my breath, Bell's other sour memory from that night was being held to 44 yards on 21 carries. As we walked off the field after the game, I went up to him and said, "Tinker, you know I'm not a redneck. You shouldn't have said that. You're a good back and I respect your ability."

"Well, Fred, maybe someday you and I can sit down and have a beer together," he said.

"Maybe. Anyway, good luck to you."

And I trotted up the tunnel.

I have to take some of the credit for Frank's success that night. In the hotel where the team stays on the eve of home games, I had him stop by the room I shared with Ritcher. A long time ago, Jim and I began a ritual of having a hamburger and a beer the night before every game. It was just something that relaxed us. For whatever reason, we believed it had a positive effect on the way we played the next day. A short while earlier, we had invited our crazy fullback, Jamie Mueller, to join us, and he remained part of the tradition. Having had that big game against the Rams, Frank also became a regular.

Considering that he's kind of a straight-arrow—he looks more like a young business executive than a football player— you wouldn't think Frank would be comfortable in a group that included two big, hairy linemen and a psychotic fullback. But he fit right in. In fact, whenever Jamie had the urge to wrestle, which usually occurred after his second sip of beer, Reich didn't hesitate to take him on. One time, as Jamie tried to lift Frank off the ground, Frank hooked his feet on to the bottom of my bed, on which I was lying at the time, and Jamie couldn't budge him. Finally, Jamie got him off the ground and threw him on top of me.

As I said, we liked to use that time to relax.

I was also Frank's personal passing coach. No joke. A few years ago, during training camp, I actually gave him written reports about his foot placement, release, follow through, and all of the other mechanical elements of throwing a pass. I might not be able to play quarterback, but I know how to throw a football. I have witnesses who've seen me throw one eighty-seven yards.

At first, I volunteered the information to Frank. Then, after a while, he started requesting it. He asked me to watch him every day in practice and in the games he played. For instance, after the Rams game, I told him, "Frank, you're steering the ball a little bit, you're guiding the ball. Just let it wing."

The following week, he threw for three touchdowns to

beat the Jets, 34–3. I'm not saying my advice was the sole reason he got better.

The beer and hamburger he had the night before helped, too.

The weirdest thing happened the morning after that game. As they were watching what should have been a pretty cheery video, two of our offensive assistant coaches, Nick Nicolau and Tom Bresnahan, got into a fistfight. Actually, "fistfight" is putting it mildly. After becoming upset about something Bresnahan said, Nicolau, who was about ten inches shorter and sixty pounds lighter, punched him in the chin and opened a cut that would require stitches. He also grabbed him in a headlock and rammed his head through a plasterboard wall, opening a cut in his forehead that would also require stitches.

That afternoon, it was all we could do not to laugh when Bresnahan showed up for meetings wearing a white, turban-like bandage around his head and sunglasses. The incident occurred shortly after the Bay Area earthquake, and as somebody on the team pointed out, Bresnahan looked like "one of the victims."

I loved Marv's explanation in the next day's paper: "Coaches have arguments all the time." That's right. They beat the hell out of each other like that once a day. Sometimes twice. There are blood-spattered holes in every wall in the stadium.

Some outsiders feared the fight would be a major distraction while we prepared for a home date with the Dolphins. As we demonstrated with a 31–17 victory, our sixth straight over Miami, it wasn't.

The only thing that was bothering me at that point was Levy's insistence on platooning his older defensive linemen—Leon Seals for Art Still and Jeff Wright for me. Although we kept our starting jobs, the backups seemed to be getting more and more playing time each week while we were getting less and less. It wouldn't have bothered me if it were productive, but it was extremely counterproductive.

We'd be on a roll defensively, then, all of a sudden, one or both of us would come out and our continuity would fall apart. We just seemed to lose something. Supposedly, the idea was to give us a rest so we'd be fresh in the late stages of the game. But neither of us was getting tired. I know I wasn't.

The paycheck I collected Monday morning would be the same whether I was on the field or the bench. It would have made more sense for me to have been satisfied with doing less work for my money. But although I didn't say too much about it publicly, I was furious. I was burning up inside because I wanted to be out there full time. I couldn't stand the thought of watching from the sidelines when I felt perfectly fine, when I knew I could have been out there helping us win.

For eleven years, I survived on pride. Pride was, is, and always will be the foundation of my game. I never quit—not in a single game, not on a single play. I may have been part of a lot of losing games and losing teams, but I never allowed myself to accept defeat. To me, being replaced by Wright so often was a form of defeat. Chuck Knox always used to say, "Don't ever leave the glove down; someone else might pick it up." Over the years, a number of nose tackles had been brought on to the team to take that glove away from me, and I always refused to give it up. I wasn't going to start then.

If I had, it would have been the same as quitting and I wouldn't have had anything left for the rest of the season, or the following one. My will to win would have disappeared. All it takes is to quit once. After that, it's easy to do it all the time.

In Wright, I saw myself ten years earlier—a young punk looking to shove an old man out of his way, with the complete backing of the head coach. Knox was behind me as I worked to unseat Mike Kadish. Levy was behind Jeff. I saw my reflection in the kid's eyes, and it really terrified me. I just couldn't back down.

And with all due respect to Wright, there was no com-

THE DROP 239

paring our performances. I was outplaying him, and I had
always been of the belief that, as long as they're healthy, a
team leaves its best players on the field. Period. Jeff's a good,
young player who had been pretty impressive as a rookie in
1988, but slipped in his second season. Besides, with my
being much more power-oriented, I was better suited for our
defensive scheme, which was designed so that the nose man
tied up the middle and allowed the linebackers to make the
tackles. Jeff's smaller and his forte is quickness. Against a
big, strong center—which is what most teams have—he gets
pushed around a lot.

After his 3-0 Cinderella story, Reich stepped aside and
Kelly came back. For whatever reason, we reverted to the
inconsistent form we had displayed before Kelly's injury.
First, we were ambushed by Atlanta, 30–28. Then we mauled
the Colts, 30–7. But a week later, we lost at New England,
33–24, allowing the injury-gutted Patriots to score 20 points
in the final 8:46.

Actually, we started letting that game get away from us
early in the third quarter, while holding a 10–6 lead. Despite
having lost Cornelius Bennett on the first play with a knee
injury, we were in control up to that point, especially on
defense. Then all of a sudden, we allowed the Patriots to
ram the ball down our throat on an 11-play, 75-yard touchdown drive that lasted 6:18. They just pounded away with
eleven straight runs—five by big John Stephens, five by Robert Perryman, and one 15-yarder for the TD by Patrick Egu.
It was our lowest defensive moment of the season. There
isn't a more demoralizing way to give up six points than to
have a team just plow right through you.

And we were demoralized.

We were all getting the shit knocked out of us up front.
A guard would hit me straight ahead, and a tackle would
come over and take me out. On top of that, our linebackers
were playing too soft and tentative. They were five yards
deep and flowing with each run, allowing the ballcarriers to
cut back for healthy gains while the linebackers were being

cut off by blockers. Instead of flowing, they should have been filling the spots we were leaving open on the line. That was something our coaches figured out afterward, and once the proper adjustments were made, it didn't happen again.

We took advantage of a fumble for one touchdown and an interception for another to build a 24–13 lead with 8:46 remaining. The Patriots came back to make it 24–20, and much to my surprise, we got into a passing mode and quickly turned the ball over on downs. The Patriots got a field goal to cut the margin to 24–23. Now, in a full panic, we started throwing again, and Maurice Hurst intercepted and returned the ball 16 yards for a touchdown.

I couldn't believe my eyes when I looked up at the scoreboard and saw us trailing, 30–24, to a team that was missing its top three defensive players—Andre Tippett, Garin Veris, and Ronnie Lippett—and had a bunch of other guys banged up. Hell, their quarterback, Steve Grogan, was playing with a neck brace after off-season surgery that had threatened his career. After Kelly fumbled while being sacked, New England killed off more than a minute and put the game out of reach with a field goal in the final seconds.

We were in dire need of a psychological lift. The following week we got it by dominating Cincinnati, 24–7, at home. We had been waiting eleven months to claim our revenge after the Bengals stomped all over our Super Bowl dreams.

In case we needed any added incentive, Marv stoked the fire by showing us a "motivational" videotape the night before the game. It consisted of action and Bengals' celebration scenes from that AFC Championship game, as well as anti-Bills comments Cincinnati players made then and the week before our rematch. There was one shot of cornerback Lewis Billups saying how we hadn't beaten the Bengals "in twenty years." Billups needed a little history lesson; we had beaten them in 1983.

Judging by the way everyone was glaring at the screen with clenched jaws and fists, it was clear the tape had had its desired effect. We felt the fire. We were ready to play the

game that night, in the lobby of our Buffalo hotel. Arthur
Still, a vegetarian, got so excited, he talked about ordering
steak from room service. And Ritcher went completely over
the edge. After we fell asleep, I woke up to the sound of his
huffing and puffing as if he were about to do a giant bench-
press. I turned on the light and looked over at his bed, and
there was Jim, with his eyes closed, taking deep breaths and
blowing out short ones.

Suffice to say he was ready.

As always, the Bengals came out with their hurry-up offense. It backfired on them because Art and I were having
our best game to date, and with the hurry-up, there was no
time for us to be substituted. We stayed on the field and were
able to maintain some sort of defensive continuity. In fact,
the only series I was out was the one on which the Bengals
scored. Their center, 300-pound Brian Blados, practically
carried Jeff on his back all the way downfield. I was hoping
that performance would, once and for all, convince Marv to
do less substituting through the balance of the season.

With that victory, all of us were certain we had finally
become the team everyone thought we would be.

But the next thing we knew, we were falling to pieces.
Again.

First, Seattle beat us, 17–16, in our third and last Monday
night appearance of the season. I found out early in that
game Marv hadn't been swayed to give me more playing
time by what he had seen the previous Sunday. After one
play on which I caused a fumble, Ted Cottrell, our defensive-
line coach, came up to me and said, "You're out the next
series."

"What?" I yelled. "I just caused a fumble. I'm making
things happen. Why am I coming out?"

Had it not been for my respect and admiration for Ted, I'd
probably have lost it completely. I got a grip on myself. I
knew it wasn't his decision to put Jeff in. I knew it was
coming from Marv.

The following Sunday, in our final home game of the year,

we lost to New Orleans, 22–19. The Saints were going no-where, so they started John Fourcade at quarterback instead of Bobby Hebert. Before joining the Saints, Fourcade had bounced around the USFL, the Canadian League, and even Arena Football. Not exactly Hall of Fame credentials.

Yet he shredded us for 302 passing yards and two touch-downs. I should say we shredded ourselves.

For instance, on the Saints' opening drive, we had them in a third-and-eleven situation at our 12-yard line. We were applying good pressure on Fourcade, but he was still able to throw a touchdown pass to tight end John Tice. Why? A line-backer who was supposed to have dropped ten yards to the middle of the end zone decided to drop only three and then came up to rush the quarterback, leaving Tice wide open.

On the Saints' second drive, Fourcade, avoiding another strong pass rush, completed a 54-yard touchdown pass to Dalton Hilliard. Why? Because when the linebacker who was supposed to have had man-to-man coverage on Hilliard saw the receiver get tangled in traffic for a couple of seconds, he decided to rush instead of remain in coverage as he was supposed to.

Then, in the second quarter, we had the Saints in a third and twenty-three at their 14. Again, good pressure was being applied. Fourcade rolled to his right and completed a 41-yard pass to Brett Perriman. Why? As Fourcade began mov-ing out of the pocket and it looked as if he were going to take off, one of our safeties came up to meet him. That left Perriman all alone for the catch. When a quarterback is 23 yards from a first down, a safety shouldn't worry about com-ing up to make the tackle; the odds of someone else's making it in time are pretty strong.

Meanwhile, Kelly was intercepted three times as our re-cord fell to an embarrassing 8-6.

More controversy filled the air in the days that followed. On a cable-TV program from Rochester, New York, that aired the night before the Saints game, Thurman Thomas called quarterback the weakest area of our team. Two nights after the game, on another cable show, he explained that he was only giving Kelly a taste of his own medicine for publicly criticizing Ballard and other players over the past two seasons. He wanted Jim to know how it felt.

The day after we played New Orleans, Bill Polian, our street-tough GM, caught some heat of his own while addressing the Quarterback Club. He said anyone in the media with complaints about our coaching, play-calling, or quarterbacking could "get out of town!" A lot of fans thought Polian was referring to them, as well as the media, and told him to follow his own advice.

Outbursts such as that didn't speak well of our poise as an organization. Nor did the public finger-pointing and bickering that involved Kelly and Thomas. Nor the fight between the assistant coaches. Reporters and fans began asking questions like, "How are you able to cope with all of the dissension and turmoil?"

I began to get the impression that, in everyone's mental picture, our dressing room looked like a war zone. That there were foxholes and barbwire around our lockers. That we had to check for mines on our way to the shower. That we drank from canteens and ate K rations.

To the outside world, we were too torn apart to make a serious run at Super Bowl XXIV.

It wasn't quite that bad on the inside. In pro football or any sport, no situation is ever as harmonious or turbulent as it appears. The dressing room is the eye of the hurricane. All of the swirling winds around it are, to a large extent, created by a giant fan known as the media. Sure, we had some dissension, but it wasn't anywhere close to the level the media said it was. Of course, if the media reported exactly what went on in our dressing room each day, people would be bored to death.

So, they took Kelly's comments about Ballard, they took Thomas's remarks about Kelly, and they took the fight between Bresnahan and Nicolau and rehashed them. They turned them sideways and upside down. They looked at them from every possible angle, which, as a result, kept the issues alive. Kept them boiling for the public. True, controversial things were said and done, but there's a big difference between that and having every single guy on the team at each other's throat—which was not at all true.

We're talking about the NFL. You have some very violent guys on every club. You have some very large egos. You have people from every walk of life, with every kind of personality. Disagreements are commonplace. Look at the Bears. Jim McMahon was at the center of a lot of internal problems with them in 1985, yet it was the best team they ever had. And the reason they overcame those internal problems was that they remained focused. They continued to work toward a common goal. You can be hugging each other and flashing peace signs all over the dressing room, but it won't make a damn bit of difference if you aren't focused.

That, more than the dissension, was the biggest thing wrong with us—we just weren't focused. We became a bunch of individuals, pulling in all different directions, rather than a group pushing as one. I can't say exactly why that was happening, although it probably resulted from our 12-4 finish in 1988. As is often the case when you've had a successful season, a lot of players start to believe they were the primary reason for that success. All of a sudden, helmets have a little tighter fit than the year before.

Compounding all of the talk about dissension in our dressing room was our performance on the field. In week fifteen, we went up against another backup quarterback, San Francisco's Steve Young, and came away with another loss. Taking over for Joe Montana, Young directed the 49ers to three second-half touchdowns on the way to a 21–10 victory. Kelly had his third consecutive poor game, and second in a row in which he was intercepted three times.

Afterward, I told reporters, "When you keep cutting your throat, eventually, you run out of blood."

Still, we managed to have enough blood left to cope with the minus-11° windchill in Giants Stadium and bury the pathetic Jets, 37–0, in our regular-season finale. The win gave us a 9-7 record and our second straight division championship. It also kind of whitewashed the three-game losing

streak and controversy that preceded it. The feeling among
the team was, "Okay, we've faltered and we've flapped. Now,
that's all in the past. Now, we are in the playoffs. Now, we
have a chance to get into the Super Bowl."

I felt we had more direction than in previous weeks. We
may still not have been as focused as we should have been,
but we were more focused than at any other time during the
season. I sensed a genuine desire on everyone's part to go
all the way.

We would face the Browns in the playoffs at Cleveland
Stadium, by far the worst sports facility on the planet. I can't
stand the place. It's supposed to have natural turf, but there's
nothing natural about finding craters and sand everywhere
you step—unless you're an astronaut. There isn't a single
blade of grass anywhere. It's dirt, with a little hay sprinkled
on top, spray-painted green.

You would have thought, Buffalo against Cleveland on a
cold January afternoon in that dump of a ballpark, it was
going to be a real defensive struggle. It was a struggle all
right—for anyone trying to keep up with the offensive yards
and scoring.

I had wanted my performance to make a real statement
that day. I had wanted Marv to know that having me off the
field wasn't good for our defense—that there was a reason I
had lasted in the league eleven seasons and played in five
Pro Bowls. Sure enough, on Cleveland's first drive, which
ended with Matt Bahr's missing a 45-yard field goal, I was
involved in two big plays back-to-back. First, I combined
with Art to dump running back Kevin Mack for a 2-yard loss.
Then, I knocked down a Bernie Kosar pass. I just threw down
the center, Gregg Rakoczy, to my left, stepped right, and got
a piece of the ball just as Bernie released it.

The first sign that we were in for a real shootout came late
in the first quarter, when Kelly hooked up with Reed for a
72-yard touchdown. The Browns made it 7–3 as Bahr made
a 45-yarder just before the quarter ended. Then, early in the
second, they went up 10–7 on a 52-yard scoring pass from
Kosar to Webster Slaughter. We entered the game wanting

to challenge Kosar, one of the slower-footed quarterbacks around, with all-out blitzes and man-to-man coverage. But on that play, he got the pass off just before he was about to be buried, and Slaughter, having used a stutter step to freeze cornerback Nate Odomes, was wide open for the catch.

We struck back a couple of minutes later when Kelly found James Lofton, whom we had acquired early in the season as a free agent, for a 33-yard TD. But just before halftime, our secondary bit on a play-fake by Kosar, and he threw a 3-yard touchdown pass to tight end Ron Middledon to give the Browns a 17–14 lead.

Despite what I felt was a strong showing on my part, the substituting continued through the first two quarters. At one point, I grabbed the arm of Walt Corey, our defensive co-ordinator, and said, "Walt, this is not a preseason game. This is for all of the marbles. Go with your best players. Put me out there."

But as we took the field for the third quarter, Ted Cottrell came up to me and said, "I've got to play Jeff more. That's what Marv wants."

I just shook my head and sighed. It would have been different if Wright were the better of us. If that were the case, he should have been in there the entire game and I should have been on the sidelines the entire game. But I got the feeling we were being alternated just for the sake of being alternated. It made no sense. It frustrated me to no end.

Early in the second half, we fell behind, 24–14, after Slaughter was somehow left by himself to catch a 44-yard touchdown throw from Kosar. One play after our fullback, Larry Kinnebrew, fumbled, I got the ball back for us by using my helmet to knock it out of Mack's arm. Mack was trying to run to my left, so I stepped to that side while jamming Rakoczy. Then, as Mack tried to cut back, I threw Rakoczy the other way, caused the fumble, and Mark Kelso recovered at the Browns' 21-yard line. A short while later, Kelly threw a 6-yard TD to Thomas to make it 24–21.

It had become clear that this was the "Jim and Bernie

Show," and the rest of us were extras. Each was having a phenomenal game, and there was no sign either would cool off.

On the kickoff after Thomas's score, Eric Metcalf broke a 90-yard return for a touchdown. Scott Norwood's kickoff was short, which didn't help matters. But we also had one cover guy out of his lane, and that gave Metcalf all the room he needed to go the distance and put the Browns ahead, 31–21.

A 30-yard field goal by Norwood at the start of the fourth quarter cut the margin to 31–24. But Bahr answered from 47 yards midway through the fourth, on a drive that ate up nearly seven minutes, and the Browns again led by 10.

Still, we had 6:50 left. With Kelly playing as he was, I knew it was plenty of time for us to rally. And he proceeded to hit six of his next seven passes to move us to the Cleveland 3, from where he fired a scoring toss to Thomas with four minutes remaining. It was here that I probably never hated that horrible turf more, because, while making his approach for the extra point, Norwood slipped and drove the ball into the butt of our long-snapper, Adam Lingner.

Instead of trailing 34–31, we were down 34–30. Missing that one point changed our entire approach to the rest of the game. Not only did we need to get the ball back in a hurry, we needed to score a touchdown and win, as opposed to tying it with a field goal and forcing overtime.

The defense did its part, forcing the Browns to go three downs and out. With 2:41 showing on the clock, one time-out, and the two-minute warning to play with, Kelly and the offense took over at our 26. From there, his mastery took over.

Nine- and seven-yard passes to Ronnie Harmon gave us a first down at our 42 at the two-minute warning. After three incompletions, Kelly faced a fourth and ten with 1:36 remaining. Bang! He found rookie Don Beebe for a 17-yard completion that gave us a first down at the Cleveland 41, forcing the Browns to call their first time-out of the half with 1:16 left. Two plays later, Kelly hooked up with Thomas for

9 yards, prompting the Browns to use their second time-out with a minute showing. After an incompletion, Kelly, facing fourth and one, threw to Reed for a 10-yard gain to the Browns' 22. Kelly quickly lined everyone up and spiked the ball to stop the clock at 34 seconds.

By this time, members of Cleveland's highly regarded defense were talking to themselves. Bud Carson, the Browns' head coach and a longtime defensive genius in the NFL, became so frustrated, he had yanked off his headset and whipped it to the ground. Obviously, none of the information he was getting from above was doing any good.

After failing to connect with Beebe on second and ten, Kelly fired to Thomas to give us a first down at the 11. He again slammed the ball down to stop the clock at 14 seconds, leaving us with three downs to get into the end zone.

On the sidelines, we all held hands, just as we had in 1981 when Joe Ferguson guided us to that miracle victory over the Patriots. All of the finger-pointing and bickering was forgotten. We were pulling for the offense. We were pulling for each other.

Victory—and a return trip to the AFC Championship Game—appeared to be ours when Kelly dropped back and fired a perfect pass to his left. All alone in the end zone, Harmon reached with both hands for what would have been, should have been, the game-winning catch. But . . . but . . . the ball slipped through his fingers on a play that will forever be known around Buffalo as The Drop. In fact, it was the ninth Kelly pass of the day that failed to stay in a receiver's hands. Had they been added to his 28 completions, his 405-yard day, already an NFL-career best, would easily have gone over 500.

We all felt like dying right then and there, but we did have another chance.

This time, Kelly, looking for Thomas, threw toward the middle of the end zone. This time, linebacker Clay Matthews intercepted.

End of game. End of season.

CHAPTER

ELEVEN

LET'S MAKE A DEAL

TWO DAYS AFTER the Browns game, we returned to Rich
Stadium for the dreaded task of cleaning out our lockers for
the off-season. Every year, you hope it'll come later than the
year before—like the day after you've ridden down Main
Street in a Super Bowl parade.

But like all of the previous ten clean-out days at Rich, this
one arrived much too soon.

By then, I had replayed The Drop in my head about a
zillion times. I kept hoping once, just once, my mental videotape would show the ball being caught, and we would win
and begin preparing for the AFC Championship.

No such luck.

I was never more heartbroken to see a season end. It was
a different feeling from the one I had had after our 1988 AFC
title loss to Cincinnati. Although it was painful to stub our
toe on the doorstep of Super Bowl XXIII, the expectations

for the team were much greater before the 1989 season than before the '88 campaign, and that made for a much greater letdown.

I also felt, when the Bengals game was over, that I had another year to look forward to with the Bills. I was far less certain of that as time expired at Cleveland Stadium.

So, when I cleaned out my locker—a monumental undertaking, to say the least—I wasn't only doing it for the off-season; I thought I might be doing it for good. Or, shall I say, for bad. Besides removing every single thing on the inside, including my poster of Larry Bird (which usually hangs year-round), I also took the nameplate from over the top of my dressing cubicle.

Nothing official had been said or done, but I just didn't like the odds of my wearing a Bills uniform for a twelfth season and third decade. Too many signs pointed to my departure.

First of all, after the '88 season, which I ended with my fifth Pro Bowl appearance, Bill Polian told me I was going to be placed on the Bills' list of unprotected players in the NFL's Plan B free-agency system. That meant that between February 1 and April 1, 1989, any team could have signed me or any of the league's other unprotected players without owing our original clubs so much as a dirty sock. As a Plan B free agent, you get a two-month taste of freedom, as opposed to having your contract expire while your exclusive negotiating rights are available to the rest of the NFL for the unreasonable price of two first-round draft picks. If you don't sign elsewhere, you stay put, providing you're still wanted.

Teams can protect a minimum of thirty-seven guys and often play Russian roulette in trying to determine their contributions to this annual flea market of flesh. They'll look at someone's age and salary, assume both are high enough to discourage any takers, and leave him unprotected with the idea he will return after April 1. Plan B is also a nice, backdoor way for teams to get rid of aging veterans. They'll tell a player they don't want back, "If you get an offer, you'd better take it."

The Bills didn't say that to me then. They said they wanted me back; they just felt safe that, because of my age and salary, I wouldn't be signed by another club. But when they found out, just before submitting their unprotected list in January '89, that there was a heavy demand for experienced nose tackles, they changed their minds and protected me.

Still, I was dumbfounded. How, I wondered, could they have even considered leaving me unprotected after a Pro Bowl season?

It wasn't until the '89 season began that I finally found the answer. Although he still wanted me around, Marv Levy didn't think I could produce at the level I had a year earlier. He thought it would take two nose tackles to do the job I had done solo for nine years, and he began substituting for me with Jeff Wright. When he insisted on doing so even after it was clear Jeff couldn't get the job done, I realized I was being phased out.

Levy confirmed the doubts I had about my future with the Bills when, a couple of days before the start of Plan B 1990, he telephoned me at my house in Waltham.

"Fred, I just wanted you to know we're not going to be protecting you this time," he said.

"I figured as much," I said.

"I also think you should know that we want to begin playing the younger guys more. It looks like we're going to go with Jeff as the starter and try to get another nose tackle in the draft."

"That's your choice. But younger is not always better. You should evaluate guys on the basis of their performance, not their age."

"Well, with more of a chance, we feel Jeff will do better. He just needs more playing time."

"Fine."

"Okay. And listen, if no one picks you up, you can always give us a call in April."

"Fine."

"Bye, Fred."

"Bye."

The conversation lasted all of about thirty seconds. The way I figure it, that's an average of less than three seconds for every year I had been with the team. I suppose, if I had had ten or fewer seasons under my belt, I'd probably have received a nice, warm fax saying, "To whom this may concern: You're unprotected!"

Of course, at least Marv told me I could call him in April. That same week, he told Joe Devlin and Art Still, both of whom were also left unprotected, they weren't in the team's plans for the '90 season and would be released if they didn't hook on with anyone else.

At thirty-five, Joe was the oldest player on the squad. At thirty-four, Art was the second oldest. I figured I didn't have much cause for comfort nearing my thirty-third birthday.

I didn't even wait to get together with my agent to talk about my future in the NFL.

On February 1, I began making telephone calls to see if there was any interest in a more-than-slightly-used, but still very reliable, nose tackle. Following a list of teams I felt needed help at the position yet were still Super Bowl, playoff, or on-the-threshold-of-being-playoff contenders, I dialed the San Francisco 49ers, Denver Broncos, Cincinnati Bengals, Los Angeles Rams and Raiders, and New England Patriots. The Indianapolis Colts weren't on the list, but they called me, so I told them I'd listen to whatever offer they might make, too.

The thing that impressed me about the 49ers was the swiftness with which they responded to the message I had left with their player-personnel office. At ten o'clock the next morning in Waltham, which was seven o'clock in San Francisco, I received a call from Neal Dahlen, who oversees football operations for the 49ers.

"We want you, Fred," were the first words out of his mouth. "The owner [Eddie DeBartolo, Jr.], the coach [George Seifert], and the general manager [John McVay] have talked, and we're interested. We think there's a place for you on our team."

I couldn't believe my ears. The best team in the world, the four-time Super Bowl champions, opened its arms to me at a time when the Bills, to whom I had given eleven years of blood, sweat, and loyalty, left me dangling in limbo. I felt like a kid who, after being thrown out of his house by his parents, was invited to live in the biggest and best house in the neighborhood—with more food.

It turned out San Francisco was in dire need of a nose tackle. Michael Carter, their Pro Bowler at the position, was about to undergo major foot surgery, putting his status in doubt for the '90 season. Jim Burt, whom the 49ers had picked up during the '89 season, had chronic back problems. And Pete Kugler had retired.

As soon as word began to spread the 49ers were interested in me, most of the other teams backed off. When it comes to bidding on a player, no one wants to lock horns with DeBartolo. With most owners, it's a matter of dollars and cents; with Eddie D, it's just cents—and good sense. He has built the best team in football and will spend whatever it takes to keep it there.

Only New England and Indianapolis were still in the running. I would spend the next couple of weeks visiting each of the three clubs. I felt like a high school senior again, making recruiting trips. The difference was, the NFL teams didn't have to say, "*Pssst!* We'll give you some money under the table if you play here." They essentially come to you with a wheelbarrow of cash and say, "Is this going to be enough to get you to play for us?"

The first stop was the Patriots. That wasn't really a trip, per se, because my off-season home is a stone's throw away from them. Their GM, Pat Sullivan, was very interested in me, but the head coach, Raymond Berry, wasn't. A short while later, Berry would be replaced by Rod Rust, and he shared Sullivan's opinion.

Next, I traveled to San Francisco. The organization's spare-no-expense attitude was obvious the moment I saw the Marie P. DeBartolo Sports Centre in Santa Clara. It's a two-story, 52,000-square-foot building situated on eleven acres of land.

When I walked inside, I couldn't get over how much cherry wood I saw. It was everywhere.

I was taken upstairs to see Eddie D's office (he wasn't in at the time). There was, of course, more cherry wood, six TV sets, and a floor made from pigskin.

"So that's what you do with the offensive linemen who don't make the team," I said to Dahlen.

Huge sliding glass doors led to a deck that overlooked the practice field. The deck surrounded the entire building. I thought, what a great place for barbecues!

I spoke with Seifert for a while, and he really made me feel at home. In fact, he even let me sit in his office chair. (I sat in Eddie D's chair, too, although I made sure to wipe it clean afterward.)

My final visit was to Indianapolis.

"We want you here," said superslick Ron Meyer, the Colts' agent-turned-head-coach.

In the back of my mind, I was hoping the Bills would have a change of heart—that they would tell me I would continue to be their starter and guarantee me one more year on the team. So I called Polian, figuring maybe, just maybe, he would say exactly that. Instead, he only reaffirmed what I had been told by Marv: I'd be welcome to return, but with no assurances I'd start or even be around to collect my base salary of $650,000.

After hearing much more positive talk from the other teams, that was extremely hard for me to swallow.

That was when the finality of my career with the Bills began to set in.

After weeks of negotiations, my agent, Jack Mula, came to me with two offers to consider: a one-year contract from the 49ers worth $750,000—$250,000 to sign, a $500,000 base, plus relocation expenses and other incentives; a two-year contract from the Patriots that would guarantee me close to a million dollars and a coaching job after I retired as a player. Both were attractive.

In the end, I figured my better chance to finally slip a Super

Bowl ring onto one of these fat fingers was with San Francisco.

But in my heart, that was, like the vehicle that brought me there, Plan B.

Plan A had always been to help bring a Super Bowl to Buffalo.

I know it might sound silly, but my wife and I cried real tears on that March afternoon I signed with the 49ers. They weren't tears of joy, although they had absolutely nothing to do with how we felt about my joining a new team. We were just mourning the loss of the old one.

Eventually, I must realize I am not a Buffalo Bill anymore. But it won't be easy. Not many guys can say they have played eleven years in the NFL, certainly not many nose tackles. And hardly anyone can say he played eleven years for the same NFL team. I'm not talking about hanging around; I'm talking about playing and starting through the thickest and thinnest of times.

I'm a loyal, emotional guy. When I commit myself to something, I *commit*. My only regret was that, in the end, I didn't feel the same sense of loyalty from the Bills.

Not the city of Buffalo, but the Bills.

For more than a decade, Buffalo has been my town. The fans have been part of my family. You always hear the phrase "These are the greatest fans in the world" when a player's ears are still ringing from the crowd noise after a game. But when Buffalo fans leave the stadium, they don't just go home and become normal citizens again. They are still fans. In or out of the stadium, in or out of the season, they are still bleeding Bills red, white, and blue.

There is nothing like it anywhere else in the world.

A franchise is a franchise. It can be moved at any time of the day or night. But when you've spent a third of your life in one place, you just can't simply pick up and walk away. Those emotional ties are linked by steel cables, not flimsy thread.

Some might say the position I play has a lot in common

with the town in which I played it for eleven years. Both require their residents to be a little bit tougher and a little bit stronger than those in other places. And you can't survive in either one without a sense of humor—without the ability to laugh.

Laugh in the face of pain. Laugh in the face of adversity.

I have had 300-pound offensive linemen knock me to the dirt, look down, and notice a smile on my face.

"What the hell are you so happy about?" they ask.

"I look at it this way," I tell them. "If I don't laugh, I might start crying."

I also think back to what my father told me about not taking life too seriously:

"If you do, it'll eat you alive."

My intention is to have as much fun playing football in San Francisco as I did in Buffalo. I just hope the chicken wings aren't cold by the time they reach the West Coast.